KINTYRE
IN THE
SEVENTEENTH CENTURY

Published by the Kintyre Antiquarian and Natural History Society.

Text and photographs copyright 2001 the Kintyre Antiquarian and Natural History Society.

First published in Great Britain in 1948.

All rights reserved. No part of this publication may be reproduced, stored in a retrieval system, or transmitted in any form or by any means, electronic or mechanical, including photocopying, recording or other information storage system, without prior permission in writing from the publisher.

Front cover: Blades in the Heather - a Century of Conflict.

Back cover: The Rock of Dunaverty, Southend.

ISBN 0-9541852-0-X

Printed by Spectra Print, Cambuslang, Glasgow
Typeset by Spectra Print, Cambuslang, Glasgow

KINTYRE
IN THE
SEVENTEENTH CENTURY

ANDREW McKERRAL

CIE MA FSA Scot

Republished in 2001 by
The Kintyre Antiquarian and
Natural History Society

with photographs by
George Stewart of Dalbuie

The Council of the Kintyre Antiquarian and Natural History Society suffered exceptional loss from the number of Office-Bearers who died in the closing months of the Millennial Year. This publication is dedicated to their contributions, severally, to the life and spirit of Kintyre.

Honorary President
Reverend John R H Cormack MA., BD. 1916-2000
Minister Emeritus of Castlehill Church and of the Lowland Church in Campbeltown.

Honorary Vice-President
Mrs Efric A Wotherspoon FSA Scot. of Campbeltown. 1913-2000.

Syllabus Secretary
Mrs Catherine (Cath) J Miller FSA Scot. of Peninver. 1910-2000.

CONTENTS

		PAGE
LIST OF ILLUSTRATIONS		vi
OUTLINE MAP OF KINTYRE		vii
FOREWORD		viii
PREFACE		ix
I.	INTRODUCTION	1
II.	THE LAST MACDONALDS OF DUNNYVEG	14
III.	THE ERECTION OF THE BURGH OF LOCHHEAD	20
IV.	EARLY EVENTS IN THE BURGH OF LOCHHEAD	26
V.	THE COLKITTO RAIDS	37
VI.	GENERAL DAVID LESLIE'S MARCH THROUGH KINTYRE	42
VII.	THE MASSACRE AT DUNAVERTY	48
VIII.	LESLIE'S RETURN MARCH	55
IX.	THE EPIDEMIC OF PLAGUE	60
X.	THE PLANTATION OF LOWLAND LAIRDS AND CAMPBELLS	68
XI.	BIOGRAPHICAL NOTES ON THE LOWLANDERS	74
XII.	SOME EARLY EVENTS OF THE PLANTATION	82
XIII.	THE PERSECUTION AND THE PENTLAND RISING	93
XIV.	THE EARL OF ARGYLL'S REBELLION OF 1685	100
XV.	THE RURAL SCENE: AGRICULTURE AND INDUSTRY	110
XVI.	EDUCATION	124
	APPENDIX I HIGHLAND PERSONAL NAMES	133
	APPENDIX II LOWLAND NAMES	143
	APPENDIX III OLD LAND MEASURES	149
	APPENDIX IV A STEELBOW CONTRACT OF 1710	152
	INDEX	153

ILLUSTRATIONS

	An outline map of Kintyre.	vii
1.	The Ralston monument at Kilcolmkill.	7
2.	James Graham, 5th Earl and 1st Marquis of Montrose.	8
3.	Archibald Campbell, 8th Earl and Marquis of Argyll.	9
4.	Saddell Castle, leased as a residence to William Ralston in 1650.	10
5.	Saddell Castle, an early 16th C. tower-house on the E. Kintyre shore.	27
6.	Tarbert Castle: the tower-house from the SW.	28
7.	The Tower-house at Tarbert Castle, from the NW.	29
8.	Skipness Castle, a castle of enceinte commanding the NE Kintyre coast.	30
9.	The 16th C. Tower-house in the courtyard of Skipness Castle.	63
10.	The Old Parish Church and churchyard at Killean.	64
11.	The family vault of the Macdonalds of Largie in Killean Church.	65
12.	St.Columba's Church, Southend, the former parish-church of Kilcolmkill.	66
13.	The graveyard of St.Columba's Church, by the shore at Southend.	83
14.	The headstone of Neil McNeil of Carskiey (d.1685).	84
15.	The memorial of Ranald MacDonald of Sanda (d.1679).	85
16.	Dunaverty Bay, Southend, looking SE to Sheep Island and Sanda.	86
17.	The site of Dunaverty Castle, scene of the siege and massacre of 1647.	119
18.	Rhunahaorine Point in Largieside, site of the battle of 24th May, 1647.	120
19.	The Glens of Antrim in the north of Ireland, from Southend.	121
20.	The Jura Bens outlined by a summer sunset.	122

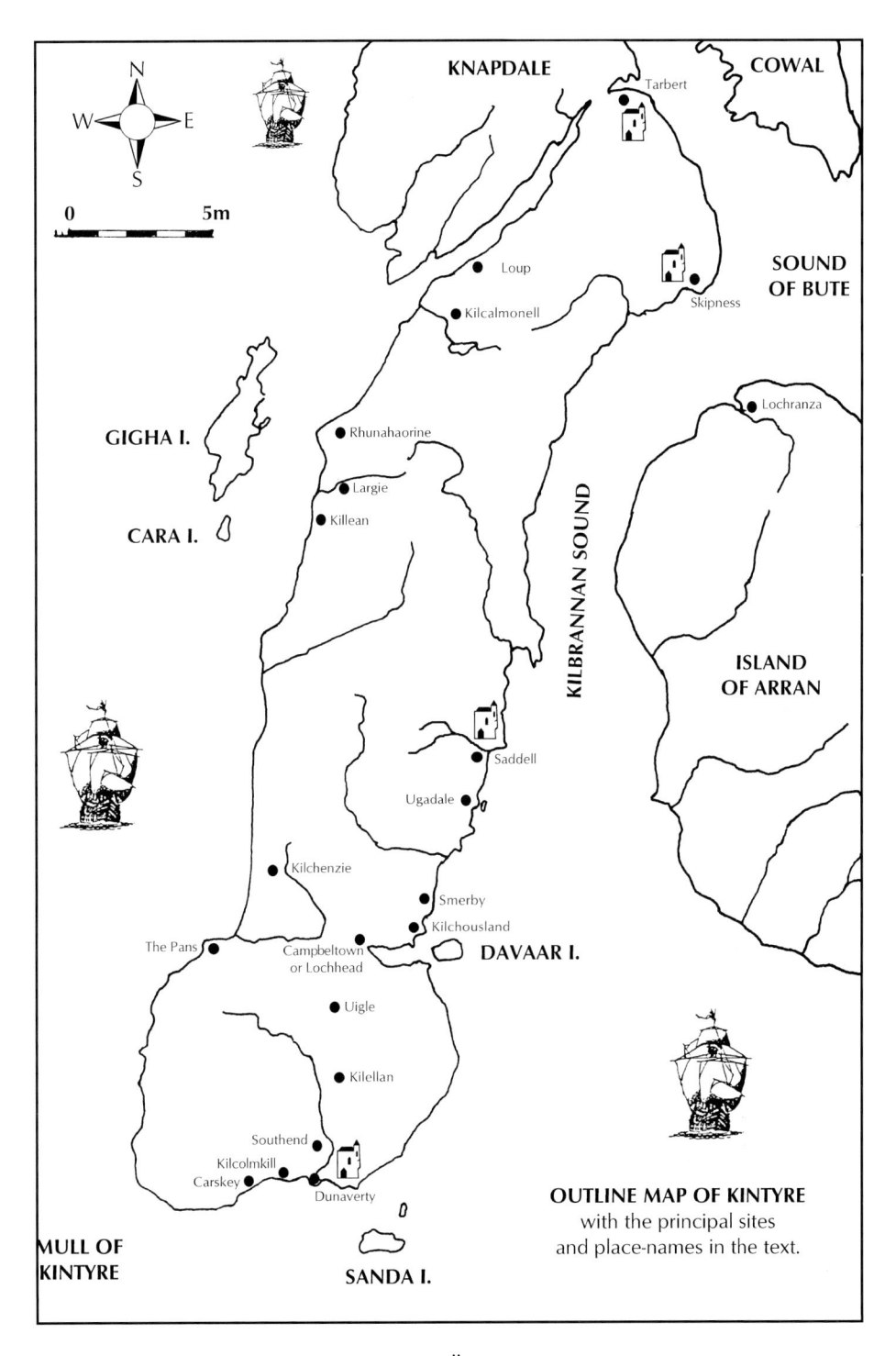

OUTLINE MAP OF KINTYRE
with the principal sites
and place-names in the text.

FOREWORD

Kintyre was the original home of the Scots of Dalriada. This book gives a short summary of its early history and then deals in greater detail with the events of one of its most important centuries - the seventeenth. It relates the causes of the fall of the Macdonalds of the Isles, the rise of the great family of Argyll, the foundation of the Burgh of Lochhead or Campbeltown, the stirring events of the Colkitto raids, the campaign of General David Leslie, the massacre of Dunaverty, and the visitation of the plague. Perhaps most important of all it gives for the first time, the real causes and circumstances of the plantation of the district by Covenanters from Ayrshire and Renfrewshire directed by the Marquis of Argyll.

The author was a native of Kintyre with a life-long interest in its history. He was a member of the Kintyre Club and the Kintyre Antiquarian Society, a member of the Scottish History Society and Fellow of the Society of Antiquaries of Scotland.

Ian MacDonald. Historian

Sheanakill, Clachan, by Tarbert

PREFACE

The study of History, whether national or local, is one the value of which is universally acknowledged. In the words of the celebrated Dr Johnson, "whatever makes the past, the distant, or the future, predominate over the present, advances us in the dignity of thinking beings." In Scotland, in particular, intense interest in the past has always been a national characteristic. "That is the mark of the Scot," says R.L. Stevenson in *Weir of Hermiston*, "that he stands in an attitude towards the past unthinkable in Englishmen, and remembers and cherishes the memory of his forebears, good and bad, and there burns alive in him a sense of identity with the dead, even to the twentieth generation."

Local history, in particular, whilst it deals with matters which are generally considered to be too trivial or unimportant to receive the attention of the national historian, nevertheless, by reason of the intimacy of its appeal, makes a special call on our attention. It supplements and enriches national history.

There is perhaps no district in Scotland, of equal historic interest, which has received such scant attention from local historians as has Kintyre. The little book by Peter Macintosh, printed in Campbeltown about 1850, interesting as it is as a record of old traditions, can scarcely be regarded as serious history. The work *Glencreggan*, by the English clergyman who wrote under the pen name of Cuthbert Bede, about the same time as Macintosh wrote, makes no claim to being more than a pleasant tourist's guide, incorporating some fragments of local history collected by the author during his fleeting visits to the district. Short sketches, not always reliable in their details, are to be found in the *Old* and *New Statistical Accounts* of the parishes, which publications are, in any case, not easily accessible to present-day readers.

The present work had its origin in a desire on the part of the author to obtain a fuller knowledge of the history of his native district, a desire stimulated by the praiseworthy efforts of the Kintyre Antiquarian Society in recent years. Failing to obtain much assistance from modern publications he turned to the original sources, without, at first, having had any idea of proceeding to publication. On the advice of some Kintyre friends, however, he finally decided to expand the notes into a book, in the hope that the material might be of equal interest to others, and the result is now placed before his readers.

It was decided, partly from reasons of personal interest, and also because of the greater accessibility of records, to confine the account to the events of what must be regarded as one of the most important centuries of Kintyre history, the seventeenth. This century saw the displacement of the old lords of the land, the Macdonalds, by the new and powerful family of the Argylls; it witnessed the stirring episodes of the Montrose Campaign - the Colkitto raids, the campaign of General David Leslie, the unforgettable events of the siege and the massacre at Dunaverty, the epidemic of Plague. It was also the century of the Lowland Plantation, an event which has left such a deep impress on the racial and cultural life of its people, and of the ill-fated rising of the Earl of Argyll. Perhaps the most important of all its events was the coming of the Lowlanders, and it is hoped that the information which it has been possible to obtain on the details of this event, and which now appears in print for the first time, may be of special interest to those Kintyreans who, either at home or abroad, are descendants of the pioneers of the plantation.

The principal claim made for the short account here presented is that it is based on a study of contemporary documents. The author has also deposited in the public library of Campbeltown typed copies of rentals for the years 1633, 1636, 1643, 1651-52, 1666, 1678 and 1683-84, and a few other documents transcribed from originals in H.M. Register House and the National Library of Scotland.

have great pleasure in acknowledging help and encouragement from many sources. I am indebted to Mr Duncan Colville, Kilmaho, for the loan of various papers, and for his kindly reading the manuscript of this book, and making useful suggestions; to Mr Archibald McEachran, Kilblaan, who placed at my disposal his stores of local historical knowledge, and to Mr Latimer McInnes, Briarlea, Campbeltown, for much kind encouragement.

To the authorities of the Free Library, Campbeltown, I have to return thanks for the loan of books and manuscripts. To Dr William Angus and the staff of the Historical Department of H.M. Register House, Edinburgh, and to Dr Henry Meikle and the staff of the National Library of Scotland, I owe many favours and much assistance, at all times generously and courteously given.

CHAPTER 1
INTRODUCTION

The peninsula of Kintyre is the forty-mile-long breakwater of the Firth of Clyde, which extends from the isthmus of Tarbert in the north, to the rocky headland of the Mull in the south, and which, in the quaint phraseology of Camden's *Britannia*, "thrusteth itself greedily towards Ireland." From the point of the Mull to the nearest point on the Antrim coast, the distance is less than twelve miles. Across these narrow waters of the North Channel there must have been a traffic in both men and merchandise long before the age of recorded history, and no part of Scotland has had such a close connection with Ireland, a connection exhibited in the place-names and personal names of Kintyre, and in its folk-songs and folklore.

The discovery of a Neolithic flint workshop at Campbeltown, some forty years ago, has disclosed the fact that this was the first known locality on the Scottish mainland to receive human colonisation, and the district has most probably been peopled uninterruptedly from that far distant time down to the present day. The name Kintyre is from Gaelic *ceann*, a head, and *tir*, land, and the meaning of the word is accordingly obvious. Adamnan, the biographer of St Columba, called it *Caput Regionis*, a name which has the same meaning of "headland." To Ptolemy, the Greek topographer of the second century, it was *Epidion Akron*, that is, the nose or promontory of the *Epidii*, an ancient British tribe who inhabited it at the time he wrote. The root of this tribal name is the ancient Celtic *epos*, a horse, and the *Epidii* were probably so called because they had taken the horse to be the badge or totem of their tribe, or because they were horse breeders or trainers. The word *epos* is Brythonic Celtic, and would appear to indicate that these people spoke a form of Celtic more akin to Welsh than to Gaelic which, in fact, is the view now held of the language of the ancient Britons by such scholars as Watson and MacBain.

From a reference in Tacitus it is probably the case that the district was visited by the Roman general, Agricola, in the summer of A.D.82. He is supposed to have gone on a tour of reconnaissance, but, on finding the west coast unsuitable for the passage of his legions he returned, and Kintyre knew no Roman conquest or occupation, and so exhibits no Roman remains.

The Ancient Britons, or Picts, as they came to be called, were most probably the people who have left material remains in the shape of the *duns*, or stone hill forts, of which there are more than forty in Kintyre, including one specimen in excellent preservation at Borgadale, near the Mull. They were also most probably the people who erected the many standing stones found in the district.

The Scots, a Gaelic-speaking people from Ireland, had begun to colonise Kintyre during the early centuries of the Christian era, and about the year A.D. 500 they came, under their leader Fergus, and founded the small kingdom of Dalriada in the west of Scotland. Two important results followed on their coming. The first was the introduction of the Gaelic form of Celtic, which gradually replaced the

Brythonic form previously spoken by the older inhabitants, and which became later the language of the court and the people all over Scotland. The Gael and the Gaelic both came from Ireland, most probably to Kintyre in the first instance. W.J. Watson, basing his conclusions on a study of the language of our oldest place-names, makes the remark, "I hold with Kuno Meyer that no Gael ever set foot on British soil, except from a vessel that had put out from Ireland."

Another result of the coming of the Scots, and one of the greatest importance, was the introduction of Christianity. The Scots themselves were at least nominally Christians on their first arrival, and it is possible that Kintyre may have been visited by Christian missionaries before St Columba arrived in A.D. 563. The considerable number of its place names beginning with *Kil*, from Latin *cella*, a cell or church, testifies to the activity of these early missionaries, some of whom came from Ireland and some from Iona.

During the period of the Kingdom of Dalriada, Kintyre formed one of its *tuaths*, or tribal territories, others being Cowal and Lorne. The *tuath* of Kintyre was possessed by the tribe of Gabran or Gowran, the grandson of King Fergus, and it saw a good deal of civil war and tribal dissension. In the year A.D.712 it was attacked by Sealbach, leader of the tribe of Lorne, who in that year as the Irish annals disclose, besieged *Aberte*, the principal stronghold of Gabran; this being the first mention in history of the famous Kintyre fortress of Dunaverty. From the tribe of Gabran was descended Kenneth MacAlpin, the first king of the united kingdom of the Picts and Scots, and ancestor of the long line of subsequent Scottish kings. Kintyre may thus justly claim that it was the cradle of the Scottish monarchy. The Scots, unlike their predecessors the Picts, have left no material remains in the district.

A Norse settlement of Kintyre began, probably about the year A.D. 800, and appears to have been fairly extensive, especially around the sheltered harbours of the east coast. Its existence is not revealed by any material remains, for the Norse, like the Scots, left no monuments or inscriptions; but it is made evident from the existence in the district of Norse, and Norse-Gaelic place-names, such as Amod, Ormsary, Borgadale, Cattadale, Sanda, Uigle, Smerby, Torrisdale and Skipness. These are scattered throughout the whole length of the peninsula, while names beginning in *Penny*, although Gaelic in origin, clearly date back to the days of the Scat or tax in silver pennies which had to be paid to the Norse overlords. Some of the old Kintyre personal names, such as Torquil, Imar or Ivar, Rannald, and Godfrey, also testify to the ancient connection between the two races, which appear to have intermarried freely, producing the mixed race known as the *Gallgael*, or foreign Gael; so called by the pure Celts of those parts where the Norse had not penetrated. They are stated to have spoken broken Gaelic in a *patois* which an Irish writer referred to as the *Giog-gog* of a Gallgael. The Kintyre Gallgael fought alongside the Danes or Norsemen, and against the Irish, at the famous battle of Clontarf in Ireland, in 1014.

Norse rule was sometimes exercised by a local lord, and sometimes by the Earls of Orkney, but in 1098 the King of Norway, Magnus Barefoot, invaded the West

Highlands, and successfully consolidated all the scattered Norse possessions under his rule. Kintyre was regarded by the Norse as being, next to Man, the most valuable of the Western Isles, and King Magnus claimed it as one of these and as part of his dominions, by having a small ship dragged overland across the isthmus of Tarbert, he himself holding the tiller.

Magnus Barefoot is stated to have expelled, as a result of his successful campaign in 1098, many of the Gallgael chiefs from their possessions. Among those so expropriated was a chief named Gillebride, father of the famous warrior Somerled. The latter, however, in the early part of the twelfth century, turned the tables and drove out these newcomers from Kintyre and from other parts of Argyllshire. He then apparently endeavoured to set up an independent kingdom of his own, and so came into conflict with the Scottish kings. The claims of Magnus Barefoot and Somerled to Kintyre were never, however, admitted by these kings, and when King David I founded the Abbey of Holyrood, in 1128, he bestowed upon it, among other endowments, the half of his tithe, pleas, and gains of Kintyre and Argyll. A little later he bestowed the other half of the dues on the Abbey of Dunfermline, but in this latter case there is a proviso that it would be paid when it was received, which appears to indicate quite clearly that he was not then in receipt of these revenues. In the year 1164 Somerled led an expedition against Malcolm, King of Scotland, and was killed at Renfrew on the Clyde. Local tradition states that he was buried in Saddell Abbey in Kintyre, which had been founded in the year 1160 by his son Reginald.

After the death of Somerled his Kintyre lands were inherited by Reginald, and by the descendants of the latter during the century 1200-1300. They called themselves Lords of Islay (*Dominus de Ile*), after the island where they maintained their headquarters. The thirteenth century was one of great importance in the district. During that century the old Celtic Church of Iona gave way to that of Rome, of which latter church Reginald and his descendants were strong supporters and generous patrons. Although Reginald gets the credit for having founded the Cistercian Abbey of Saddell in 1160, his father Somerled may have also had some share in it. Reginald also founded the Benedictine Abbey at Iona, about the year 1200, and a convent of nuns there. He gave liberal gifts of cattle and money to the monks of Paisley, and he himself finally became a monk, and his wife Fonia a nun. His son Donald repeated his father's gifts to Paisley, and he and his wife also embraced the religious life.

Angus Mor, son of Donald, was the first of Somerled's descendants to acknowledge the superiority of the King of Scotland over his Kintyre lands, for when, in or before the year 1249, he bestowed the church of Kilkerran in Kintyre on the Abbey of Paisley, the gift was made "for the weal of the soul of my Lord Alexander, the illustrious King of Scots, and of his son Alexander," the reference being to Alexander II and Alexander III. He also named his eldest son Alexander, in honour of the King, and this would appear to mark the first use of this name, or its Gaelic form

Alaster, among the West Highlanders. After the surrender of all Norse territory to the King of Scotland in 1266, Angus became a vassal of the Scottish king for his island possessions as well, and, as a great baron of Scotland, sat in the Parliament which settled the Crown on the Maid of Norway in 1284. It was most probably during his time that the parish boundaries were settled, and the earliest of the old parish churches built, the ruins of which can still be seen at Kilcolmkill and other places. They probably replaced the smaller churches or chapels, ruins of which also exist here and there in Kintyre, and of which there was probably one in each of the old townships or *ballys*.

Angus Og succeeded his father Angus Mor. He is the chief who is entitled, somewhat prematurely, Lord of the Isles in Sir Walter Scott's poem of that name. He gave Bruce refuge and hospitality in his Castle of Dunaverty in the summer or autumn of 1306, and later brought a strong force of West Highlanders to assist him at the crowning victory at Bannockburn. His elder brother, Alexander, had taken the side of the English, for which he was forfeited and imprisoned by King Robert, and is stated to have died in captivity in Dundonald Castle.

Angus Og was rewarded by King Robert with extensive grants of the forfeited estates of the Macdougalls of Lorn, but, in view of its strategic importance as the key to the Isles, the King caused him to surrender Kintyre, which he then bestowed upon Robert the Steward, the King's nephew. He also caused a new castle to be built at Tarbert, in a strong strategical position there, and appointed John de Lany its first Constable. De Lany's accounts of the castle of Tarbert for the year 1325 form the first complete *Exchequer Roll* of Scotland, and are of fascinating historical and antiquarian interest. King Robert was then living at Cardross on the Clyde, and the accounts reveal that he took a keen personal interest in the building, paid frequent visits to ascertain the progress made, and actually supervised personally the giving out of the piece-work contracts.

John, son of Angus Og, having acquired the Northern Isles by a marriage with their heiress Amie Macruarie, proceeded to take the title Lord of the Isles (*Dominus de Insularum*) , which was also borne by his three successors in the Lordship. Later he divorced his first wife Amie and married Margaret Stewart, daughter of King Robert II, who, as we have seen, had had the lands of Kintyre bestowed on him by Robert I. In 1377 King Robert II bestowed these lands on John, Lord of the Isles, and his wife Margaret, the King's daughter, so that they once more returned to the race of Somerled.

During the century of their power the princely house of the Lords of the Isles ruled as practically independent sovereigns. The maintained large and powerful fleets and navies, and had their own judges and judicial system. They even aspired to challenge the authority of the Scottish kings, and made separate treaties with the English monarchs. All the Stewart kings, from James I down to James IV, endeavoured to curb their power, and they finally fell, in the person of the last and weakest - John, fourth Lord - who was forfeited first in 1475, and finally, after a brief reinstatement, in 1493.

During their sway the lands of Kintyre had been given out in grant to several of their vassals, of whom the most important and most powerful were the Macdonalds of Dunnyveg and the Glens, otherwise known as the Macdonalds of Islay and Kintyre, and also as the Clan Iain Mhor, because they were descended from John Mor Tanister, a brother of Donald, second Lord of the Isles. This man had strengthened the position of his family by marrying, about the year 1400, Marjorie Bissett, heiress of the estate of the Glens in Antrim, a union which must have drawn closer still the connection between Kintyre and Ireland.

After the first forfeiture of John, 4th Lord of the Isles, in 1475, King James III took prompt steps to strengthen the position of the Crown in Kintyre. By the year 1481 a Sheriffdom of Tarbert had been created, when the comparatively limited powers of the Constable of Tarbert Castle became merged in the wider jurisdiction of the sheriff, which covered all North Kintyre. This Sheriffdom lasted down to 1633, when it was merged in that of Argyll, and all sixteenth century charters refer to Kintyre as being "in the Shire of Tarbert." In the same year, 1481, a Stewardry of South Kintyre, that is of the peninsula south of a line joining the modern town of Campbeltown to Machrihanish, was erected by the King, and Charles MacAlexander, or Macallaster, of Loup was appointed Steward, with headquarters in Dunaverty Castle, and received a grant in life-rent of forty merklands, mainly in South Kintyre. The Crown Steward had virtually the powers of a sheriff.

After the final forfeiture of 1493 King James IV took steps to fortify the remaining strongholds of the district, and to retain them in the keeping of his own servitors. In 1495 he placed the keeping of the Castle of Skipness in the hands of his Comptroller, Sir Duncan Forestare, who received a grant of lands in Skipness and the neighbourhood. In 1498 the old castle of Ardcardle, remains of which can still be seen near the modern fishing village of Carradale, was placed in charge of Sir Adam Reid of Starquhyte and Barskimming in Ayrshire, who was head of the Reids of North Ayrshire, and who also had a grant of lands in its vicinity.

King James himself visited the West Highlands in the summer of 1493, and on that occasion he bestowed the order of knighthood on John Cathanach Macdonald of Dunnyveg, who apparently took this honour as a portent that his lands in Kintyre, which he had lost at the forfeiture, as also the keeping of the ancestral Castle of Dunaverty, were to be restored to him. When, however, King James again visited Kintyre in the summer of 1494, he stayed at Dunaverty Castle, and, far from returning it to Macdonald, he installed his own governor and re-fortified it with cannon. At this Sir John appears to have taken mortal offence, and when the King was in his boat, preparatory to his departure, and attended by a small bodyguard only, Macdonald took the castle by surprise and hanged its governor over the walls in sight of the King. He then fled to the Glens of Antrim, but a few years later he and others of his family were betrayed by their kinsman, MacIain of Ardnamurchan. Their fate is recorded in the contemporary *Annals of Ulster* as follows:

"A great deed was done in this year by the King of Scotland, James Stewart. Eoin Mac Domhnail, King of the Foreigners' Isles (*i.e.* of the Gallgael), and Eoin Cathanach his son, and Raghnall the Red and Domhnail the Freckled, sons of Eoin Cathanach, were executed on one gallows the month before Lammas."

MacVurich, in his *Red book of Clanranald*, gives a somewhat different account of the number of those put to death, and does not include Sir John's father. He states that they were hanged on the Boroughmuir, and their bodies buried in the Church of St Francis in Edinburgh.

In 1498 King James IV again visited Kintyre, and caused a new castle to be built at Kilkerran, or the modern Campbeltown, some remains of which can still be seen by the loch-side. From it he issues several charters - *apud novum castrum in Kyntire* - in the summer of that year. While there, the King's attention appears to have been drawn to the condition of Saddell Abbey, then in a state of dissolution, and its lands appropriated by laymen. In order to restore the lands to the Abbey as a religious corporation, the King issued a precept to the Bishop of Aberdeen, Keeper of the Privy Seal, to expedite a charter confirming all previous grants of land from the time of Reginald downwards. The Abbey, however, was never reconstituted, and the last mention of any of its abbots occurs in the year 1467. Some ten years later it was described as having been deserted by its monks from a time beyond the memory of man, and a new charter by King James annexed its lands to the Bishopric of Argyll, with power to the Bishop to build castles. This he appears to have begun to do at once, for a Royal letter, dated February 1511-12, reveals that the Castle of Saddell, which still stands, had been erected by that date.

After the forfeiture of 1493 Archibald, 2nd Earl of Argyll, the same Earl who led the right wing of the Scottish army at Flodden, and who fell there in September 1513, was appointed Crown Chamberlain of the forfeited lands. In July 1505 the Earl, accompanied by the Bishop, came to Ceannloch-Kilkerran, and there drew up a rental of the Crown lands of Kintyre, and a set of accounts of these lands. This is the earliest Kintyre rental in existence, and is of great historical value and interest, in that it gives in details the names and extents of each holding, the names of their occupants, and the rents paid by each. From this rental we are enabled to obtain a clear picture of the principal Kintyre families in the fifteenth century, some notes on which are now given.

The *Macallasters of Loup* occupied the estate of that name on West Loch Tarbert, and had also tacks of other holdings in Kintyre. Branches were the Macallasters of Tarbert, and the Clan Allaster Beg of Arran. As we have seen, Charles Macallaster of Loup was Crown Steward of Kintyre in 1481, and the family was in existence down to the nineteenth century, but are now represented by that of Macallaster-Somerville of Loup and Kennox in Ayrshire.

The *Macrannaldbane*, later Macdonalds of Largie, possessed, in 1505, these lands by charter from the Lords of the Isles, and were descended from Ranald Bane, a son of John Mor Tanister and Marjorie Bissett of the Glens. They were represented in 1505 by Donald Macrannaldbane, who had taken part in the insurrection of The

1. In the graveyard at Kilcolmkill, Southend, a much-weathered monument carved with the Arms of Ralston and commemorating William Ralston of that Ilk, a leader of the Lowland Plantation in Kintyre, who died c.1691.

2. James Graham, 5th Earl and 1st Marquis of Montrose (1612-50), in 1649.

3. Archibald Campbell, 8th Earl and Marquis of Argyll (1607-61), c.1644.

4. Saddell Castle stands on the shore of Kilbrannan Sound at the mouth of Saddell Water. At the end of the 16th C. Saddell passed to the Earls of Argyll, and was leased to William Ralston of that Ilk in 1650.

Donald Dhu in 1501, but had received a pardon under the Privy Seal, and was allowed to retain his lands. His descendants lost them for a time during Montrose's wars of the seventeenth century, in which they took the Royalist side, but had them restored in 1661, and later descendants are still in possession of the estate.

The *Mackays of Arnicle and Ugadale* were one of the oldest Kintyre families of consequence, and possessed a genealogy going back to the eleventh century. In 1329 Gilchrist Mackay received a charter of his lands of Ugadale from King Robert the Bruce, having previously been in possession of other lands, probably of Arnicle. In 1505 the family head was John Mackay More, who was Mair of Fee, or Sheriff Officer, of North Kintyre. The male line became extinct about 1680, and the family was absorbed by marriage into that of the Macneills of Tirfergus and Lossit, who then acquired the Ugadale estate in addition to their own.

The *Maceachans of Tangy* are a family of which we have little early record, but it is most probable that they were feuars of the church lands of Skierchanzie, or Kilkenzie, which in pre-Reformation days belonged to Iona. As church lands were not detailed in the rental of 1505, this connection cannot be traced therein, but the names of several of the family occur as tacksmen of secular lands in the same locality. In 1623 Charles MacEachan of Tangy, who was later factor to Lord Lorne, received a charter of the lands of Tangy and others from the Bishop of Argyll. They retained their estate down to 1709, when it was conveyed to Robert Semple.

The *Maceachrans of Kilellan* were the Mairs of Fee of South Kintyre, and were represented in 1505 by Colin of Kilellan, who, in 1499, had received a charter of his lands of Kilellan, and of his office of Mair of Fee, from King James IV. He is almost certainly the Colin who, with his spouse Katherine, is commemorated in the fine but injured Celtic Cross which lies in Kilkerran cemetery, and most probably was either a brother or nephew of Ivar Maceachran, Rector of Kylreacan (probably Kilneachtan in Islay), who is commemorated on the Town Cross of Campbeltown. They lost their estate temporarily during the Montrose wars, but recovered it from the Marquis of Argyll in 1659, and Kilellan was possessed by them down to about 1740, when the male line came to an end in Neil Maceachran.

The *Macneills of Carskey* are the earliest family of that name to occur in the record, and were represented in 1505 by Hector Mac Ian MacGillecallum, who was occupier in that year of the 12 merkland of Carskey and the 4 merkland of the Mull. The family of Macneill held Carskey in the male line down to about 1824, when Colonel Malcolm Macneill died. Macneills of Tirfergus and Lossit, a related family, do not appear in the 1505 lists, nor before the middle of the seventeenth century.

The *MacVurichs*, or *MacMurchys*, were the Bards or Seannachies of the Clan Donald in Kintyre, and were represented in 1505 by John MacVurich, who occupied, free of rent, in return for his services as Bard, an 8 merkland comprising Brecklate, Gartloskan, Cattadale, Gartvain, and Keprigan. Later in the century they disappeared as bards, but individuals of the name, most probably descendants, occur as tacksmen in later rentals.

Macoshenogs were Harpers to the Clan Donald in Kintyre, and in 1505 were represented by Murdoch, or Muriach, who held rent-free for his service as Harper a 4 merkland comprising Brunerican, Amod, Drumnarianach, Dalsmirren, and Lagnadamh. Descendants were later proprietors of the estate of Lephenstrath, which they retained down to the year 1819. They changed the family name to Shannon.

The *Omeys of Kilcolmkill* were an ecclesiastical family, one of which, Cornelius Omey, was Rector of Kilblaan parish at the Reformation of 1560, and two others were among the early Protestant ministers of Kintyre. Duncan Omey became minister of Kilcolmkill in 1611, and Donald Omey of Kilkerran about 1632. In 1505 the family was represented by John Omey, or Ofey, who was tacksman of Cristlach, Kilhattan, and Dalnaeccleis. In 1622 Duncan Omey received a charter of the lands of Kilcolmkill from the Bishop of Argyll, and the family held this estate until 1819, when it was sold by Samuel Omey, the last of the line.

Of the above, only Macrannaldbane of Largie and MacEachran of Kilellan are stated in the rental to have possessed charters to their lands in 1505, and although these "sheepskins" gradually came into use, at the date in question, and in days antecedent to it, little value appears to have been placed on them in the Highlands. Most of the land appears to have been held by tacksmen in what was called "native tenancy," that is a kind of hereditary tenancy in which the rentaller was allowed to continue so long as he paid his dues, and rendered his services to his chief. How deeply rooted in the soil these Kintyre tacksmen were may be realised from the fact that many remained in the same holdings from the year 1505 down to the nineteenth century.

It is clear from a study of this rental that there was no single dominant clan in Kintyre, in the sense of a single chief and his following who were his own kith and kin, and who bore his surname. There was a multiplicity of surnames, although that of the leading family - Macdonald - does not appear in the 1505 rental at all. This may be due to the fact that the Macdonalds of Dunnyveg were under forfeiture, that those of Largie did not use the surname at this date, and that the family of Sanda had not yet been founded. The more important of the families mentioned above no doubt functioned as small clans or clanlets. Thus in 1594 we find the Macneills of Carskey executing a Bond of friendship with the Macdonalds of Dunnyveg, apparently on a footing of equality. Intermarriage between these families was frequent, and most of them were related to their neighbours.

Fresh assedations of the Kintyre lands were made by the Crown in 1506, on three-year leases, and again in 1541, after they had been inalienably annexed to the Crown in 1540, a state in which they remained down to 1617. In the rentals of these two years, which are still extant, it is seen that all the old tenants, excepting those of Clan Iain Mhor, were retained on the land. A few incomers are to be noted. In 1506 Andrew Macfarlane, chief of the Macfarlanes of Arrochar, received a tack of lands at Askomel near Kilkerran, and in 1542 Robert, Duncan, and Andrew Macfarlane received Kintyre tacks under the Crown. In 1541 a Governorship of

Kintyre had been created, and Alexander Cunningham, Master of Glencairn, appointed Governor with power to exercise the offices of Sheriff and Justiciar, and with headquarters in Dunaverty Castle. The Macfarlanes were related to his family, and their receiving these tacks may have been due to his influence.

Another family, whose coming to Kintyre during this century was of far greater consequence than that of the Macfarlanes, was that of the Campbells of Argyll. As early as 1502 Sir Duncan Forestare had surrendered his grant of the lands of Skipness into the hands of Archibald, the second Earl, and these lands were re-granted in 1541. In 1576 they also obtained the superiority of the church lands of Iona at Skierchanzie, and in 1584 of those of St Ninian's, otherwise known as of Macharioch and Sanda, which had belonged to the Priory of Whithorn in Galloway. Early in the seventeenth century they rounded off their control of Kintyre by obtaining a charter of the lands of the Lordship itself. The circumstances under which the Argylls came to receive this last and greatest grant, and the consequences which resulted from it, form the main theme of this book, and will be related in due course. Before doing so, however, it will be necessary to consider in some detail the main course of events in Kintyre during the latter half of the sixteenth century, for it was in these that the events of the seventeenth century had their roots, and it is by them that they can best be explained.

CHAPTER II
THE LAST MACDONALDS OF DUNNYVEG

As has been already stated, after the affair of the hanging of the King's governor at Dunaverty in 1494, two of the family of Dunnyveg escaped to their estate of the Glens of Antrim, and eluded capture there. Alexander, the eldest, appears to have remained in the Glens until the death of King James IV at Flodden in 1513, but returned to Scotland after that date, and took part in some of the stirring adventures of the period. For a time he was received back into favour in the place of his rival Archibald, 4th Earl of Argyll, and in 1532 was actually put in command of a Scottish army of seven or eight thousand men sent to Ireland to fight the English.

It was, however, his son James who restored the house of Dunnyveg to its former prestige and power. He had been noted by King James V as the most likely leader of the West Highlanders, and had been brought to Edinburgh, and his education entrusted to Alexander Henderson, Dean of Holyrood, under the eyes of the King. During the Regency he was in favour and, in 1545, received a grant of a great tract of lands in Knapdale, Kintyre, and elsewhere, to be incorporated into the Barony of Bar in North Kintyre. He was killed in Ireland in 1565, fighting against the O'Neills. His wife was Agnes Campbell, sister of the Earl of Argyll, who after his death received a gift of the Ward of the Barony of Bar; but a few years later this amiable and accomplished lady, known in the English annals as the Lady of Kintyre, married Turlogh O'Neill, afterwards Earl of Tyrone. When she set out to marry O'Neill in the island of Rathlin, she had a bodyguard of seven hundred of the men of Kintyre.

It is with Angus MacDonald of Dunnyveg, son of James Macdonald and the Lady Agnes Campbell, that our history is, however, more immediately concerned. From his time began the deadly enmity between the Macdonalds and the Campbells which fills such a large page of West Highland history. His first feud, however, was not with the Campbells, but with his brother-in-law, Sir Lachlan Maclean of Duart, whose sister he had married, and had arisen over a dispute in connection with the possession of the Rinns of Islay. They alternately devastated each other's lands, pillaging, slaying, and burning. Macdonald employed English mercenaries to fight Maclean, and the latter hired one hundred Spaniards from the *Florida*, one of the stranded ships of the Spanish Armada, to fight Macdonald. Their adherents also took sides. Following the Macdonalds were the Clanranald, Clanian of Ardnamurchan, Macleods of Lewis, Macneills of Gigha, Macallasters of Loup, and Macfies of Colonsay, and on the side of the Macleans were Macleods of Harris, Macneills of Barra, Mackinnons, and Macquarries. The whole of the West Highlands was set aflame and, as an old historian said, "they did vex constantly one another with slaughters and outrages to the destruction almost of their countries and people." In this half century there is no doubt but that the West Highlands reached the lowest depths of misery and disorder. The very churches did not escape destruction, and as late as 1635, when the Earl of Antrim made a bid to obtain the lands of Kintyre, one of the conditions agreed to was that he would repair "the ruinatt churches."

To such a state of affairs the Scottish government could not turn a deaf ear. In 1589 Macdonald and Maclean received pardons under the Privy Seal to enable them to go to Edinburgh and discuss means of settlement. Arrived there, they were, in violation of their safe conduct passes, placed in prison and brought to trial, but refused to plead, and threw themselves on the King's mercy. Finally they were liberated on paying fines which, according to one account, amounted in Angus Macdonald's case to £20,000. James Macdonald, son of Angus, was retained as a hostage, and Campbell of Calder was made surety for Angus Macdonald, and Campbell of Ardkinglas for Maclean.

In 1592, however, Calder was assassinated, and this restraint on Macdonald's conduct was thereby removed. In 1594 a summons of treason was served on him, and he was forfeited. Whether the sentence of forfeiture was actually put in execution at this time is, however, doubtful, for some years after the date we are now considering he is still referred to as Lord of Kintyre, and he was in actual possession of a good part of its lands in 1605, but probably only as a Crown tenant.

In 1596 the government decided to take more drastic measures for the subjection of the Highland chiefs by the dispatch of a military expedition. Formidable preparations were made, and the array of the kingdom called out. These brought about the speedy subjection of all the chiefs except Angus Macdonald, so that the expedition became one directed against him and his Kintyre vassals. The government had allowed his son James to return to the West Highlands, in order to persuade his father to submit, and Angus, hoping to get better terms, had surrendered all his lands to his son, who returned to Edinburgh with terms, but too late to prevent the dispatch of the expedition.

Under the command of Sir William Stewart of Houston as King's Lieutenant, it reached Lochhead-Kilkerran in late October, and on 1st November 1596 Sir William held a court there. Angus Macdonald, attended by his principal Kintyre tenants, made his submission, and a roll of the tenantry was prepared. "Quhilkis personis and everie ane of thame being present in proper persone offerit thair dewtefull obedience to the said Sir William Stewart of Houston ... and faithfullie promesit to be ansuerabill to his Hienes lawis, and to observe kepe and fulfill the samin, ilkane for thair awin pairtis respective as becummis dewtefull and obedient subjectis, and for the better keping and observeing Farquhar McCay, John McGacharne, and Hector McNeill, thrie of the chief of thair clanis, faithfullie promittit band and obleist thame ... to be transportit be him (Sir William) to the law cuntrey; and thair to remain during his Majesteis will and pleasure." The three hostages were John Mackay of the Ugadale family, John Maceachran of Kilellan, and Hector Macneill of Carskey. As an example of the state to which the country had been brought by these disorders the King's Lieutenant reported that, out of 139 merklands in North Kintyre, 36½ were waste, and out of 205 merklands in South Kintyre 45 were waste.

In the following year, 1597, Angus Maconald went to Edinburgh to hear the King's will, which was that he was required to find security for the arrears of the Crown rents, to remove his clan and followers from Kintyre and the Rinns of Islay, to confine himself to other parts of Islay, and to surrender the Castle of Dunnyveg to the King's men before the 20th May.

Matters were now complicated by a sudden claim to the Kintyre estates, made by James Macdonald of Dunluce, an Irish cousin of Angus, who attempted to claim these lands on the grounds of the alleged illegitimacy of Angus. Dunluce was invited to Edinburgh by King James VI where, although he spoke no English, his handsome carriage and gallant demeanour made him the favourite of the hour. The Privy Council, however, rejected his claim, and he returned home a disappointed man, albeit with a salute of guns from the Castle rock. As some return for the trouble and expense to which he had been put, King James gave him a grant of thirty merklands in Kintyre, his principal seat to be at Culilongart in Glenbreckrie, and bestowed upon him the Order of Knighthood. In his charter he is referred to as *eques auratus de Culilongart*. He did not live to enjoy even this small favour, for he was assassinated in Ireland a few months later, a not unfitting retribution for the treachery which he had meditated on his Scottish cousin.

In 1598 James Macdonald, son of Angus, now Sir James Macdonald of Knockrinsay in Islay, who was still retained in Edinburgh Castle as a hostage for his father Angus, was again liberated, in order to try to bring the father to terms. Angus was at this time residing in his house of Askomel at Ceannloch-Kilkerran, where he had given refuge to the two sons of the tutor of Loup, whose father had been slain by young Macallaster of Loup. Sir James MacDonald took sides with Macallaster, and coming with him, accompanied by an armed following, to the House of Askomel at the dead of night, he set fire to it, although he knew that both his father and mother were inside. The father escaped badly burned, but was seized by his son, put in chains, and taken a prisoner to Smerby, where he was detained for several months. In excuse of this atrocious act it has been stated that Sir James actually possessed a written warrant in the King's name for the arrest, if not for the assassination, of his father, but the truth has never properly come to light.

The next year, 1599, Sir James made offers to settle the longstanding dispute on his own behalf. He offered to make the whole of his clan and followers leave Kintyre, so as to place these lands at the King's disposal, and promised to refrain from molesting any new tenantry introduced on to them. He also offered to surrender the Castle of Dunnyveg in Islay, to be placed under a Crown governor, as well as sixty merks of land in its vicinity, for the support of its governor and garrison. He then asked that the remaining three hundred merklands of Islay should be granted to him in heritage at a duty of £2 the merkland, out of which he agreed to pay his father Angus a yearly pension of one thousand merks. These offers, which appear very fair, came, however, to nothing. The forces against the Macdonalds were too strong. Campbell of Calder coveted Islay, and the Earl of Argyll coveted Kintyre, and both finally had their wishes satisfied.

In 1603 Angus Macdonald, fearing that his son Sir James was plotting his destruction, had him arrested by the Earl of Argyll as agent for the government, and from this date until 1615, a period of twelve long years, Sir James remained a prisoner in Edinburgh Castle.

In 1605 it was found necessary to send another military expedition to Lochkilkerran, this time under Lord Scone, Comptroller of Scotland, as King's Lieutenant. Before the expedition set out, Angus Macdonald met the Comptroller in Glasgow, and made certain fresh offers, the terms of which have been lost, so that it cannot be said whether they were more comprehensive than those made by his son Sir James in 1599 or not.   Lord Scone reached Lochkilkerran in September, and on the third day of that month held a court "on the hill called Knockbae," similar to that held by Sir William Stewart in 1596, again received the submission of Angus Macdonald and his vassals, and prepared a fresh roll of the latter, which shows that all the old Highland tenants of Kintyre were still on its lands in 1605. Lord Scone's report showed that a further deterioration of the land had taken place since 1596, and that in 1605, out of 151½ merklands in North Kintyre, 62 were now waste, and out of 203 merklands in South Kintyre, 51 were waste.

During the next year Angus Macdonald addressed the Crown in two documents, protesting that he had received no answer to his offers of the previous year, and pointing out that he had now paid up all his arrears of rent and feu-duties, and had received the Comptroller's discharge for the same.   He faithfully promised to continue to do so in future, and also "to set fordward and asist sic reformatioune of the barbaritie of thir cuntries of the Wast and North Iyles of His Majestie's Kingdome of Scotland, as it sall pleas his hienes best to devyse."

But for the Macdonalds the die had already been cast, for in November of this year, 1606, Lord Scone and the Earl of Argyll drew up at Perth a set of conditions on which the Earl was to receive a feu of the Crown lands of Kintyre. The Earl agreed to pay for these lands according to the best rental of the time of King James V, to find caution to make his new tenants keep the peace, to appear at the King's courts, to find "landit gentlemen of the in-country" as cautioners for the King's duties, to take on feu other lands of the Isles on similar conditions, to expel all broken men of the surnames of Macdonald and Maclean, and to set none of the lands to anyone of the name of Macdonald.   In the next year a letter, unsigned and undated, was sent to the Privy Council, requesting that the lands of Kintyre should be given to the Earl for his services in subduing the Macgregors and other turbulent clans.   The Council considered it, and although expressing the opinion that trouble would arise from the Macdonalds, "scoolmaisters and fosteraris of all barbaritie," if the request were granted, nevertheless considered that the Earl was the most suitable person to possess these lands, in view of the fact that he held the heritable offices of Justice-Colonel and Chamberlain.   A charter in feu-farm issued in due course, and the vexed question was settled at last, Argyll receiving a legal title to the lands of Kintyre which, as Sir James Macdonald stated, had been in the possession of his forebears for six hundred years.

Some show of resistance appears to have been made by Angus Macdonald on receipt of this news, but this seems to have come to nothing, and Gregory expresses the opinion that it was probably intended to prevent the men of the Lowlands from following a royal commissioner to the Isles.

On receipt of the news that the lands of Kintyre had passed to the Argylls Sir James Macdonald made an attempt to escape from his imprisonment in Edinburgh Castle, but failed, and was re-taken. In 1609 he was brought to trial for breaking ward, and for the attack on his father's house at Askomel in 1598 - a charge of treason. His own father and mother testified against him through the Earl of Argyll, but did not appear at the court in person. He was found guilty and sentenced to be beheaded, but the sentence was never carried out because, it has been surmised, he had in his possession a warrant from the King for the arrest and imprisonment of his father in 1598, and that, in return for suppressing this evidence, the exposure of which King James dared not face, he was given a promise that the capital sentence would not be carried out, and that he might ultimately receive a pardon. He remained in Edinburgh Castle under sentence of death until 1615, the year in which the Islay rebellion broke out. On hearing, according to his own statement, that Campbell of Calder, who was his own brother-in-law, had received a warrant to have the sentence carried out, he made another attempt to escape. This time he was successful, and, making his way through the Perthshire Highlands, he soon got among his own clansmen in the west, and reached the Island of Islay. There he and his followers retook the Castle of Dunnyveg by a stratagem.

Sir James then proceeded to Kintyre, through which he sent the fiery cross, and his followers captured what Gregory calls "the King's Castle at Kinloch," which must have been the new castle built by the Earl of Argyll, on the site still called the Castlehill, a year or two before, and after he got his charter of the Kintyre lands. This rebellion, however, was ultimately suppressed, and Sir James had to flee, first to Galway in Ireland, and later to Spain. There, by a strange turn of fate, he foregathered a few years later with his old rival, who had now also fallen into disfavour, and had suffered forfeiture and exile. It is pleasant to record that they buried the hatchet, and perhaps even entered into a joint plot for the future. In 1620 Sir James Macdonald was recalled by King James, granted a pardon, and awarded an annual pension of one thousand gold merks. So far as is known he never returned to Scotland but died in London, and is said to have been buried in St Martin's church there.

After his escape in 1615 Sir James wrote a number of letters to the Bishop of Argyll, the Earls of Craufurd and Caithness, and other Scottish noblemen, explaining his reasons for breaking ward, mainly the danger to his life from Calder, and expressing his regret at having had to do so, and his desire to faithfully serve His Majesty as a loyal subject. At his trial in 1609 he was described as "a monster of iniquity from his youth upwards,", but these letters give no indication of his having possessed such a character. They indicate, on the contrary, a man possessed of a considerable sense of dry humour, and of an innate kindliness of heart which was perhaps warped by the barbarity of the age and circumstances in which he had to live. He makes kindly enquiries after his friends, and in particular after his wife, Margaret Campbell, who had sat by his side during his trial in 1609. His whimsical humour appears in a letter to the Earl of Tullibardine, who had been sent on the hunt after him when he escaped. "Truly the tyme hes beine, when I wald never a luiked thatt your father sone suld persew me so hardly of my lyfe ... bot I am much obleist to your lordship, for in faith ye maid me to be ane better fuitt-man, in one hour, nor I thocht to have beine in ane yeir." He was clearly proud of his prowess in capturing Dunnyveg Castle, and explains his tactics on that occasion in a letter to the Earl of Craufurd. "I trust in God," he states, "that all the Campbells in Scotland, without His Majestie's power, shall not recover it so long as they live."

He was a man of considerable culture and reading, and in the same letter to Craufurd deplores the loss of his books. Some had apparently to be left in Edinburgh when he escaped, but others were lost "at the onset in Atholl." He requests the Earl to be good enough to try to recover them for him: "the thrie conversiones of England, Burne's book, and it that Phillip sett out on the controverted heades, it ye saw Makcartney wrotte, the Mekle old Cornikle, in wrett." The first three appear to have been theological works, and the last a history in manuscript. Sir James Macdonald was the last of the male line of the old leading family of the Macdonalds of Kintyre. His father Angus is said to have died at Rothesay in October 1614, and to have been buried at Saddell.

CHAPTER III

THE ERECTION OF THE BURGH OF LOCHHEAD

The two military expeditions to Lochkilkerran in 1596 and 1605 do not appear to have achieved results in proportion to the time, trouble, and expense incurred in dispatching them.   In the year 1597, however, a step was taken which, although the times prevented it from having immediate results, was destined to have far-reaching consequences.   In that year the Scottish Parliament passed an Act which decreed that "our soverane Lord has for the better entertaining and continuing of policy within the Highlands and Isles statute and ordained that there be erected and built three burghs and burgh towns in the most convenient and commodious parts meet for the same: to wit: one in Kintyre, another in Lochaber, and the third in Lewis, to which burghs and the inhabitants thereof our Sovereign Lord and Estates aforesaid shall grant all privileges which His Highness or his predecessors has granted to any other burghs or the inhabitants thereof within his realm ... to be holden in free burgage of his Highness in such form and manner as His Majesty's most noble progenitors of worthy memory has granted of old to the erection of other burghs of his realm".   The burghs so created were Stornoway, Fort William, and Campbeltown or Lochhead.   The intention was to make all three Royal burghs, but, of the three, only Campbeltown attained to that status a century later.

No steps were taken to put this project into execution in Kintyre until the Earl of Argyll obtained a charter to its lands in 1607.   This was Archibald the seventh earl, known to Highlanders as *Gilleasbeg Gruamach*, or Archibald the Grim.   He was born in 1575, the son of Colin the sixth Earl and Annas Keith, widow of the Regent Moray.   From his early youth he had been employed by the Government as its agent in suppressing rebellious clans, and in endeavouring to maintain law and order in the Highlands.   While engaged in these duties he and his relations had acquired great estates, and the Campbells doubtlessly acted on the scriptural adage that it is not wise to muzzle the ox that treadeth out the corn.   But to say that personal gain was their main or only motive is as untrue and as unfair as to say that the Macdonalds were monsters and schoolmasters of iniquity, as they were described by the Government of the day; and there can be no doubt that the pacification and civilisation of the West Highlands, the appalling state of which in the sixteenth century has been already referred to, was mainly the work, and stands to the credit of, the House of Argyll.

The Earl's charter to the Crown lands of Kintyre was granted in feu-farm, that is to say, he had to pay feu duties which are enumerated in the charter in oatmeal, malt, cheese and marts, as was the custom of the time.   Later they appear to have been commuted into money payments.   In the year 1609, however, the Exchequer passed an Act discharging him, at least temporarily, of the feu duties of his Kintyre lands, on condition that he would, within five years, "plant a burgh, to be inhabited by Lowland men and trafficking burgesses, within the bounds of Kintyre."   This represented a further step, this time a very concrete and important one. Not only was a burgh to be founded, but it was to be a Lowland burgh. In other words, what was called in those days a Plantation was intended.

It is to be remembered that at this time Plantation, as a means of settling political and other disputes, was in the air, so to speak. About the year 1600 an attempt had been made to plant the Island of Lewis with people from Fife. It failed completely, partly because of the resistance of the Macleods, and partly because of the inferior character of some of the planters. About 1610 there began the great Plantation of Ulster, by Scots and English settlers. The Lowland Plantation of Kintyre, which began during this century by the foundation of a Lowland burgh at Lochhead, was therefore quite in the spirit of the times. The Earl accepted the responsibility for the erection of the burgh, and gave as his cautioners for fulfilling this engagement his brother Sir John Campbell of Lundie, and Sir John Campbell of Calder.

It must not be supposed that the object of Government in founding these burghs was entirely altruistic. King James VI's financial resources were at a low ebb, and he was looking around for means to replenish an empty exchequer. His attention had been drawn to, and his cupidity aroused by, the economic possibilities of the Western Highlands, especially in connection with herring fisheries, by interested parties who no doubt hoped to get a share of the spoil. Some time before the year 1595 a highly-coloured account of the Western Isles, by an unknown author, had been prepared for the information of His Majesty. In this, some of the lands in islands like Islay are shown as paying rents which were not merely an economic but a physical impossibility.

The Earl of Argyll lost no time in making a beginning with the erection of the burgh, for we find him granting, in this same year 1609, two charters to a sub-vassal, John Boyll of Ballochmartin in the Greater Cumbrae. Boyll was a cadet of the Boylls, or Boyles, of Kelburn, the head of which family became, about the end of this century, the first Earl of Glasgow. Boyle's charters, copies of which are preserved in the National Library of Scotland, are of very great local and antiquarian interest. The first, which is dated at Inverary the last day of April 1609, bestowed on him the 3 merkland of Eskamull Beg and the 2 merkland of Wagill. For the first he was to pay as feu duty three pounds Scots money, one boll of oatmeal, one boll of bear, two stones of cheese, and two stones of butter "of good and sufficient merchandise," also one mart, two wedders, and four poultry, and these were to be delivered yearly "at the castle or fortalice of Keanloch-Kilcheran to be built beside the toune of Campbeltoune." For the lands of Wagill, now Uigle, he was to pay four pounds money, half a boll of oatmeal, two bolls of bear, one stone of cheese, and half a mart, and he was to provide four carriages of a horse every year from the said Castle of Campbeltoune to any place within the bounds of Kintyre not exceeding eight miles. He was also forbidden either to lease or to feu any of the lands of his grant to persons bearing the names of Macconnell or Macdonald, Maclean, Macleod, Macallaster, or Macneill.

Boyle's second charter granted to him three acres of land, "where it shall be expedient to the said John, upon the north part of the river of Lochhead, together with another acre of land for building and planting, with the houses of old formerly built about the same, except the house and yard possessed of before by Angus MacConnell of Dunnavage, within the burgh of Campbeltoun, and with the pasture of six horses upon the forty shilling land of Lochhead etc., with free power to brew and sell wine, ale, and aquavitae by them or their tenants within the Sheriffdom of Tarbert or any part thereof, and to no other but to the burgesses and inhabitants of Campbeltoune." For this land he was to pay "ane good and sufficient mart at the feast of Martimess," and also "the carriage of one horse be the space of eight myles from Lochhead," when it would be asked for.

One or two points in these charters are worthy of our attention. The castle referred to in the first was that known as the House of Lochhead. It is clear from this charter that it was not yet built in 1609, but its erection must have begun immediately after this, as it was captured by Sir James Macdonald in 1615. It occupied the site still called the Castlehill, and is sometimes referred to as an old Macdonald stronghold. There is no evidence to support this view, and such as we do possess points to its having been a new castle, built at this time by the Earl of Argyll, for the protection of the new burgh and its inhabitants. The second point is that in these charters of 1609 we meet for the first time with the new name Campbeltown, and it is seen to have been applied, not by the inhabitants in honour of the Earl, but by the latter, to mark the connection of his family with the new town about to be erected. It did not come into use at this date, however, and the older name of Ceannloch-Kilkerran, or the English form Lochhead, was that by which the burgh continued to be known down to about 1680.

The erection of the Burgh of Lochhead, beginning about 1609, was undoubtedly the first step in the Lowland plantation of Kintyre, and John Boyll of Ballochmartin the first of the planters. In the year 1636 he received a further grant of the lands of Kilbreid and Cunachan near Campbeltown. These grants were undoubtedly meant to give him a status and hold in the district, and to enable him or any other of his family, to act as what was in those days called an Undertaker, that is the man on the spot who would make the necessary plans and put the scheme on its feet. Such evidence as we possess points to the earliest incomers to Lochhead being from Bute and the Cumbraes. The Ayrshire and Renfrewshire contingent came later. The connection of the Boylls with Campbeltown is now almost forgotten, but it existed down to the year 1701, when Finella Boyle and her spouse, Archibald Macallaster in Towart in Arran, resigned their lands on the water of Lochhead into the hands of Archibald, Earl of Argyll, superior thereof.

The position of the Earl of Argyll in Kintyre during the ten years 1607 to 1617 is somewhat obscure. Professor Masson, who edited the volume of the *Privy Council Register* which covers this period, came to the conclusion that his charter of 1607 was a mere draft, which means, in other words, that he was not properly infefted at that date. This view would appear to receive support from the fact that John

Boyll did not obtain sasine of his Kintyre grants until the month of May 1618, and sasine was necessary for the completion of the infeftment. In the year 1609 we find Argyll obtaining a Decreet of the Lords of Council to eject a list of Kintyre tenants. There are fifty-three names in the list, and all the old tenants - Macneills, Macallasters, Mackays, Macoshenags, Maceachans and Maceachrans and others are included. This Decreet effectively disproves the statement made by Hill in his *Macdonnells of Antrim* that a "clean sweep" of all the old inhabitants of Kintyre had been made in the year 1599, and their places taken by Presbyterians from Ayr and Renfrew in that year.

If we accepted the Decreet of 1609 at its face value we would, however, come to the conclusion that a general clearance was made, or intended to be made, at this date. That such did not take place is, however, proved by subsequent rentals, where the names of the old Highland tenants occur side by side with those of Lowlanders. Some of the more important of them, such as the Macdonalds of Sanda, Macneills of Carskey, Macoshenags of Lephenstrath, and Maceachans of Tangy, actually received charters to their lands from the Earl's successors in this and the subsequent century. The events which followed soon after - war, transportations, and disease - must have greatly thinned their ranks, and made a plantation by Lowlanders more easy of accomplishment; but such evidence as we possess leads us to the conclusion that there never was at any time a planned clearance of the old stock, as erroneously stated by Hill, and that the Kintyre plantation was not accompanied by the deliberate inhumanities which had characterised those of Ulster and Lewis. In fact, the example of the last would have been enough to deter the Earl and his successors from such a course, even if they had had the will and power to set about it.

In 1613 we find the Earl's agents discussing the commutation of his Kintyre feu duties into their money equivalents, and in the same year the Earl represented that, owing to the expenses to which he had been put in the service of Government, he was unable to fulfil his contract to erect a new burgh at Lochhead within the specified period. He asked for an extension of time, but this was refused, and in the year 1615 the King wrote to his Commissioners of Rents to the effect that, unless the contract was fulfilled, the duties of Kintyre for the previous eight years, that is from 1607, the year of the Earl's charter, were to be paid by him. From this we may conclude that, even if his feudal infeftment was incomplete, he had been drawing the Kintyre rents from the date when he got his charter; but it is more probable that Masson's view is incorrect. In this year the district was overrun by Sir James Macdonald, and the Castle of Lochhead taken by his following, and these events no doubt would put a stop to the negotiations for the time being.

It is clear from what has just been said, that, with the exception of the building of the new castle at Lochhead, little progress in founding the new burgh could have been made before the year 1617. A description of Kintyre which, from internal evidence, must have been written between 1609 and 1617, is extant, and is probably by Timothy Pont, the well-known Scottish cartographer. From it we take the following extract: "eight mylls from Saidill upon the same syde is the Logh of Kilkerrane ... upon the Southsyde of the Logh there is a church which is called Kilkearrane and ane ancient castle which K. James the fourth builded. At the end of the Logh there is a certain village and a new Castle which the Earl of Argyll builded laitlie." Boyll's charters showed that, even before the erection of the new burgh of Lochhead, there had been some houses on the Askomil side, probably connected with Angus Macdonald's house of Askomil, set fire to by his son James in 1598. It was perhaps the place called Castle Mail.

The above description probably depicts the new burgh of Lochhead in its very embryonic stage. There was one church only - the old church of Kilkerran - of which Captain White, about 1870, found some remains within the present cemetery. Near that also was the old castle built by King James IV in 1498, then, as now, in ruins. At the head of the loch, on the Castlehill site, was the new castle built shortly after 1609 by the Earl of Argyll, either on his own account, or as the agent of Government, of which no trace now remains. Near that castle was a small clachan or hamlet, which became the future Campbeltown.

Whatever the Earl's position may have been in Kintyre between 1607 and 1617, it was clarified in the latter year by an Act of Ratification of the Scottish Parliament. His first Countess, Agnes Douglas of Morton, had died in 1607. By her he had a son Archibald, now Lord Lorne, and afterwards the famous Marquis of Argyll. In 1610 the Earl married again, Anna Cornwallis, an English lady, and a Catholic. By her he had several children, of whom the eldest son James received the title of Lord Kintyre, and afterwards of Earl of Irvine. In the charter of 1607 the succession to the Kintyre lands was to pass to Lord Lorne, but in the Ratification of 1617 it went to Lord Kintyre instead. When the intention to make this arrangement became known it was strongly opposed by Lord Lorne, by the Earl's brother Colin Campbell of Lundie, and by others of his cautioners and debtors, who had look to the Kintyre estates as a means of getting their debts paid. Their objections were met to some extent by inserting a proviso that the lands of Kintyre were to be burdened with the debts owing to Lundie, Calder, and others. The act also disannexed the lands of Kintyre from the Crown, and reconstituted the ancient Lordship in Argyll's favour. It included all the lands of the peninsula except those of Kilcalmonell and Skipness, which belonged to the Lordship of Knapdale, and it included also the Island of Jura. Its boundaries were "from the Mull to Alt-na-sionnach," the latter being a small stream on the south side of Kilcalmonell parish, shown in Blaeu's atlas of 1654, but not in later maps. Dunaverty Castle, on its southern shore, was denoted as its principal messuage.

Argyll at once made out a charter of these lands in favour of his son Lord Kintyre, then a mere child six years of age, but reserving to himself the life-rent. The Earl's subsequent career was strange in the extreme. In 1617, when King James VI visited Scotland, he was high in the royal favour, and carried the Crown at the State opening of Parliament on 17th June of that year. Two years later he was a denounced rebel and exile. He had asked for and obtained a royal licence to leave the country and go to the Well of Spa for his health. Once abroad he turned Catholic, probably at the request of his Countess, and, what was a greater offence in the eyes of the King, he entered the service of the King of Spain, and is stated to have distinguished himself in the campaigns against the Dutch. His licence was revoked, and he was summoned to return. Failing to comply with this request he was, with sound of trumpets, declared traitor and rebel at the Mercat Cross of Edinburgh on 16th February 1619. In 1620 Sir James Macdonald was recalled from Spain, pardoned, pensioned, and narrowly missed coming into his own again. The King wrote to the Privy Council in his favour, but through the influence of the Council he was debarred from entering Scotland. He died later in London in 1626.

Later Argyll made his peace with the King, and in November 1621 he was declared, by open proclamation at the Mercat Cross of Edinburgh, the King's free liege. He never, however, returned to Scotland. The control of his great estates, except Kintyre, passed to Lord Lorne, and the responsibility for law and order was entrusted to a group of Campbell barons. That of Kintyre had been, in 1618, placed under Campbell of Kilberry, with the assistance of Hector Macneill of Carskey, and the keeping of the House of Lochhead was entrusted to the latter. While in Spain the Earl had resigned his lands of Kintyre to his son James, who had this resignation confirmed by a charter of King Charles I on 12th February 1626. Then, or a few years afterwards, James, Lord Kintyre, came to reside at the House of Lochhead, which apparently he preferred to his principal messuage of Dunaverty, and the very early history of the new burgh is largely centred round this young nobleman.

CHAPTER IV

EARLY EVENTS IN THE BURGH OF LOCHHEAD

The land on which the burgh was built comprised the old sixteenth-century holdings of Askomel More and Kinloch. At the beginning of the century the first had been in the possession of the Mackays of North Kintyre, and the last in that of the Maceachrans. At the time when the burgh was founded a good deal of these lands had been in the hands of Angus Macdonald, and probably used by him as "bordland" or home farm land for his house at Askomel. The site was well chosen for a burgh on account of its excellent harbour, which was one of the best in the west of Scotland, and which must have been used by foreign ships from time immemorial. In Adamnan's *Life of St Columba* we read of an occasion when the Saint paid a visit to a place called *Caput Regionis*, which is Latin for "head of the land," and that when there he met and conversed with the captain of a ship from Gaul. Dr Reeves, the editor of Adamnan, identifies *Caput Regionis* with Kintyre, and the place where the Gaulish ship was as Lochkilkerran.

From this harbour a curious expedition set sail in 1627 in George Masson's ship. This was a company of Highland archers, raised by the Laird of Macnachtan, and intended to be employed in the Duke of Buckingham's expedition for the relief of La Rochelle in France. It was commanded by Captain Alexander Macnachtan, and among the soldiers were some who appear to have been Kintyre men, bearing such well-known local names as Macsporran, Maclarty, Macmillan, Macneill, and Macallaster. It had two pipers and a harper. As we shall see, archers were actually employed in the Highland regiments of the Scottish Army a good many years after this date, and during the Civil War in England. We do not know where the expedition went to, but we are told that it was too late for La Rochelle.

A few years later we find Lord Kintyre, then a young man of about twenty years of age, in residence at Lochhead Castle. We learn from some old accounts that the castle had a garden, which, according to the custom of those days, would be a walled enclosure situated at some distance from the castle itself. It had a gardener named Thomas Gillies, whose annual pay in 1643 amounted to 8 bolls of oatmeal valued at £6, 10s. Scots each, and paid out of the multures of Machrimore Mill in Southend parish. A new house for the gardener cost £46, 13s. 4d. to build. We have mention also of Lord Kintyre's footman, John McKinlay, of his cook or chef, James Stewart, and of a "post" whose name was McInower, and who was most probably in private employment as messenger for the castle. An official whose duties were of a grimmer nature was the hangman, whose wages or "fiall" was two bolls of oatmeal. The hangman was in those days a usual appendage of all barons who had powers of pit and gallows. His existence, and that of his office, are commemorated in the local place-name of Gallowhill.

Lord Kintyre was a young man of an adventurous and high-spirited nature, and The Bailie and Chamberlain of Kintyre were ordered to keep the Castle of Lochhead in

5. Saddell Castle, built by David Hamilton, Bishop of Argyll, for defence of the Barony of Saddell, comprises an early 16th C. (1512) tower-house incorporating a barmkin wall and outbuildings. The castle has been saved from ruin by late 19th and 20th C. restorations.

6. Tarbert Castle: the tower-house from the SW. The original 13th C. castle was developed by Robert I from 1325-29; while construction of the tower-house was probably begun at the instance of James IV in 1494.

7. The tower-house at Tarbert Castle, viewed from the NW. In 1652, the castle was held, briefly, by Cromwellian forces. During the Argyll Rebellion of 1685, the castle was garrisoned by the insurgents, but recaptured for the crown by Walter Campbell of Skipness.

8. Skipness Castle, of 13th to 16th C. construction, is a castle of enceinte and holds a commanding prospect of the Arran and Bute coasts from Kintyre. This view, from the SW, shows the Latrine Tower and crosslet-loopholes on the W curtainwall, and the entrance Gatehouse on the S curtain.

acquired great credit for a gallant exploit in the year 1631. A pirate ship had been taking toll of merchantmen in the western seas, and plans were laid to capture it. Under Lord Kintyre's command a ship was prepared, described as "ane great boat weill manned and appointed with all warrelike furniture." The crew appear to have been local men. In this he set out and, having encountered the pirate, brought him to action. A desperate battle, described in the records of the trial as "ane sharp and cruel conflict," took place, which resulted in the complete victory of Lord Kintyre and his men and the capture of the pirate ship. Those of the pirate crew who were not killed in the action were handed over to Lord Linlithgow, then Lord High Admiral of Scotland, at whose hands they no doubt met the usual fate of captured pirates. We are not told what the nationality of the pirate was, but at that date some were Dutch and some English. The result was reported to the Privy Council of Scotland, and the Council accorded to Lord Kintyre its thanks "for his honourable and worthie carriage in the matter." The accounts show that subsequently pensions were being paid to the families of some local men who had been killed in the action with the pirate ship.

Lord Kintyre, however, does not appear to have been too happy in his position at Lochhead. His half brother, Lord Lorne, as we have seen, disapproved of the estate becoming his property, and the two appear to have been on a footing of enmity. Hence Kintyre, for this reason perhaps, and also for the reason that he sought a wider sphere of action for his adventurous spirit, decided to get rid of his estates. Hill, in his *Macdonnells of Antrim*, states that he made a first offer of them to his half brother Lorne, but the statement is not supported by any evidence. A clause in his charter of 1626 expressly forbade him to sell or alienate the lands of Kintyre to any Macdonalds, yet, in defiance of this condition, he entered into negotiations with the Macdonalds of Antrim for the transfer to them of these lands.

The Antrim Macdonalds, or Macdonnells as they spelt their name, were a junior branch of the Macdonalds of Dunnyveg and the Glens, and were descended from Sorley Buy, a younger brother of James Macdonald, father of that Angus of whom we have already had some account. This man had taken possession of the estate of the Glens of Antrim, which ought legally to have belonged to Angus, and had founded a new branch of the Macdonalds. They were more fortunate that their Scottish cousins, and in 1620 Rannald Macdonnell of Dunluce had been created the first Earl of Antrim. It was to his son Viscount Dunluce, that Lord Kintyre granted, at Dunaverty Castle in January 1635, a charter to the lands of the Lordship of Kintyre, including the Island of Jura. The ceremony of sasine appears also to have been gone through there in the presence of certain witnesses, one of whom was Mr Donald Omey, minister of Kilkerran.

Lord Kintyre's action was at once reported to the Privy Council of Scotland, most probably by Lorne, and the Council took prompt and energetic measures to stop the transfer. A man named William Donald, a messenger, was sent from Edinburgh to Lochhead to stop the infeftment, but was told that he was too late, as sasine had been granted two days before his arrival.

their hands. Lord Kintyre had given a written warrant to Dunluce to enter this house, and to break open the door if he could not find the key. It was occupied, at Lorne's instance, by a party of soldiers, commanded by William Stirling of Auchyle, who was at this date Lord Lorne's man of business and confidential adviser. A proclamation to the people of Kintyre warned them not to attend any courts which the Macdonalds might set up, nor to give suit and service at such. The notary employed by the parties in the case, John Nicholl by name, was summoned before the Council in Edinburgh, and questioned by them, when it transpired that, although the ceremony of sasine had taken place, the actual Instrument of Sasine had not yet been handed over to Dunluce's attorney. All that he had given them was a mere minute of the ceremony, and this document, from the Glenarm archives, is printed by Hill in his book. Nicholl was warned by the Council, on pain of death, not to issue the Instrument or have it registered.

The Council then reported the steps they had taken to King Charles I. The King replied, stating that he acquiesced in the action taken, thanked the Council for its prompt measures, and recommended to them "that if the Lord Kintyre hath done anie thing contrare to our royal intention you use your best endeavours to make it ineffectual." The council then called before them Dunluce's attorney, Archibald Stewart of Blackhall, who had been instructed to bring all the documents of the case. Stewart produced a contract and disposition, as well as two charters. He was informed by the Council that it was His Majesty's pleasure that these should be destroyed, and they were therefore ordered to be "cancelled, riven, and destroyed" in the presence of the Council. Only four years later the first Bishops War broke out, and King Charles found himself in arms against his Scottish subjects, and seeking the aid of Antrim to invade the west of Scotland, offering, it is stated, the lands of Kintyre as a bribe. Had they found their way into the hands of the Macdonalds in 1635, so as to give them control of its castles, matters might have turned out very different from what they did, and the prompt action of the Council probably changed the course, not only of Kintyre history, but of that of Scotland as well.

In the following year, 1636, Lord Kintyre resigned his lands into the hands of the Crown which, in fact, was the course which he should have adopted from the start, and the Crown bestowed then on Lord Lorne who, a year or two later, became the first and only Marquis of Argyll.

Lord Kintyre's subsequent career was one of much interest. In the year 1642 he obtained from King Charles a licence and commission to raise a regiment of Scots Guards, 4500 strong, to serve under the King of France. It may be remarked that, during the first half of the seventeenth century, the raising of these levies of Scotsmen for foreign service had assumed the proportions of a national industry. Some fought on one side in the Thirty Years' War and some on the other; some chose one side on principle, but others were willing to offer their swords to the highest bidder. The methods of recruitment of Lord Kintyre's regiment are illuminating, and afford an early example of those of the press-gang of later times, except that in this case the men impressed were forced to fight for a foreign state in whose quarrels they had no interest.

Instructions were issued to judges, officers, and magistrates to assist in the recruitment, or answer at their peril. The Privy Council issued orders to all sheriffs "to take and apprehend all idle persons and vagabonds," and impress them into its ranks, and ministers and kirk sessions were required to prepare lists of all such people in their parishes. Recruiting officers haunted taverns in Edinburgh, and seized half-tipsy persons, some of whom appealed to the Council to prove that they were neither idle nor vagabonds.

At last the regiment, 1500 strong, was recruited and sailed from the Port of Leith. Before departure it was inspected by the French ambassador, who did not appear to be impressed with the men's appearance, and described them as mere "garcons." The regiment took precedence in the French Army after the French and Swiss guards, and remained in service down to the year 1662, when it was disbanded. It is of peculiar interest to Kintyre, firstly because it was raised by a man who was intimately connected with the town of Lochhead or Campbeltown in the very early years of its existence, and secondly, because there is evidence that it was into its ranks that the men taken alive at the massacre of Dunaverty in 1647 were impressed. The influence of the Marquis of Argyll had been enlisted in its recruitment, and in 1643 his son, Lord Lorne, afterwards Earl of Argyll, was one of its captains although only fifteen years of age. Lord Kintyre died in 1645, at the early age of thirty-four years, and was succeeded in the command of the French regiment by Sir Robert Moray, one of the most accomplished Scots of his generation, and one of the founders of the Royal Society of England.

When the Marquis took over the Kintyre estate in 1636 a careful rental of the whole estate was prepared. This, unfortunately, does not give the names of the landward tenants, but includes those of the indwellers of Lochhead, and from this list we get a glimpse of the state of the burgh in that year. There were only thirty householders, and of these less than half bore Lowland, or at least non-Kintyre, names. They were Colin Stirling, Adam Stewart, James Stewart, John Allan, William Kelburne, William Anderson, Robert Stirling, James Cunningham, Alexander Weir, John Burnes, James Kincaid, Alexander Harvie. The rest were *macs*, but some of them probably also incomers. Some of the above had been in Lochhead as early as 1618, which may be taken as the true year of the effectual foundation of the burgh, and of the first attempt at a Lowland Plantation. Witnesses to a sasine dated 28th May 1618 included Colin Stirling, James Stewart, John Allan, and Alexander McOnlay, described as "all in Lochkilkerran and burgesses of Rothesay." This is the first list of Lowland names to appear in the record.

The average rent of the houses was £6, 13s. 4d., but one occupied by John McEachran, clearly a Kintyre man, paid £12 or instead a barrel of herring. A Tolbooth, or Court and Jail, had been erected by this date, and the vaults under it were let to two of the burgesses. This building, most probably on the site of the present Town Hall, was in use down to 1754, but in that year was described as being in so ruinous a condition that prisoners could escape from it, and so evade punishment, and it was replaced by the present building in 1757. There is no mention of a mill, although one was certain to have been in existence. Most of the burgesses kept cows, and they jointly rented the farm of Crosshill for grazing, and possibly also to grow corn. For this they paid the curious rent of six quarts of aquavitae. This was the parent of whisky, distilled spirit flavoured with the roots of certain plants, and was prepared by special aquavitae makers. Whisky making on a commercial scale did not begin until the eighteenth century. It may be remarked that the old Scots quart was a much more generous measure than that of to-day, and was between eight and nine imperial pints.

When what was called the first Bishop's War broke out in 1639 it was fully expected that the Earl of Antrim, to whom King Charles is stated to have offered the lands of Kintyre as a reward for his services, would invade the west of Scotland. Lochhead was a most likely place for him to attempt to land. It was the principal place and harbour in the territory which he desired to possess, and there were no doubt a good many adherents of the Macdonalds among the Highland population. To meet this possibility the Marquis constructed a defence work on the north side of the loch, called in the records of the time the Fort of Askamylnemoir. It was not a stone castle, but an entrenched camp, and was garrisoned by a force of some four hundred men under Campbell of Auchinbreck, and fortified with cannon. In April 1639 the Synod of Argyll ordained that Mr James Campbell should go and preach to Auchinbrecks's company there, for the space of three weeks.

The victory of the Covenanters at Newburn-on-Tyne in 1640 put an end to the war, and removed the threat from Antrim. In 1641, however, there broke out the rebellion in Ireland, and King Charles and his Scottish subjects, in face of the common peril, became reconciled again. The Marquis took his regiment to Ireland, and Sir Duncan Campbell of Auchinbreck was also there. The fort at Lochhead, however, appears to have been maintained, for we find the Marquis receiving further permission to keep it manned from the Privy Council in 1642, because "of the great rebellion in Ireland with the which diverse of the Clan Donald, speciallie Coll McGillespick's sonnes and others followers of the Earl of Antrim, have joyned themselves ... and because of the known inmitie of the said Earl of Antrim and the Clan Donald aganis the said Marquess of Argile and his friends." How long it was manned cannot be said, but General David Leslie found seven cannon in it when he marched to Dunaverty in 1647. Its existence is commemorated in the names Trench Point and Fort Argyll.

We may now glance at the state of ecclesiastical and scholastic affairs in the early days of the burgh. The period 1606 to 1638 is known as the First Period of Episcopacy in Scotland. In the first of these years King James I had restored the bishops to their ancient powers and dignities. The Bishops' Courts, or Commissaries, were revived, and these took to do with matters such as divorce, slander, and registration of wills and testaments, now dealt with in our civil courts.

Otherwise the Church retained the Presbyterian form established by Andrew Melville. Ministers wore the black Genevan gown, the kirk sessions and presbyteries still functioned, but General Assemblies were forbidden. There were ten pre-Reformation parishes in Kintyre, but owing to lack of funds the number had to be reduced by amalgamation. In 1617 an Act of Parliament united in one charge the old parishes of Kilkerran, Kilchousland, and Kilmichael, and in another those of Kilcolmkill and Kilblaan. The Kintyre ministers traceable during this period were Mr Maurice Darroch in Kilcalmonell (he died in 1638), Mr Murdoch McWhirrie or McCurrie in Killean; Mr Malcolm Macoshenag in Kilkivan; Mr Donald Omey in Kilkerran, and his brother Mr Duncan Omey in Kilcolmkill.

The minister most intimately connected with Lochhead during the period of Episcopacy was Mr Donald Omey. He was a member of the Southend family of Omeys of Kilcolmkill, who had been tenants there from an unknown date, and later proprietors of that estate from 1622 to 1819. He graduated M.A. at Glasgow University in 1622, and in 1624 was sent by the Bishop to Ardnamurchan. He was the first Protestant clergyman to be sent here, and his presence was greatly resented, as the chief of Clanranald sent an armed man into the church who interrupted in the middle of his discourse, and bade him begone if he valued his life. The case was reported to the Privy Council, and King Charles personally intervened to support the authority of the Bishop.

Mr Omey, however, had to leave, and we find him at Kingarth in Bute in 1626. He appears to have come to Kilkerran as early as 1632, for in that year he took a feu of land in the burgh. Although the parishioners of the three old parishes had petitioned Parliament to get a new church built to serve all three as early after their union as 1621, no action was taken to get this done at the time, and Mr Omey preached in each of the old churches of Kilkerran, Kilchousland, and Kilmichael, once in every third Sunday. He was described by the Bishop at the time of the Ardnamurchan case as "ane learned, modest, and good teacher." When Presbyterianism was restored, in 1638, both he and his brother Mr Duncan conformed to the new order, and both attended the first meeting of the Synod of Argyll in 1639. He was dead before October 1640, but his brother Duncan was alive for some years later. The estate of Kilcolmkill went to Mr Donald Omey's descendants.

The Synod of Argyll took commendably prompt measures to end the awkward state of affairs existing at Lochhead, and at its meeting in October 1642 resolved that a new church should be built there to serve the united parishes. The work seems to have been put in hand at once, and the new church, the first Presbyterian-built church in Kintyre, was erected by 1643, on a site near the New Quay Head. It is stated to have been built in the form of a Genevan Cross, and to have had seating accommodation for about four hundred persons. A churchyard or cemetery was also opened at the church. In later times this was referred to as the Old Gaelic Church of Campbeltown. It continued in use down to 1778, when it became ruinous, and the congregation, during the time of Dr John Smith, used the new Lowland Church, built at the Castlehill in 1780, until the present Highland

Church was built in 1804. The new parish was called Lochhead, and the old churches at Kilkerran, Kilchousland, and Kilmichael were no longer used. Mr Omey was the last minister to preach in them.

A school had been opened at Lochhead as early as the year 1622, for in that year we find mention of John Spang, schoolmaster at Lochhead. His unusual name was borne by a family of Glasgow burgesses, one of whom, Mr William Spang was, about twenty years later, minister of the Scots Kirk at Campvere in Holland. It is possible that John Spang may have been a relation, but we have no other record of him. This is the first mention found in the record of a school in Kintyre. It probably continued in existence down to 1643, when we find that a certain Thomas Neere (probably McNair) was schoolmaster; but it and most, if not all, of the small burgh must have been swept away during the troubles of the ensuing five years, of which some account follows in the next chapter.

CHAPTER V

THE COLKITTO RAIDS

The events of the next four or five years in Kintyre may be described as the backwash of the great civil war then being waged in England and Scotland. When, in 1644, the Marquis of Montrose took up arms on behalf of King Charles I he found an ally in the Earl of Antrim, who sent a force of some 1500 men to his assistance. This was commanded by Alexander, or Allaster, Macdonald of Colonsay, a cousin of Antrim. The Colonsay Macdonalds were, like the Antrims, a branch of the family of Dunnyveg, but senior to the Antrims, being descended from an elder brother of Sorley Buy who had founded the Antrim branch. At this date the family of Colonsay were represented by the father and several sons. The father's name was Coll MacGillespeg Vic Coll Macdonald, but he is better known by his soubriquet or nickname of *ciatach*, which is the Gaelic for "left handed." Coll *ciatach* became to English historians Colkitto, and the name is frequently applied to his son Alexander, or Allaster.

The father, old Colkitto, had a stormy and not too reputable career. He had been in the Islay rebellion of 1614-15, and had surrendered Dunnyveg Castle and a considerable number of his adherents to the Campbells, who promptly had a good many of them hanged. He had also been among the rebels in Ireland in 1641, when he and some of his sons were arrested by the Marquis of Argyll who, in 1642, reported to the Privy Council that he was holding the father and four sons, including John and Donald Gorm Macdonald, in ward at great trouble and expense to himself, and who requested to have the advice of the Council in the matter. The latter granted him the sum of forty merks weekly for the maintenance of these five persons and of their five keepers; The names of the other two sons are not recorded. They appear to have been released, or to have escaped, by the year 1644. Old Colkitto was at this date about 76 years of age.

The character of his son Alexander, who commanded Antrim's contingent and such other Highlanders as joined him, in Montrose's campaigns, has been variously estimated; the estimates, as was usual at this time of high feeling, depending on the political colour of the writers. To the Covenanters he and his Irish and Highlanders represented the Devil and all his works. Sir James Turner, himself a Royalist at heart, although for a time employed by the Covenanters, loathed and despised Allaster for his desertion of Montrose. He describes him as a drunkard; a man, he says, "besotted with brandy and aquavitae," in which matter, to judge by contemporary reports, Turner should have been a good judge. The contemporary Royalist writers like Spalding, and the later Macdonald protagonists, picture him as a hero, although it is hard to ascribe heroic qualities to one who deserted his chief Montrose, and left his own people, including his father, to their fate. He appears to have been an intrepid and skilful officer under Montrose, and gradually won the confidence of the Scottish Highlanders, although at first they regarded him as a person of little consequence.

He and his contingent fought with Montrose for over a year, and greatly contributed to his victories. For his services he was knighted by Montrose in the name of King Charles, but detached himself and his force from his chief after the battle of Kilsyth in 1645, and then proceeded to wage a private war against his old enemies the Campbells, and to make one more attempt to win back the Macdonalds' old patrimony of Islay and Kintyre. When King Charles ordered Montrose to lay down his arms in order to avoid further bloodshed, Sir Alexander Macdonald refused, and a later offer to come in under protection, given by General David Leslie, was also refused. Thus he and his followers were rebels in a double sense, firstly to the Parliament of Scotland, and secondly to King Charles, and Turner describes them as a crew of graceless and rebellious desperadoes.

When the Montrose war first began the Marquis of Argyll, now in the plenitude of his power, and in a sense the uncrowned King of Scotland, had the most extensive powers granted under a commission of the Scottish Parliament, to quell the rising. He was empowered to raise his Majesty's subjects and arm them; to call upon the chiefs and heritors of the west to assist him, and to punish those who refused; to appoint commanders, to take over ships and their captains, and to pursue the enemy by land and sea, and with fire and sword, until every one of them was expelled, apprehended, or destroyed. The victory of Montrose at Inverlochy in January 1645 had, however, placed the lands of the Campbells at the mercy of their enemies, and for two years Sir Alexander and his father, old Colkitto, worked their will on their inhabitants. Sir Alexander acted like a king on his own account, granting a commission to his father "to command in chief over the lands of Yla and all uther lands unto me belonging," to defend the Castle of Dunnyveg with the assistance of Captain Daniel O'Neall, and to be responsible to him (Sir Alexander) for the rents and feu duties of Islay for the time being.

From contemporary records we get an idea of the damage done to Argyll's country. It was raided from end to end. Houses were burnt down, their inhabitants slain, the crops destroyed, and the cattle driven off. When General Leslie marched through Kintyre in 1647 he reported that he was unable to get any cattle to maintain his troops in food. As early as January 1645 there had been want in the country, as we find the Parliament dispatching 1500 bolls of meal and 300 bolls of malt "to the garrisons and cuntrie people in Argile." The worse year appears to have been 1646, and by the end of it Kintyre was a smoking ruin. In January 1647 the Marquis and Campbell of Calder reported to the Parliament that they had received no rents from their lands in Kintyre and Islay respectively for the past three years, and they were accordingly exempted from paying their feu duties to the Crown for these years, and yearly until the rebels had been ejected. At the same time an Act of the Parliament awarded the Marquis £15,000 sterling for the damage done to his estates, and £30,000 sterling among the other heritors of Argyllshire who had been sufferers.

The Parliament also recommended to the General Assembly to give orders to the several presbyteries throughout Scotland to persuade the people in all congregations throughout the land to make a voluntary contribution to assist the poor people of Argyllshire, whose homes and property had been destroyed. The total amount subscribed is not revealed, but must have been considerable, as out of it the Synod was able to set apart 10,000 marks for the foundation of schools - a matter to which reference will be made later on under the head of education. Proposals for the proper distribution of the sum collected were made by the Marquis to the commission of the Assembly in March 1647. Two-thirds was to be assigned for the immediate relief of relatives of those killed in the raids, and of the poor and aged, and one-third to purchase seed grain. No provision was made for Kintyre, no doubt because, while central Argyll had been merely raided, Kintyre had been taken possession of by Macdonald, and was in his power, so that nothing could be done there.

The Synod records reveal the state to which the country had been reduced. The minutes of the meeting of 8th September 1646 record that "all the absents excused because of the troubles of the countrey and of their being scattered and chased fra their dwellings, ... the presbyterie of Kintyre being under the power of the rebels, and none being resident in the presbyteries of Argyle and Lorn but such as were sheltered in garesones, and no ruleing elder present."

What gave even more concern to the Church was an attempt to reintroduce the Roman Catholic faith. On 10th September 1646 the Synod addressed the Commission to the effect that "with the enemy there are a number of freiris and seminary priests who are going about Kintyre and some of the Isles using all diligence and endeavour to seduce the people to poprie; and many not only in Kintyre but also of the adjacent isles, even of the better sort, already following their ways and not only countenancing but embracing their superstition." The Commission at once reported this to the Committee of Estates, expressing the opinion that "for well-nigh three score years have we not heard of so bold attempts against religion ... our spirits have been much afflicted to heare that our brethren there ... should have their houses burnt with fire, be spoiled of their goods, many exposed to nakedness and famine etc. ... but to see the remanent that is left have their soules made a prey to Anti-christ is bitter as death."

The action taken by the Committee was the dispatch of General Leslie's expedition in the summer of 1647. It is possible that at this date Protestantism had but shallow roots in Kintyre. There is no record of a Protestant minister placed there prior to 1611, and we are told that in 1615, the year of the rebellion in Islay, most of the inhabitants of that island were still Catholic, so that it is quite possible that, in 1646, there were still many old people in Kintyre who had been brought up as Catholics, and who would not perhaps need much seducing to make them return to the older faith.

The incomers at Lochhead may be assumed to have fled when the Colkitto raids began, but from later lists we know that some at least of the burgesses returned when the troubles were over. The school was swept away, for we find that a proposal to start a school was made again in 1649. The church built in 1643 appears to have escaped destruction, but was probably vacant during this period of trouble. The old minister, Mr Donald Omey, died in 1640, and in 1642 the Marquis of Argyll presented Mr Neil Campbell, who had been Bishop of the Isles during the first period of Episcopacy, to the charge. We have no record, however, of this serving the cure, and the next minister traceable is Mr Dugald Darroch, who had previously been minister of Kilcalmonell, but was inducted to Lochhead in 1649.

Of the leading Highland families in Kintyre some joined the Macdonalds out of old loyalties and racial ties. All were, either by reason of Argyll's superiority, conferred by his charters, his feudal vassals, or were bound to him by other ties. In the year 1625 the Marquis, then Lord Lorne, had been made responsible for the behaviour of Macdonald of Largie, and in that year Lorne and Largie had signed a Bond of Maintenance whereby Lorne agreed to protect Largie "from generation to generation," and Largie, in token of this warrandice, agreed to pay yearly to Lorne a sum of £80 Scots. This sum had been paid by Largie down to the year 1643, and payments were actually renewed later in Charles II's reign when both Largie and the Earl of Argyll had their estates restored to them. In spite of this bond, however, Angus Macdonald of Largie joined his kinsman Sir Alexander Macdonald, and was made a Captain in his army. His estates were forfeited, but restored to him again by the Parliament of 1661.

Another Kintyre family of Macdonalds were those of Sanda. They were represented at this date by Archibald Mor, the chief, and his son Archibald Og, the latter of whom had married a daughter of Campbell of Glencarradale. They were Argyll's vassals for their lands of Macharioch, in view of his feudal superiority thereof. Both joined Colkitto, and both lost their lives at Dunaverty in 1647. Their estates were forfeited, but restored at the same time as those of Largie.

Some of the other leading Highlanders were probably forced to join Sir Alexander's forces under duress. There is some reason to suppose that this may have been so in the case of Angus Maceachran of Kilellan, the then representative of a very old Kintyre family which had held the office of Mair of Fee for many generations. He, too, was Argyll's vassal for his lands of Kilellan. He met his death at Dunaverty, having previously handed over the title-deeds of his estate in a small red box to Sir James Turner, with a request that he would deliver them to the Marquis of Argyll. The latter restored the lands of Kilellan to his son Colin in the year 1659.

Of the other families we have no direct evidence. The Macneills of Carskey were at this time tacksmen of the Marquis, and during the Islay rebellion were definitely on the side of Government and the Campbells and, as we have seen, Hector Macneill of Carskey had been in charge of Lochhead Castle in 1618. The living representative in 1646 was Malcolm Macneill. The Carskey lands appear to have escaped the general destruction, and it is possible that he may have joined the Macdonalds to preserve his life and property. It is perhaps significant that the year of his death, as recorded on his tombstone, was 1647, which might indicate that he was one of Leslie's victims, but this can be only conjecture. We know that a number of the Mackays of North Kintyre, and also of the Macallasters of Loup, followed Sir Alexander Macdonald, and that some of them met their deaths at this time.

Against those men the church, then extremely powerful, took the strongest action possible, and passed on them sentence of excommunication.

It must not be supposed that this sentence was merely ecclesiastical in its results and designed only to deny to those on whom it was passed the benefits of religion. The power of the Church at this date was closely intermingled with that of the civil arm, and excommunication could involve forfeiture of land and movable goods, and even seizure and imprisonment of person. No person in the communion of the Church was allowed to have any dealings with, or to give any assistance to, an excommunicated person. It was a form of religious and social boycott at its mildest, and very much more at its harshest. The records show that, curious as it may appear to-day, it was passed on Protestant and Catholic alike.

In Kintyre the following adherents of the Macdonalds were excommunicated by the Synod of Argyll in September 1646: Archibald Mor Macdonald of Sanda; Archibald Og Macdonald of Sanda his son; Duncan Mackay in Crossibeg; Adam Mackay his son; Archibald Macneill buie; John Macdonad, Largie's grand uncle; Ranald Macdonald nephew to Sanda; Mr John Omey (presumably a student or minister, and member of the Kilcolmkill family, but cannot be traced further); John Gearre Macneill. The name of Angus Maceachran of Kilellan, killed at Dunaverty in the following year (1647), is not among the excommunicated, the inference being that he must have joined the Macdonalds at a later stage.

In addition to the sentence passed on the above, the Church deposed from his office and stipend - *tam a beneficio quam ab officio* - Mr John Darroch, who had been minister of Kilcolmkill, now Southend, since 1642. The Synod records state that "Mr John Darroch ... confessed himself guilty of very grosse complyance and that he hath been for a long tyme a preacher to the rebels." Why this should have been regarded as an offence is not easy to understand. His wife was a Campbell, and it is most probable that anything he did was done under duress. He was reinstated a few years later, after expressing contrition for his conduct, but did not return to Kilcolmkill. Kilblaan was also included in his charge, and he was the last minister to preach in that church, of which all traces have now disappeared.

CHAPTER VI
GENERAL DAVID LESLIE'S MARCH
THROUGH KINTYRE

The defeat of Montrose at Philiphaugh by General David Leslie in September 1645 had broken the back of Royalist resistance, but during 1646 the Marquis of Huntly in the north, and Sir Alexander Macdonald in the west, were still holding out for the cause, and in the spring of 1647 the Scottish Parliament took steps to subdue these two leaders. Early in that year the National Army had been remodelled and, in the interests of economy, greatly reduced. The New Model Army, as it was called, consisted of seven regiments of infantry and fifteen troops of horse, and was placed under the command of General Alexander Leslie. The infantry was composed of the two Highland regiments of the Marquis of Argyll and James Campbell of Ardkinglas, of a strength of 1000 men each, and of the Lowland infantry regiments, five in number, consisting of 800 men each. The troops of cavalry each consisted of eighty ruters or horsemen.

The strength of the whole army was thus about 7500 men in all, and of this a part was retained near the capital, to protect the Parliament, and, in the words of Bishop Guthry of Dunkeld, to act as a check on those "who groaned for the King." The remainder of the army, commanded by Lieutenant-General David Leslie and Major-General John Middleton, was sent to the north to deal with Huntly. After Huntly's fortresses were taken Middleton was left in the north to keep guard, while General Leslie separated from him with a part of the force, to deal with Sir Alexander Macdonald in Argyllshire.

Leslie chose Dunblane as a temporary headquarters to prepare for the expedition to the west. The force with which he invaded Kintyre has been variously estimated. Jean de Montereul, at that time French Ambassador in Edinburgh, where he had been trying to effect a tripartite agreement between France, the Scots, and King Charles I, stated in a letter to Cardinal Mazarin that it was over 8000 men. This, however, is a clear over-estimate, for, as we have seen, the whole National Army did not exceed that number and Leslie had only a part of it under his command.

Baillie, another contemporary historian, records that it was only a small army, ill-provided and not equipped with tents. From Leslie's own dispatches we learn that when he separated from Middleton he took with him the two Highland regiments and six troops of horse. This would appear to have been the force that went into Kintyre, and its size is more in accordance with Baillie's statement that it was only a small army. Sir Alexander Macdonald was reported to have had only about 1500 men and two or three troops of horse. Leslie had thus a superiority in numbers, but he had to face the possibility of reinforcements being sent to Macdonald from Antrim, and his anxiety about this is expressed in his dispatches.

Some preparations had been made by the Government for the Campaign, but on the whole the record is one of shocking inefficiency on the part of those responsible for supply. A consignment of gunpowder was ordered to be sent from Dumfries to Dumbarton, thence to Tarbert, to be picked up by Leslie when he got there. This never reached him. Some naval vessels under the command of Captain Louis Dick, son of Sir William Dick, then Lord Provost of Edinburgh, were to accompany Leslie on his long march down the peninsula, and were intended for the dual purpose of warding off any attack by Antrim's forces, and of preventing the escape of Macdonald's. It never, for some unexplained reason, arrived, although after earnest solicitations by Leslie from Dunaverty, some boats appear to have been sent from Portpatrick and Saltcoats.

The Highland infantry of 1647 were clad in the belted plaid, that is the older form of kilt and plaid, all in one piece, pleated as a kilt round the middle and fastened by a belt, with the remainder flung over the left shoulder in the form of a plaid. Their essential arm was the claymore or broadsword, but a proportion may have been supplied with muskets, and some with bows and arrows. The latter archaic armament in the Highland regiments was the cause of much surprise when these fought in the Civil War in England a year or two before, but an English observer testifies to the skill of the Highlanders as archers, stating that they could bring down a running deer. The cavalry had "five shots," a carbine and four pistols, two of the latter by the side of each horseman, and two at his saddle bow. A proportion probably still carried the lance, which had been retained in the Scottish Army long after it was abandoned in England.

Leslie tells us that he was eager to set out from Dunblane, because the pestilence had broken out in the neighbourhood, a remark the significance of which will be noticed later. He had, however, to wait until the summer grass had grown sufficiently to feed his horses, and until the Marquis of Argyll was freed of his duties at the Committee of Estates in Edinburgh.

At Dunblane he was joined by James (afterwards Sir James) Turner, who signed on as Adjutant. Turner was a son of the minister of Dalkeith, and had himself been meant for the Church, to which end he had studied at Glasgow University. He graduated M.A. in 1631, and in his Memoirs remarks somewhat drily that this title "was undeservedlie bestowed on me, as it was on many others before me, and hath been on too many since." He had, however, changed his mind, become a soldier and, like the Leslies, had been a soldier of fortune in the continental wars. He is portrayed by the historian Burnet as a man of fiery temper, "naturally fierce, but mad when he was drunk," which is stated to have been frequent. He has been described as "every inch a soldier," and he wrote a learned treatise on the military art entitled *Pallas armata*. He is most probably the real prototype of Sir Walter Scott's Dugald Dalgety in the *Legend of Montrose*. Although at this time employed by the Covenanters he was himself no Covenanter, and he lets us know that his purpose in joining Leslie's army was to punish Macdonald for his desertion of Montrose. In the next reign he was employed against the Covenanters, to whom he became particularly hateful, although that is no reason why we should accept at face value their estimate of his character. He continued in the employ of the

Covenanters, and under Leslie, until he was taken prisoner at the Battle of Worcester in 1651. During a period of imprisonment he wrote his *Memoirs*, which form one of the important historical records of this period, and one of the principal authorities for the events about to be described.

When the Committee of Estates rose, Leslie was also joined by the Marquis of Argyll, for the purpose, Turner tells us, of guiding the army through the passes leading to the West Highlands. In view of the vast powers granted by the Parliament to Argyll, and held by him under this Commission of Lieutenandry, Turner's remarks are, to say the least, an understatement. So also is his remark that Argyll was "bot a Colonel" and so under Leslie, a mere subaltern of Leslie, as one writer has said. This is the narrow view of a purely military expert who was unaware, or had perhaps overlooked, the greater powers granted to the Marquis. He was, of course, Colonel of his own regiment of Highlanders, but he was very much more.

Another name deserving mention, because of the notoriety which has attached to it, was that of Mr John Nevay, or Nevoy, the chaplain of Argyll's regiment. He had previously been the minister of Loudon in Ayrshire, and had been a member of the General Assembly Commission and one of those appointed to revise the Scottish psalmody. He appears to have been one of the more fanatical divines, whom those times produced in considerable numbers. The part he played in the principal event of the campaign, which has earned for him considerable obloquy, will be mentioned later. In the next reign he was exiled to Holland, where he died. During his exile he maintained a considerable correspondence with friends in the west of Scotland, some of which is still preserved in our National Library.

The army, then, with which Leslie set out to attack Sir Alexander Macdonald, whose forces were then in Kintyre, consisted, according to the best evidence available, of two Highland regiments of 1000 men each, if up to strength, raised sometime before by the Marquis of Argyll and James Campbell of Ardkinglas respectively, and several troops of horse, each troop consisting of 80 horsemen. Leslie may have had six troops, and according to his own dispatches had certainly three. The names of only two of his cavalry leaders - Colonels Strachan and Urry - have come down to us. With this small army Leslie rose from Dunblane on the 17th of May 1647.

Baillie tells us that the May of that year was one of the stormiest and wettest in human memory, and, as the army had no tents, the marching must have tried even the seasoned Highlanders. Neither Turner nor Leslie give us details the route taken after leaving Dunblane, or in Argyllshire, but we know that Inveraray was reached on the 21st, and that a halt to rest the army was made there on the 22nd. On the next day, the 23rd, Leslie marched again, and as this was a Sunday he had to make the necessary excuses to this Covenanting employers, and to emphasise the fact that the exigencies of the public service made it a work of necessity. How far he marched on this day is not stated, but he had probably sent scouts ahead to discover the whereabouts of Macdonald, and these probably reported that the passes leading into Kintyre were undefended, for on the next day, Monday the 24th, he made a forced march, the cavalry doing forty and the infantry twenty miles.

Macdonald appears to have been taken completely by surprise, and to have been unaware of his approach, and Turner makes some scathing remarks about his military inefficiency, pointing out that, had he held the passes with a few troops, Leslie would surely have been defeated, for there would not have been room, he states, to have got together more than 100 men in a body to oppose him nor to bring up cavalry in files of more than three troopers abreast. As it was, Leslie's cavalry passed right through the Isthmus of Tarbert, and discovered Macdonald's forces on the more level ground in Kilcalmonell parish. When this was reported to Leslie he at once ordered an attack to be made "with a foretroope and two more," that is with a vanguard or leading troop, and two other troops, or three troops of horse in all. Macdonald's forces were scattered in confusion, and their losses estimated at between three and four score men. In addition three of his captains, "pryme leading men," were taken prisoner. Leslie's own losses amounted to nine of his troopers killed.

The sun was nearly setting when this action, known locally as the Battle of Rhunahaorine Point, was fought and, as Leslie was unable to pursue his advantage that evening, he called off his cavalry to the main body of his army which had apparently not yet crossed the isthmus. His chief thought now was to prevent Macdonald's forces from escaping by sea. The ships under Louis Dick had not yet arrived, so he sent Campbell of Inveraw to Castle Sweyn to try to procure boats to prevent their passage to Gigha. None, however, were procurable, and Leslie had to report that Alexander Macdonald and old Coll Ciatach his father had escaped. They were accompanied by various of their officers, including Macdonald of Largie.

The engagement at Rhunahaorine, and the flight of their leader, virtually decided the fate of the Macdonalds and of the campaign and for this action Leslie received the thanks of the Committee of Estates. The army under Macdonald - a mixed force of Irish and Highlanders - included many Kintyre men, and also a large contingent of the Macdougalls of Dunolly and Raray. After this fight it appears to have retreated down the peninsula to Lochkilkerran and Dunaverty.

At this stage of the proceedings some of the local chiefs who had been under the power of the Macdonalds wrote to Argyll and Leslie, offering to submit on assurance that their safety would be guaranteed. Montereul mentions the incident, and states that they were the chiefs of the Macneills and Macallasters. He goes on to say that their offers were accepted, and that Argyll agreed to let them have their lands on much easier terms than those on which they had previously held them, on condition that they captured and destroyed the rest of Macdonald's following. This, he says, they did, and reports that all the Macdonalds, or Irish, were massacred by them. Later he had to admit that he had been misinformed, and that no such massacre had taken place. Leslie also refers to the matter, and his story is likely to be the true version. He states that their overtures were turned down by himself and Argyll on the grounds that they considered the offers to have been insincere. Had they been, he states, genuinely against the Macdonalds, they would not have allowed any of them to escape, and he leaves the matter at that. The episode, however, appears to have had a sequel which will be related in due course.

The Parliamentary Army now proceeded to pursue their enemies down the peninsula, and marched to Lochhead-Kilkerran, where the Marquis and Leslie took up their quarters in the House of Lochhead, surrendered to them by the Macdonalds, and spent a day or two there to obtain information and rest the soldiers. Lochhead was reached on 25th May, and, while he was there, Leslie appears to have heard for the first time of the departure of the Irish contingent by sea to Ireland. It would appear, therefore, although the fact is not specifically stated, that the whole of Macdonald's force came to Lochhead, and that it was from that port that the Irish sailed. Their numbers are stated to have been about 800 men, and they left in fifteen ships. They apparently did not go direct to Ireland, but touched at Islay to pick up Sir Alexander and his staff, for they did not arrive on Irish soil until 9th June, when they landed "on the sands near Cundrum in the isle of Lecall."

The remaining part of the contingent, the Kintyre men and the Macdougalls, under the command of Archibald Mor Macdonald of Sanda, who was accompanied by his son Archibald Og, Leslie learned at Lochhead, had withdrawn into the fortress of Dunaverty on the south shore of Kintyre, and, balked of his other prey, he set out for their capture there. He reached Dunaverty on or before 31st May, for on that date he wrote from there a dispatch to the Committee of Estates at Edinburgh. Local tradition states that before actually investing the fortress, Leslie halted his army for a night on the slope of the hillside opposite Keprigan, and near to where the present War Memorial stands.

In his dispatch Leslie reports his progress from Dunblane to Dunaverty, and describes the action at Rhunahaorine. Turner also describes this, but somewhat more curtly than Leslie. Leslie complains bitterly about the failure of his supply. The ships under Captain Louis Dick had not arrived, and although he had written to the Sheriff of Bute to have boats sent from that island, and to the Chancellor for those ships and boats promised to be sent from the shires of Ayr and Renfrew, he has to report that not a single boat had reached him before he got to Dunaverty. The pay of the army, also, was two months in arrears, and the soldiers had no shoes. He reports that when at Lochhead he found in the castle four pieces of cannon, and seven more in a fort at the mouth of the harbour, the reference being to the fort of Askamylnemoir, as it was then called, or Fort Argyll as it subsequently was named, constructed by the Marquis in 1639 to meet the threat of invasion by the Earl of Antrim. He does not state whether he made any use of these cannon, but apparently considered the matter important enough to be mentioned in his dispatch.

This letter of Leslie to the Committee of Estates was carried to Edinburgh by one of his cavalry officers, sent specially for that purpose - Colonel Strachan, Laird of

Thornetoun in Kincardineshire. In addition to sending the dispatch, Leslie felt his situation, arising out of the failure of his supply, to be so serious that he prepared a special set of instructions which Colonel Strachan was to present to the Committee, in order to impress on them the need for urgency. Summarised these were as follows. He was to acquaint the Committee with the manner in which the failure to supply shipping had prejudiced the public service. He had not as yet had the least assistance in this matter, "wherein if we had not been disappointed none of the Rebels could have escaped, and this country in all appearance had been totally reduced ere now." He was to represent to them that the soldiers' pay was overdue, and that there was in the army a serious shortage of provision for both horse and man. In addition, the ammunition to have been sent from Dumbarton had not yet reached him. Lastly, and a very serious matter affecting the discipline of the army, he was to announce the fact that, with the exception of himself (Colonel Strachan) and Colonel Urry, none of his cavalry commanders were at their posts, and that, accordingly, he requested the sanction of the Committee to his filling their places "by others able and sufficient who will better wait on and apply themselves heartily to the service." Having delivered the above instructions Colonel Strachan was to return to his post within two days after reaching Edinburgh.

CHAPTER VII

THE MASSACRE AT DUNAVERTY

It is probable that Sir Alexander Macdonald, after the engagement at Rhunahaorine, had come to the conclusion that his situation in Kintyre was hopeless. He had neither the forces, nor the military experience, to oppose a general of the calibre of David Leslie, and had therefore decided to extricate his army as best he could. The Irish had to get back to Ireland, and he may not have had shipping to evacuate the others. They had therefore been ordered to take refuge in Dunaverty, receiving from him, according to Turner, a promise that he would return to its relief. Local tradition records that an attempt was made, but that the ships were warned off by a piper playing a certain tune which conveyed to them intimation of their danger. Some lorists have gone further, and stated that an actual landing was made, and an action fought against Leslie's men. Had such taken place, however, it is incredible that Turner would not have mentioned it, and the story may be regarded as a myth. Turner tells us that the men who went into the castle - the Scottish contingent - were the best of Macdonald's force.

The Castle of Dunaverty was at this date legally a Campbell stronghold, as it was appointed in the charters to be the principal messuage of the Lordship of Kintyre, but it must have been captured by the Macdonalds during the Colkitto raids. It was built on the top of the mass of Old Red Sandstone rock which stands at the mouth of Coniglen Water, and, having a precipitous sea front about a hundred feet high, and a deep chasm extending along its landward side, it was a position of great strength in the days of ancient and medieval warfare. It had a history extending back nearly a thousand years from the date we are now considering, as the *Annals of Ulster* record that Aberte was besieged by Sealbach, King of Dalriada, in the year A.D. 712. Its name means the fort of the *Abhairtach*, a powerful tribe in ancient Ireland and Scotland. It was besieged and stormed by John Bissett on behalf of King Henry III of England about the year 1250, and was garrisoned by King Alexander III of Scotland in order to meet the invasion of King Haco of Norway in 1263. Alexander's captain surrendered the fortress to Haco, who put in command of it a Norwegian named Guthorm Backa-Kolf.

A little later it was in the hands of Angus Og of Islay and Kintyre, and in it he entertained King Robert the Bruce for three days in the autumn of 1306. In September of that year it was stormed and captured by the English, who expected to find Bruce there, but he had escaped to Rathlin or, some say, to Orkney. During the times of the Lords of the Isles it was held for them by their kinsmen the Macdonalds of Islay and Kintyre, but on the forfeiture of the island lords it passed into the keeping of the Scottish Crown. It was visited by King James IV in the summer of 1494, and we have already mentioned its surprise seizure by Sir John Macdonald at that time, and the hanging of the royal governor over its walls in the sight of the king.

In the reign of King James V it was rebuilt by John Scrimgeour, Master of Works to the King, and apparently finished at a cost of at least £500 Scots in 1542, in which year the Master of Glencairn, who had been appointed Governor of Kintyre, took up his headquarters in it, accompanied by certain trained gunners. The Earl of Sussex claimed to have fired it in his raid on Kintyre in 1558, but the damage done was probably slight, and the castle in which the Macdonalds now took refuge appears to have been that built by Scrimgeour about a hundred years earlier.

We have no exact information about its dimensions or design. Turner, unlike the garrulous Dugald Dalgetty of Scott's novel, merely tells us curtly that it was "environed by a wall," and that it had no water on the top of the rock except what fell from the clouds. This contradicts the traditional story that its water supply was led in a pipe from the neighbouring hills, a fact which, had it been true, would scarcely have escaped Turner's attention. The *Old Statistical Account* of Southend parish, by the Rev. David Campbell, states that it had a fosse or ditch, and two or three surrounding walls, one within the other. Turner tells us that the water supply of the garrison was derived from two "stripes" of water, apparently outside the wall or walls. These were most probably two branches of the Coniglen Water, which in those days meandered over the flat land near to where Southend village now stands, and did not enter the sea by its present straight channel, which was only cut in the year 1817. The two stripes of water were defended by a trench in which were placed a party of the besieged.

The circumstances of the siege and massacre are somewhat obscure and, as Turner is the only eye-witness who left a written account, we are largely dependent on his statements, although not necessarily compelled to accept them all. In his *Memoirs* he states that the besieged "had fair conditions offered to them for their persons and baggage if they would give over the house; this they stifflie refused to do, expecting relief which Alaster had falsely promised." These offers, if actually made as Turner states, were presumably made as soon as Leslie had arrived at the fortress, and if they were refused then, as Turner holds, the besieged, by the laws of war, forfeited any claim to mercy.

Whatever may have been the case, Leslie felt himself compelled to proceed to storm the place, and, in accordance with his usual tactics in such cases, began by an assault on the trench protecting the water supply of the besieged. The brunt of this attack appears to have fallen on the Marquis of Argyll's regiment. The trench was captured, and forty of the besieged killed in defending it. On Leslie's side six men only fell, but the Major of Argyll's regiment, Mathew Campbell of Skipness, was killed. Like Leslie, Turner, and others, he had been a soldier in the wars of Gustavus Adolphus. He was buried in the church or churchyard of Lochhead, that is the church built in 1643, and subsequently known as the old Gaelic Church of Campbeltown, and it is interesting to note that Mr Dugald Darroch, who came as its minister two years later, in 1649, was his son-in-law, having married his eldest daughter Aylis Campbell. A monument was erected in the church to Skipness's memory, which bore the following incription:-

> A captain much renowned,
>
> Whose cause of fight was still Christ's right,
>
> For which his soul is crowned.
>
> So briefly then to know the man,
>
> This stone tells all the storie;
>
> On earth his race he ran with grace,
>
> In heaven he reigns in glory.

After the capture of the water supply Leslie was not under any necessity of taking the castle by storm. All he had to do was to keep it invested until thirst had done its work. The weather, which had been wet and stormy in May, became hot and sultry in early June, and this accelerated the surrender. "Inexorable thirst," says Turner, made them seek a parley, and he was sent to speak with them. Leslie's terms were that they were to surrender at discretion, and Turner points out that he was somewhat surprised at the nice distinction which he made when he said that they must yield to the Kingdom's mercy, and not to his. Having no alternative but to die of thirst, they finally surrendered and came out, Turner says, to the number of 300 men. He does not mention that there were any women or children in the fort.

Leslie, Argyll, and some of the other officers then apparently held a council of war to decide what should be done with them. Two days were taken up this in the discussion and, if we are to believe Turner, he besought Leslie to spare their lives, and Leslie appeared to be always agreeable to do so. In the long run, however, other counsels prevailed, and they were ordered to be destroyed. "They were put to the sword," says Turner, "every mother's son, except one young man Mackoull, whose life I begged, to be sent to France." The single exception was John Macdougall or Mackoul, of Dunolly, who apparently owed his life to Turner's intercession. He lived to bring his case before the Parliament of 1661 and recovered his lands.

There is a local tradition that the besieged were tied in pairs and flung over the rock, but there is no reason why we should not take Turner's statement that they were put to the sword in its literal sense, and conclude that the army was simply let loose on them, and hacked them to pieces. Skulls showing sabre marks have been dug up near the rock and, about a century ago, an old fisherman at the waterfoot of Dunaverty used to keep one in his house for exhibition to visitors.

Some at least of the chiefs were hanged on a gibbet, or shot, including the two Macdonalds of Sanda. Montereul, describing the massacre in a letter to Mazarin, states that "Baron Sance [that is, Macdonald of Sanda] of the Clan Macdonald, who commanded the fortress, was hanged and as the gibbet was found to be too short, so that his feet touched the ground, he was subsequently shot." The Macdonalds of Sanda are stated to have been buried where they fell on the old lands of Machricastel, now part of the farm of Machribeg, and later a walled tomb was erected on the spot which bears this inscription:-

'This enclosure was erected by the Rev. Douglas Macdonald, XIIth Laird of Sanda, in 1846, to mark the spot where his ancestors Archibald Mhor and Archibald Oig, father and son, were shot and buried after the battle of Dunaverty in 1647. Other human remains found on the battlefield were interred here by him.'

Turner mentions two incidents which are worthy of our attention. Among the leading men executed was included Angus Maceachran, laird of Kilellan. After the surrender, and while his fate was still in the balance, he handed over to Sir James Turner a small red box, "full of writtis and evidentis belonging to himself," with the request that Turner would deliver them to the Marquis of Argyll. The box, presumably, contained charters and other papers relating to his estate. Turner did so, and after the execution of the Marquis of Argyll in 1661, he had prepared and witnessed at Edinburgh a declaration to the effect that he had done so. It is pleasing to know that Maceachran's trust in the Marquis was not belied, for in 1659 Argyll restored the lands of Kilellan to Colin, the son of Angus.

The other is the strange episode of the men in the cave. One hundred men, whom Turner describes as "country fellows," that is local men or natives of the place, were found to be taking refuge in a certain cave. Who these men were, or where the cave was, we can only surmise. They may have been stragglers of the Macdonalds who failed to get into the castle in time, or for whom there was no room within its walls. They were smoked out of the cave, in Turner's words, "as they do foxes." Turner states that their lives were spared, but they were taken as prisoners of war, and handed over to Captain Campbell the Chancellor's brother, that is to a brother of the Earl of Loudon, who was at this time Chancellor of Scotland. Montereul throws some fresh light on the incident, to which he also refers in one of his letters to Mazarin. He states: "The consideration of his Majesty's [that is the King of France's] service saved a hundred men that the Marquis of Argyle and David Leslie gave to one of Sir Robert Moray's Captains."

The seizure of these men, and their transportation to France, was one of the charges against the Marquis at his trial in 1661, and is contained in Article 7 of his indictment. He was therein charged with "having slaughtered and murdered the number of 260 of them, or therby, thay being undir your trust, assurance, creadit, or power, and did dispoise of the rest of them, at your own hand, without any lawful warrand, to captanes William Hay and Archibald Campbell, to serve in the Frenche service." The last named captain has been identified as Sir Archibald Campbell, brother-german to Sir John Campbell of Lawers, who became first Earl of Loudon in 1633, and who was Lord Chancellor of Scotland in 1647. Sir Robert Moray succeeded Lord Kintyre in 1645 as colonel of the French regiment of Scotsmen raised by the latter in 1642, and it would thus appear that either Hay or Campbell, or both of them, were at this time captains in the French regiment. It is quite clear, therefore, that it was into this regiment that the men taken alive at Dunaverty and Dunnyveg were impressed, and condemned to an enforced exile of fifteen years, until it was disbanded in 1662. Local tradition agrees with the historical record that this was the period during which they were abroad.

Doubtlessly many never returned, and some who did so are stated to have discovered that their wives, who had long given them up as dead, were found to have married other husbands.

Evidence by another eye-witness is to be found in the Acts of the Scottish Parliament. In the year 1661 John Macdougall of Dunolly, Allan Macdougall of Rarae, Dougall Macdougall of Donnach, and John Macdougall of Dagish, obtained an Act and Decreet of the Parliament against the Marquis of Argyll, James Campbell of Ardkinglas, and others. John Macdougall of Dunolly was the young man mentioned by Turner as the sole survivor of the besieged at Dunaverty in 1647. The Act stated that the Macdougalls and others "had risen in arms to the number of 500 with the Marquis of Montrose and Sir James Lawmont, and that they were pursued to the fort of Dunaverty in Kintyre, which not being able to hold out, there being one message sent in to these within the fort that if they did not come forth against ten hours the next day they should have no quarter, and if they came out they should have quarters. And the said John Macdougall being within the fort with his friends, who, having punctually, as was desired, at the verie hour of the day, came forth and rendered themselves, they were all by the instigation of the deceast Archibald Campbell late Marquis of Argyll, to the number of five hundred men, officers, and soldiers, cruellie and inhumanly butchered in cold blood (the said John Macdougall being then a child and in nonage was only spared)."

This account was prepared fourteen years after the event happened, and taken down from one who was a mere child at the time. Hence less reliance is to be put on it than on Turner's account. It differs from his in that it definitely accuses Argyll of breach of faith, and in that it gives the numbers of those killed as 500 against Turner's 300. Some years ago a list of names of Macdougalls killed at Dunaverty, found at Inveraray, was printed. It contains the names of ninety men in all, of whom forty-nine appear to have been *daoine-uasail* or leading men. No list of the Macdonalds and their followers has ever been discovered, and the exact total of the killed must remain doubtful.

A similar charge of breach of faith by Argyll and Leslie towards the besieged was made by Henry Guthry, Bishop of Dunkeld, in his *Memoirs*. Guthry was a Royalist, but his book gives a not unfair and very graphic picture of the events of the Civil War in England and Scotland. In it Guthry made the statement: "The country people whom he [Sir Alexander Macdonald] had constrained to join him, submitted upon quarter given them by David Leslie, but having surrendered their arms, the Marquis and a bloody preacher, Mr Nevoy, prevailed with him to break his word, and so the army was let loose upon them and killed them all without mercy, whereat David Leslie seemed to have some inward check; for while the Marquis and he with Mr Nevoy were walking over the ankles in blood he turned about and said, 'Now, Mr John, have you not gotten your fill of blood?' This was reported by many that heard it."

Turner had seen Guthry's book in manuscript, and noting these words, and the charges of bad faith, he sat down and added an appendix to his own *Memoirs* in order to rebut them. He describes the Bishop's statements as "a fearful lie" and "a most foul calumny." He denies that the victims were offered quarter before they came out, but states that they had previously refused to surrender when quarter was offered, and so had no claim on the General's mercy. "And is it not," he goes on, "a pretty story of the Bishop to say that the Marquis of Argyle, David Leslie, and Nevoy waded over their ankles in blood? Certainly they have been horribly delighted in blood that would walk in blood when they might have walked dry-shod. Could the blood of 300 men, in a hot summer day, make such a pool of blood as to come over men's ankles? But this is so far from the truth that David Leslie never saw these 300 men, dead or alive, or ever came near them, say the Bishop what he will."

Some previous accounts of the siege of Dunaverty have greatly exaggerated the length of time for which the besieged held out. In the *New Statistical Account* of Southend parish the Rev. Daniel Kelly states that the water supply failed about the 10th of July. This would imply a siege of over a month. In a paper entitled *Kintyre and the Kintyre Club*, printed in 1884, the author, Alexander Sinclair, states that the siege lasted "for several months." The publication of the Montereul correspondence some years ago, however, has enabled the point to be settled beyond any possibility of doubt. In a letter to Cardinal Mazarin dated 15th June, Montereul reports the fall of the castle, the massacre of the besieged, and the execution of Macdonald of Sanda. This was written from Edinburgh, and, allowing two days for the news to get there from Dunaverty, and remembering that two days were spent in deliberating on the fate of the besieged after they had come out, we get the 10th or 11th day of June as the probably date of the surrender, and the total duration of the siege as not more than ten days.

This massacre shocked the public conscience of Scotland at the time, and it was natural that there should have been much discussion as to the responsibility of such an exalted personage as the Marquis of Argyll, in whose case the motives for revenge must have been strong. On 9th May 1647 the Committee of Estates had addressed a letter to General Leslie to the effect that, in all matters pertaining to the pardoning of the rebels, he was to take the advice of the Marquis. Leslie must have had these instructions in his pocket at Dunaverty, and it is incredible, considering this fact, and the powers which the Marquis possessed by reason of his Commission already referred to, that Leslie would have dared to order the massacre if the Marquis had said "pardon." The Marquis was undoubtedly a crafty man, but there is no evidence that he was a cruel man, and the reason for this and other massacres, such as that at Philiphaugh, is to be sought for in the religious fanaticism of the Covenanters. Every now and again arise in the world men, or nations, or sects, who imagine that they are God's chosen instruments to set the world right. This belief the Covenanters, and their clergy in particular, held in full measure. In his evidence at Argyll's trial in 1661 Sir James Turner testified that he had never heard the Marquis advise Leslie to proceed to the massacre, but that, on the other hand, Mr John Nevay, his chaplain, had never ceased to urge it, calling down upon their heads the curses which befell Saul for not slaying the Amalekites, if they failed to slay the Macdonalds. He is actually said to have preached a sermon from the text in Samuel: "What meaneth this bleating of sheep and lowing of oxen"? in order to work on the superstitious mind of Argyll.

Such ministers drew from a contemporary historian, Sir James Balfour of Denmylne, the following criticism: "The best instruments misapplied do greatest mischief, and prove most dangerous to any state; and as of the sweetest wine is made the sharpest vinegar, so churchmen, who, by their holy function and robes of innocence, should be the sweetest of all professions, who should breathe nothing but peace, unity, allegiance, and love, if they misapply their talent and abandon themselves to the spirit of faction, they become the bitterest enemies, the most corroding cankers, and the worst vipers in any commonwealth." Twenty years later, under the misgovernment and tyranny of King Charles II in Scotland, this fanaticism became transmuted into a passion of resistance, and a struggle for freedom of conscience, which arouses our highest admiration, but in 1645 and 1647 it was, judged by present-day standards, fanaticism pure and simple, and the massacres of Philiphaugh and Dunaverty have cast an indelible stain on the pages of Covenanting history.

There is no evidence that the Castle of Dunaverty was dismantled at this date. As it was Argyll's messuage, he would not be expected to have done so unless he felt that he could not hold it. We find a few later references to it. In 1654 a sasine of lands in favour of the daughters of the Marquis was granted at Dunaverty. As late as 1683, after the forfeiture of the Earl of Argyll, and when John Boyle of Kelburn was Crown Chamberlain of the forfeited estates, one of his agents, Robert Stewart, had his headquarters there. It was most probably finally demolished at the time of the Earl's rebellion in 1685, when the Marquis of Atholl was ordered to destroy all his castles. The traces of foundations on the top of the rock, a fragment of wall running down the landward side, and some masonry near the cave called *Boes Chair*, are the only remains now left of this once noted stronghold.

CHAPTER VIII

LESLIE'S RETURN MARCH

Having disposed effectually of his enemy at Dunaverty, Leslie, accompanied by Argyll, returned to Tarbert, via Lochhead, with the intention of proceeding to Islay to deal with the remainder of the Macdonald's following who were holding out there in Dunnyveg Castle, which had been left in the command of old Coll, father of Sir Alexander. All Leslie's dispatches relating to the campaign in Kintyre and Islay in 1647 have been preserved, and some have been printed in Thurloe's *Memoirs*, except the one which he must have written describing the massacre at Dunaverty, and giving his reasons to the Parliament for the action taken on the besieged. There is good reason to think that this, compromising, as it may have done, either or both Argyll and Leslie, may have been destroyed, but, should it ever come to light, it may help to make clear some facts connected with the Dunaverty affair which are still obscure.

Leslie's next dispatch appears to have been written from Lochhead, just after he had sent on his army from that place to Tarbert, but it is undated, and can only be interpreted by reference to the others which preceded and followed it. He appears to have stayed some days at Lochhead, and while there was met by John Kennedy, Provost of Ayr, and Commissioner for Ayr in the Parliament, who had a licence for the disbursal of public moneys, and whose mission to Leslie was to bring the arrears of pay for the army. For this purpose, much against Leslie's will, a muster was held for the purpose of deducting the pay of those who had died or had been killed in action, and he states: "I must crave leave to shew your lordships, that it was verie hard and unusuall to have astructed us to a muster now after three moneths faylour of payment, and that diverse soldiers were killed and wounded in the service, to whom the officers had furnished moneys in their extreamities." Like all his other letters, it is a moan about the failure of supply, especially of boats, and he states that he will not have at Lochtarbert boats sufficient to take to Islay half the force he had intended to take, but that he has set out with the few boats he possesses, "giveing the businesse a hazard, and committing all to God."

The Castle of Lochhead had also been seized by the Macdonalds, but had surrendered to Leslie on his march to Dunaverty. Some of those who had been in it appear to have been the men who wrote to Argyll and Leslie after the Rhunahaorine fight, offering to submit, but whose offers, according to Leslie, had been rejected by him and Argyll on the grounds that they were not sincere. Montereul, as we have seen, described these men as chiefs of the Macneills and Macallasters. There now took place an incident, or alleged incident, at Lochhead, which formed the grounds of one of the charges against the Marquis of Argyll at his trial in 1661.

The evidence led was to the effect that, after they had surrendered the House of Lochhead, they were allowed to return peaceably to their homes. While, however,

Leslie was besieging Dunaverty they were called to successive *rendez-vous* by him, but again, after each such meeting, were allowed to return. Finally, apparently on his return march, they were called to Lochhead Castle, into which they were thrown, and on the following morning sixteen or seventeen of them were taken out and hanged. To aggravate the offence it was also charged to him that a young lad, who had just returned from the "schools" at Glasgow, probably from the university, was among those taken, and although his old father testified that the lad had never borne arms in his life, both father and son were hanged. This was denied by Argyll, through his advocates, who stated that it was the first time that he had ever heard of it, and that the charge had been concocted by his enemies in order to make him appear the more odious in the eyes of the law.

It is strange that of these men only one name is given, that of a certain Hector Macallaster and his two sons, who were all three said to have been hanged. It is strange, also, that Turner, who reported so many hangings by Leslie in the course of this campaign, makes no mention whatever of those at Lochhead. It is hard to believe, however, that the story of the young student could be easily concocted, and there is little reason to doubt that a Hector Macallaster and his two sons at least were hanged.

Peter Macintosh, in his *History of Kintyre*, mentions the incident as a tradition in his time, and states that Macallaster was of Glenlussa, and married to a sister of the Marquis of Argyll, which can easily be shown to be untrue. There were several Hectors of that name, large tacksmen in South Kintyre a little before this date, and there was also a Hector of Loup, but he was alive and an elder in 1649. He is more likely to have been one of the others.

Cuthbert Bede in his *Glencreggan*, a book which, however entertaining, must not be mistaken for serious history, also relates, with some embroidery, the story of the Macallasters. He states that when they were brought to the gallows Argyll's men asked him "Which of them shall we put up first?" and Argyll replied, "The whelps, and afterwards the old fox," and that the wife of Macallaster, Argyll's sister, who had come to beg for their lives, arrived too late, and only to see the bodies of her husband and two sons swinging lifeless in the air, whereupon she fell on her knees and invoked seven curses on the head of Argyll. This makes an exciting story but unfortunately there is no evidence that the details were as stated, although little doubt that the Macallasters and others suffered. Lord Archibald Campbell, in his *Records of Argyll*, states that a Mackay of Ardnacroish was hanged along with the Macallasters. In cases such as these, where sufficient historical evidence is not forthcoming, it is preferable to retain an open mind, and to consider part of the evidence at least as unproven.

Leslie's next dispatch was sent from the Island of Gigha, which he had reached by 23rd June. In this he tells us of his difficulties in getting his troops ferried across, and that he had only managed to take eighty horsemen in the boats. The rest were probably left at Lochhead, for he reported to the Committee of Estates that he had put that castle in the command of the Captain of his Horse. No mention is made of the arrangements made by him at Dunaverty. He got to Islay on or before 25th June, and his next dispatch is of that date from Dunnyveg. In this he states that Sir Alexander Macdonald had left for Ireland sixteen days before, carrying with him all the leading gentlemen of Islay, and some of the best of the country people or local inhabitants, and had left behind in the fort 100 Irish, and as many local men under the command of his father, assisted by his brother, promising and swearing that, as he was his son, and expected a blessing, he would shortly return to relieve him. He also reported that he had heard that there were 4000 Irish ready to return with Sir Alexander, and he implores the Committee to send him the necessary supplies of ships and materials of war. He relates also that as soon as he arrived, having summoned the fort to surrender, he had received an unfavourable answer, and therefore was now under the necessity of proceeding to storm it. He reports that only three boats from the Lowlands had as yet arrived, and that these had come from Saltcoats, and were commanded by Lord Montgomerie, eldest son of the Earl of Eglinton.

Sir Alexander Macdonald, however, did not return to relieve Dunnyveg, any more than Dunaverty, and the fall of the castle took place much sooner than Leslie expected. His next dispatch is dated the 5th July 1647, and is extremely interesting in that it contains his own account of the taking of old Colkitto. It has not yet appeared in print. Leslie's story is that he had ascertained that old Coll was in the habit of leaving the castle with an armed escort to speak with the Captain of Dunstaffnage, who was an old friend of his own, and that he had done so on 29th June. On the 30th, he had sent out one of his soldiers with a letter to Dunstaffnage, asking for four dollars worth of aquavitae. This soldier was apparently caught and examined by Leslie's orders, when he stated that Dunstaffnage would not go into the fort to drink with Colkitto, but that the latter would come out to drink with him. Leslie states: "This so fair an opportunitie of seasing upon so notorious a Traitor could not in reason be anie longer slipt, and therefore order was given that if he shold againe confer after that maner anie more, they shold lay hands on him, which fell out the next morning, being the 1 day of Julie, at which tyme he was apprehendit by Lieut Colonel Menzies and three more."

Leslie is at pains to explain that Coll came out with an armed escort, with swords, targets, head pieces, long guns, and side pistols, and that there was no question of his having had any assurance of safety from him, and of having been betrayed by him. This, however, appears to have been an opinion opposite to that held by some at the time, and even Turner states that his arrest was made "not without some stain to the Lieut. General's honour." It would, however, have been more satisfactory if Turner had stated precisely the manner in which Leslie had a stain cast on his honour, instead of making what is merely a vague accusation. The escort of four armed men, according to Leslie's account, escaped back into the fort.

For the next three days after this there was what Leslie calls "nothing but hard shooting," but on Sunday, the 4th of July, a parley was asked and granted, and a set of conditions of surrender drawn up. Dunnyveg surrendered on the 5th July 1647, and 176 men walked out. There was no massacre, as at Dunaverty, probably because Leslie's terms of surrender were accepted, but the 176 men, or those of them who did not die later of plague or starvation, were sent, as in the case of the men taken in the cave at Dunaverty, to the service of the King of France. Some of the leaders Leslie took along with himself, until he had reduced the remaining strengths in the west.

The articles of capitulation of Dunnyveg Castle have been preserved. They were drawn up between Leslie and Argyll on the one hand, and Ranald Macdonald, Daniel O'Neall, and Donald Macdonald on the other. They provided for (1) the handing over of the fort with all its ammunition and plenishing before 12 o'clock on 5th July 1647. (2) The holders to swear that they would never again take up arms against the kingdom of Scotland. (3) To leave the fort without any arms except their necessary baggage. (4) That as many as the General should choose were to go along with the army until all the other strongholds were reduced or the army left the field, and these were to be given the assurance of a safe conduct. (5) The lives of all to be guaranteed and all the local people to be allowed to proceed home, but the Irish to go to Ireland and France. (6) The leaders mentioned above were to leave Scotland unless given special permission by Argyll and Leslie to remain.

The question may well be asked why the men of Dunnyveg were not subjected to the same fate as those at Dunaverty. In this matter neither Turner's nor Leslie's accounts afford us any information. It may have been, as we have already surmised, because in this case the besieged, especially after the taking of Colkitto, were more in a mood to come to terms, and that when these were once signed the men's lives were assured. Nearly a month had elapsed since the Dunaverty massacre, and it may have been that during that time Leslie and Argyll had heard some serious criticisms from Edinburgh on the conduct of that affair, or that the wind of public opinion had begun to blow.

If Turner is to be believed, Leslie suffered from great remorse after the Dunaverty massacre. While exonerating Leslie on the legal issue, Turner makes the remarks: "It is true, on the other hand, *summum jus summa injuria*, and in such cases mercy is the more Christian, the more honourable, and the more ordinary way, in our warres in Europe. Bot I reallie believe, advise him [Leslie] to that act who will, he hath repented it many times since, and even very soone after the doeing it." Perhaps, also, by the time they had got to Dunnyveg Mr John Nevay had had his fill of blood, and had ceased to tempt the Marquis and Leslie to further slaughter.

The fate of the Macdonalds, old Coll and his son Sir Alexander, remains to be told. Old Coll, according to the evidence led at Argyll's trial in 1661, was put on board a boat belonging to Captain James Browne, with orders from the Marquis that he was to be sent to Dunstaffnage; but Captain Browne, unwilling to lose the opportunity of a fair wind, went straight with his prisoner to Leith Roads, where he handed him over to the Marquis, who had by that time returned to Edinburgh.

Argyll sent him back to Dunstaffnage, but the argument of the prosecution appears to have been that he should have been delivered to the Parliament, and made to stand his trial in Edinburgh. At Dunstaffnage he was tried "in a justice or lieutenant court judicially," sentenced to death and, on October 1647, hanged, it is said, from the mast of his own galley placed across a fissure in a rock. He was 77 years of age.

At his trial Argyll gave evidence as follows: "One thing I shall add in general, that I thank the Lord by his grace in helping me, I never took any man's life but what was done in conflict, or by order of law, for notorious crimes according to standing acts of parliament." Needless to say the other side held, and apparently still hold, an opposite view, and the *Clan Donald* historians, who wrote about fifty years ago, make the following comments on Coll's trial and execution: "Coll Ciatach under promise of safety [Leslie denied this, as we have seen] ventured outside to speak to an old neighbour of his, Campbell of Dunstaffnage, who was evidently the means of luring the unsuspecting veteran to his doom. Regardless of every consideration of honour the besiegers at once took him prisoner, not, as Sir James Turner admits 'without some staine to the Lieut. General's honour.' Such an admission by a Covenanter determines the unspeakable perfidy of the act. The execution of Coll from the mast of his own galley under the direction of 'The Master fiend Argyll,' and after so horrible a travesty of the forms of law as a trial by a Campbell jury, is a worthy sequel to conduct so lacking in the most elementary principles of good faith."

The reader will, of course, draw his own conclusions. We do not know whether it was customary in those days for the leader of a besieged garrison to come out to talk and drink with some of the besiegers. General Leslie apparently did not take the view that it was, and certainly no British Commander of to-day would have acted differently from what he did. It certainly would have looked better if Coll had been tried in Edinburgh; but it is doubtful, in view of his past record, whether in that case his fate would have been any different from what it was. Two of his sons were, according to the *Clan Donald* historians, also executed, Archibald at Skipness, and Angus at Dunnyveg. His most distinguished son, Sir Alexander, was killed in Ireland towards the end of 1647, that year which proved so fatal to the Macdonalds and their associates.

CHAPTER IX

THE EPIDEMIC OF PLAGUE

There is a vague but persistent tradition of a great epidemic of plague or pestilence having occurred in Kintyre about the middle of the seventeenth century, which took a devastating toll of the human population. The disease referred to is that known to-day as Bubonic Plague, and is quite different from Cholera, which has also been, at a later date, an unwelcome visitor. Plague is to-day essentially an Asiatic disease, now practically unknown in Europe and America. In the seventeenth century it was usually supposed to come from Holland, and, as the Dutch were then the principal ocean carriers from Asia to Europe, there may have been some truth in this view.

The symptoms of Bubonic Plague, as detailed by a modern expert, are as follows: fever, severe headache, giddiness, congested eyes, extreme mental depression, stammering, staggering gait, bodily weakness, painful swellings in the groin, armpits, neck, or other regions of the lymphatic glandular system, with an occasional eruption on the skin of so-called carbuncles or pustules. They end in death in a large percentage of cases, in the course of three to five days. The disease is due to a bacillus, the carrier of which is the rat flea. Most of the old houses in Scotland, with their thatched roofs, harboured a considerable rat population, and it is easy to understand that the disease would spread rapidly once the bacillus was introduced. The alarming nature of the symptoms, the fatal course of the attack, the absence of any known remedies, added to the superstitious outlook of the times, made this disease one of peculiar horror in the minds of the people.

We have no contemporary account of the course of the disease in Kintyre, or exact details of the extent of its ravages, and the actual date of the visitation has been given differently by different writers. Peter Macintosh puts it as occurring in the year 1666, and records the popular local tradition, as recounted by his elders in the days of his youth (about the beginning of the nineteenth century) as follows: "The old people used to say that the plague came from Ayr to Dunaverty in a white cloud, and spread over most of Kintyre. In a short time the ravages it made were dreadful, turning the houses into graves, and multitudes fleeing for their lives, not knowing whither to go - the living fled from the dead. On the farm of Kilkivan some green knolls are shown, where some houses once stood in which all the inhabitants died without any person to bury them." The houses were left until they fell in, and until nature performed for the dead the office of burial which the living were afraid to perform. Fear of having no relative to perform the office of burial in a proper manner was ever present in the minds of the old Highlanders, and it was a common precaution, taken to avoid such contingency, for people to order their coffins while still alive.

When Cuthbert Bede was collecting material for his book *Glencreggan* in 1859, he encountered some of the old plague traditions, which he recorded as follows: "When the Great Plague of 1666 had swept away its thousands in the city of

London, it visited Scotland, and was very fatal in Ayrshire. From thence it passed 'in a great white cloud' across to Cantire." Here he is either giving an account of the same tradition recorded by Macintosh, or simply borrowing from him. He tells, however, another legend of the plague which he states to have received from the man at the wheel of the steamer on his way to Glasgow, and which illustrates the fear of improper burial to which we have just referred. "You see there Carradale Glen," said his informant, "where the plantings are, and where the river comes down from the mountains ... Well, sir, in that glen in the time of the Great Plague there was a man who took the sickness; and, hearing of the people dying in their houses [as related of those at Kilkivan] he feared he should not be buried. So, this fear took such a power over him, that he prevailed on some of his friends to dig his grave, and he went and sat by and saw it done. And when it was dug he laid himself in the grave, with his sword by his side, and presently he died; and his friends covered his body with the turf. MacCaog was the man's name; and they will show you the grave to this day."

The Marquis of Lorne, in his *Adventures in Legend*, also records some of the popular traditions relating to this subject. Under the date 1661 he relates that "the visit of the Plague is very vividly remembered in the oral tales ... It spread through the whole of Kintyre and other districts suffered terribly. Two years after the Plague came there was a terrible famine. Sleet continued to come down during the Spring. Farmers were not able to plough nor crofters to dig. The corn when it came up did not ripen ... another bad year followed. The corn and hay seemed sapless, people and cattle died, and Kintyre became nearly a desert ... When the district was in this condition through famine and pestilence, MacCalein brought men from Carrick and Ayr to be farmers in Kintyre."

These traditions no doubt recall on the whole very fairly the conditions brought about by this great epidemic, but all are very far out in regard to the date, as we shall show by reference to contemporary documentary evidence. Plague had been prevalent in England from the beginning of the seventeenth century. There was a terrible visitation in 1603, the year in which Queen Elizabeth died, when some 30,000 deaths took place. Again in 1625, the year in which King Charles I came to the throne, over 40,000 people died of the disease. The city of London, we are told, was one great mortuary, and this was the worst attack that England had experienced since the Black Death in 1348.

It was from England that the plague came to Scotland. It was prevalent during the Civil War, and was carried from one town to another by the besieging armies. War has always been a potent factor in the spread of epidemic disease. It was brought to Scotland after the storming of Newcastle by the Covenanting army in 1644. The earliest mention, or one of the earliest, occurs in the *Diary* of James Burns, Merchant and Bailie of Glasgow, who records the fact that it had broken out at St Johnston, or Perth, in September 1645, and that the laird of Craigends had died of it. In the same year it was rife at Edinburgh, Kelso and Borrowstounness. In Edinburgh special huts were erected at Salisbury Crags, in which the plague patients were isolated.

In January 1646 Principal Baillie of Glasgow university wrote of "the crushing of our nation by pestilence and Montrose's victories." A year later, in January 1647, he reported that in Glasgow, despite very severe weather, "all that may are fled out of it." In the summer of that year Baillie was himself confined in the town of Kilwinning, owing to a suspicion of plague in that place, by which it was shut off for several weeks from the outside world.

It was in May of that year that General David Leslie led his army from Dunblane to Dunaverty, and he records in his first dispatch of the campaign his desire to get away from Dunblane as early as possible, owing to the fact that the pestilence had been rife in the neighbourhood. As we have seen, it had broken out at Perth as early as September 1645. It is probable, although he does not disclose any details, that Leslie suffered more casualties from plague than from war during his campaign of the summer of that year, and there can be no doubt that it was his army that brought the plague into Kintyre and Islay. This, in fact, was admitted at Argyll's trial in 1661. He was accused of transporting 200 men to the uninhabited Isle of Jura, where they perished by famine. In the course of his defence this charge was met by the statement that "the truth is that David Leslie was with his army in Ila against old Coil McGillespick, who held out a fort there called Dunavage, and by the continuing of his army there the Isle was spoiled of meat. But Coil being taken and the fort surrendered David Leslie came home with his army *and the army left the Pestilence in the country*." It is significant that Macintosh records the tradition that it first appeared at Dunaverty.

On the above evidence, therefore, we are forced to conclude that the Kintyre and Islay visitation was in 1647 and the two subsequent years, and that the infection was introduced by Leslie's army from the already plague-stricken areas of central Scotland. In England this disease reached its peak in the fatal year of 1665, when in London city alone some 80,000 persons died of it. The records, as examined by Creighton show, however, that in that year there was no plague in Scotland. When the severity of the outbreak in London became known the most stringent measures of inspection and quarantine were taken by the Scottish government, and these, as he points out, were completely successful. The outbreak of 1644 to 1648 was the last visitation that Scotland experienced of this fell disease.

As we have pointed out, there is no direct evidence available of the extent of the ravages of the plague in Kintyre in 1647 to 1648, but there is some fairly convincing indirect evidence. An old tradition states that after the epidemic only three chimneys were left smoking in what is now Southend parish. This is doubtlessly the language of exaggeration, but, if we turn to such written records as are capable of throwing any light on the subject, we get at least a partial confirmation of the statement. In a rental of 1651, that is immediately after the epidemic, we find that out of 55 holdings recorded in the rental for the old parishes of Kilcolmkill and Kilblaan, 29

9. This 16th C. Tower-house occupies the NE corner of the courtyard of Skipness Castle. The castle withstood siege by the Macdonalds during the Colkitto Raids, and following Argyll's Rebellion of 1685, the Campbell laird of Skipness successfully petitioned against the 'razeing down' of the castle.

10. The ivy-covered nave and chancel of the Old Parish Church, Killean, in Largieside, date from the 12th C. Monuments and carved stones in the churchyard range from Early Christian times, through Medieval and Post-Reformation centuries, until the present.

11. The N. aisle of Killean Church, latterly became the family vault of the Macdonalds of Largie. The estates of Angus Macdonald were forfeited after 1647, the only break in ownership since 1431, but were restored by the parliament of 1661.

12. St. Columba's Church, Southend, the former parish-church of Kilcolmkill. The E part of the building is ascribed to the 13th C., and was extended to the present length in late medieval or post-reformation times.

were entered as wholly waste and 13 as partially waste. Waste land meant land that had once been cultivated, but was so no longer, and this could only have happened if the previous occupiers had been killed in battle, transported to a foreign land, died of disease, or had been deprived of their seed corn, plough horses, and other necessaries of cultivation. No doubt all these factors were at work in Kintyre in the years 1644 to 1650, and the figures for waste land probably represent their combined effect, but the memory of the plague and its horrors appears to be more vivid than that of any of the others, and this disease probably accounted for the major portion of the damage.

The Marquis of Lorne, as we have seen, gives 1661 as the date of the plague in Kintyre, and states that it was after this, and because of it, that, in order to repopulate the wastelands, the Marquis of Argyll brought Lowlanders to Kintyre. As we have already pointed out, the correct date of the epidemic of plague was 1647 to 1648, and while it is a fact that the plantation of Lowland lairds took place immediately after that event, it is a mistaken view to think that the plague was anything more than an accidental factor in bringing it about. There is no doubt, however, that, added to the destruction by war and the depopulation caused by transportations, it made the actual eviction of existing tenants unnecessary, and so, in that sense, it was one of the factors to be taken into account. The beginnings of a Lowland plantation were, however, much earlier than the plague, and due to other causes, some account of which has already been given in the chapter dealing with the Burgh of Lochhead. With the later and more important phase we propose to deal in the succeeding chapter.

CHAPTER X

THE PLANTATION OF LOWLAND LAIRDS
AND CAMPBELLS

The first step in the Lowland Plantation of Kintyre was the foundation of a burgh of Lowland burgesses at Lochhead which was taken, as we have seen, under the authority of an Act of the Parliament of Scotland of 1597, and the scheme of founding the burgh set on foot, after 1609, by the 7th Earl of Argyll, in accordance with the conditions on which he had obtained the grant of the Lordship two years before. The second and much more important stage in the Plantation had, however, no government support, and was taken by the Marquis of Argyll, apparently on his own initiative and responsibility.

General Leslie's suppression of Macdonald resistance in 1647 had removed any further menace from that quarter. Since the Marquis had come into possession of Kintyre his tenure of it had been threatened by the Earl of Antrim in 1639, and during the Colkitto raids of 1644 to 1647. The times were still troubled, and it is not surprising that, shrewd man as the Marquis was, he should have taken steps to strengthen his position in the future. He had been the head of the Covenanting party in the State, and it was to that party that he now turned to help him out of his difficulties, by bringing some of its members to colonise his Kintyre estates. The men whom he chose for this purpose belonged to a higher position in the social scale than the Lochhead burgesses, and were lairds or barons, possessing estates in the Lowlands, and scions of some of the oldest landed families there. In addition to these, he brought many members of the Clan Campbell from other parts of Argyllshire.

The design of the Plantation was intended to secure for the Marquis a strong political and, if necessary, military backing in the district, and at the same time to introduce peaceable and thrifty tenants, who would enable him to recover the value of his estates which had been wasted by war, transportation and plague. The new tack-holders were not themselves farmers, but gentlemen whose main activities were absorbed in the political and military doings of the times, and as the tacks were of holdings much larger than a single man could work, the tacksmen, who were responsible for the rents, brought along with them many of their relations, with whom they shared the holdings, but of whom, and even of whose names, the Marquis knew nothing. In addition, these latter brought with them tenants, cottars, and others from their Lowland estates, to whom they sub-let farms. Thus the Plantation soon far exceeded in its scope the small initial attempt at Lochhead, which had been purely urban in character, and was spread over a large part of the landward area of the district. It must have been greatly facilitated by the numerous deaths of the old native tenants by the wars and plague of 1644 to 1647, but its true causes were in the political and ecclesiastical events of the period.

The man chosen to pioneer the plantation of lairds was William Ralston of that ilk, who possessed at this date estates in the parish of Beith and Lochwinnoch, and who was the principal heritor in Beith parish. He was a friend and confidant of the Marquis, and a Covenanter of the extreme sect know as the Remonstrants. The Marquis settled him in Kintyre, in the year 1650, by giving him a tack of 23½ merklands of the old lands of Saddell Abbey, with Saddell Castle as a residence. This castle had been built by the Bishop of Argyll shortly after the year 1508, when the lands of the Abbey had been erected into a temporal lordship, and annexed to the Bishopric. It had, however, been burned by the Earl of Sussex during his raid on Kintyre in the year 1558, and when Ralston arrived was in a state of disrepair, for in that year he executed an agreement with the Marquis to have it restored to its former state. He was to repair the breaches in the masonry, to provide new wooden floors, and a new roof of "firr and sklait," and to have the windows glazed and fitted with iron stanchions. The work was to be completed and "perfyted at the sight of craftsmen of skill" before 1st November 1652, the Marquis advancing 5000 merks to be paid back in three instalments. The Castle of Saddell, as it stands today, must have been that put in order by Ralston at this time.

He had eleven fellow tacksmen, making twelve in all, whose names and locations were as follows:

THE LAIRD OF RALSTON: the Mains of Saddell, the minister's manse and glebe excepted, Leppinmoir, Guystell, Plock, Kilmichell, Bradifernan, Ullodill, Tortisell, Leppinbeg, Leppincorrach, Ifernan, Ugadilluachtrach and Ugadillichtrich, all in twenty-three and a half merkland.

THE LAIRD OF DUNLOP: the fourth part of Ardnacroish and the lands of Drumgarrow, Laggan, Peninver, and Altinerve, in all a twelve merkland.

MR CUTHBERT CUNNINGHAM: three-quarters of Ardnacroish and the lands of Ballochgair, Kilchedan, and Gartgrenan, in all eleven merklands.

JAMES HAMILTON OF AITKENHEAD: Drummoir and the two Balliwillingis, in all an eight merkland.

THE HEIRS OF THE DECEASED JOHN PORTERFIELD OF HAPLAND: Achalick, Craig, and Backs, a twelve merkland.

JAMES HAMILTON OF ARDOCH: Ballenaglack, Ballinalargiemoir, Drum and Kilmacho, extent not given in the rental, but from the rent an eight merkland.

THE LAIRD OF HAZLETT (HAZELHEAD): Killeunan, Straichtrach, Strawachtrach, Belloch, an eight merkland.

JOHN CUNNINGHAM OF HILL OF BEITH: Machrihanish and Trodigall, an eight merkland.

CORNET ALEXANDER MURE: Kilchevan, Drumlemble, Ballegregan, and Schiskan, an eight merkland.

COLONEL ROBERT MURE: Achachoan, Knokurk, Ballemanach, Kildalloig, Mulmartin, Glenramskillmoir, Glenramskillbeg, an eight and a half merkland.

COLONEL PATRICK MONTGOMERIE: Kilellan, a four merkland.

CAPTAIN JAMES FORBES: the 20 shilling land of Langa.

In addition to the above, who received their tacks in 1650, we find many other names during the next quarter of a century. Thus in rentals of the Earl of Argyll of 1666 to 1669 and in other lists there occur: William Wallace in Ballimenach, a son of Colonel James Wallace; Colonel Robert Halket in Kilmichell, Achinleck, and Upper Balliwilling; John Caldwell, Younger of Caldwell, in Laggan, son of William Caldwell of that ilk; John Cunningham of Boghouse in Balloch; Forrester of Arngibbon in Killewnan; Robert Forrester in Nether Wigill or Garvachie; Alex. Forrester in Knockrioch and James Forrester in Beachmoir; Capt. James Browne in Askomelmore (1684); James Maxwell of Southbar in Ballivean from 1673, and his son Thomas Maxwell of Milnehouse in Southend (1685); James Fleming in Ballivean; James Baird in Ifernan; James Lockhart in Ewsdale; John Reid in Ewsdale; John Ryburn in Backs; Robert Menzies in Kilmichell; Robert Brakenrig in Craig; John Henderson or Hendry in Mukloch; Mr James Drummond in Kilmichell, Crossibeg, and Kilcousland; John Paterson in Balnagleck; James Brodie of Brodie was infeted in the lands of Moy in 1677, but was not in possession in 1684. The above is the earliest list of Lowland tacksmen that we possess, and some biographical notes on the more important of them will follow.

At the same time as this colonisation of Lowlanders took place there was also an extensive immigration of members of various Campbell families from other parts of Argyllshire. By far the largest extent of land given in tack by the Marquis of Argyll in Kintyre was the estate of the Macdonalds of Largie, granted to Dugald Campbell of Inverawe, a chieftain known to the Highlanders as the Maconachie of Inverawe, and who had been a faithful adherent of his chief MacCalein in the wars of the period. He received in the year 1652 a tack of 53 merklands of the forfeited estates of Largie, but must have had to surrender this in 1661, when Largie had his estates restored to him by Act of Parliament.

The rentals of 1666 to 1669 show that many other Campbells had been settled in tacks in Kintyre by that date. They included the following: Robert Campbell, late bailie of Kintyre, in Killewnan; Major William Campbell in Balligregan; Donald Campbell in Skerblingorrie; Colin Campbell in Lossit; Donald Campbell in Glenahantie; John Campbell in Puble and Inengowy; Archibald Campbell in Colinlongart; Archibald Campbell in Askamelbeg; Duncan Campbell in Putchantie; John Campbell in Machrimore; Campbell of Kernan (an ancestor of the poet Thomas Campbell) in Knockalloway and Achgeyll; George and John Campbell in Kildallig, Mulmartin, Balliwillingichter, also in Langa, Bordadow, and Kilmaho; Mr Alexander Campbell in Balligregan and Craigak; Sir Hew Campbell of Cessnock was infeted by charter in the lands of Knockriochbeg and others in 1677, but was not in possession of these in 1684.

In addition to the Campbells we begin to find in the lists between 1666 and 1685 names like MacNab, Macallum, MacTavish, and Maconachie, hitherto not encountered in Kintyre, and we may conclude that their bearers accompanied the Campbells from other parts of Argyllshire.

The first Lowland lairds and their followers, those who came in 1650, were settled mainly in the old parishes of Kilkerran, Kilcousland, Kilkivan, and Kilmichael, and at Saddell. There was no settlement of any magnitude in what is now Southend parish, at this date, and it was not until the year 1669, when the Laird of Ralston received a tack of the best lands in that parish, that a Lowland colonisation took place there.

The distribution of land between the old Highlanders of Kintyre, the Lowlanders, and the Campbells, in the year 1678 is shown in the following table which has been compiled from the Earl of Argyll's rental of that year. The figures represent the land in merklands.

Parish, etc.	Lowlanders.	Campbells	Old Kintyre Stock.	Total
Kilcolmkill	16	5	41	62
Kilblaan	17	1	19	37
Kilkivan	14	1	33	48
Kilkerran	10	14	22	46
Kilmichael	16	16	26	58
Kilchousland	40	2	2	44
Killean	21	29	22	72
Kilkenzie	5	15	14	34
Saddell	-	20	-	20
Totals	139	103	179	421

The table shows, firstly, that the centre of gravity, so to speak, of the Lowland population was, in 1678, in the parishes of Campbeltown and Southend, and secondly, that on the merkland basis of possession, the old Kintyre stock, despite the plantation, were still the principal occupiers of land. This provides a further refutation of the statement made by Hill, in his *Macdonnells of Antrim*, and already referred to, that a "clean sweep" of all the Macdonald vassals in Kintyre had been made in the year 1599.

There has been a good deal of dubiety in the past about the date when the Plantation of Kintyre began. From what we have seen the first attempt, but on a very small scale, was made when the Burgh of Lochhead was founded about 1609, while the date of Ralston's agreement with the Marquis to repair Saddell Castle, taken along with the Lowland rental of 1651 to 1652, which states that this was the second year of the tacks, places beyond any doubt the date of the main plantation of Lowland lairds as being 1650.

Another misapprehension that needs to be corrected is that the Lowlanders who arrived at this date came to avoid religious persecution in their native districts. Down to the date at which we have now arrived, 1650, there was no religious persecution in Scotland, and this could not have been the motive, either in that year, or at the time of the founding of Lochhead. The decade 1650 to 1660 was the era of Cromwellian government in Scotland, and Cromwell was no persecutor. In fact, during this decade the Presbyterian Church attained the height of its power and influence.

It was, however, a time of much political unrest, when nobody knew what the morrow would bring, and it is possible that the lairds welcomed the opportunity of having places to which their families could retire in times of war or danger, and where could these be found better than on an estate belonging to their political leader, to whom they could look for protection? As events turned out some twenty or more years later, these Kintyre holdings did become places of refuge to people in Ayrshire, Renfrewshire, and other parts of the Lowlands, when the active persecution of Charles II's reign began, and the Highland Host was let loose among them to plunder and destroy. This, in fact, constituted the third phase of the plantation, to which we shall have occasion to refer later on.

On the side of the Marquis of Argyll, it was clearly to his advantage to have on his much contested Kintyre estates a body of men on whose allegiance he could put implicit trust, and, as later events proved, he was not disappointed. From the material point of view also, he stood to gain by having his lands occupied by sober, peaceable and industrious tenants, such as the Covenanters and their families were. The statement has been made that he granted them estates in Kintyre, but this is quite erroneous. They had their own estates in the Lowlands, and in Kintyre they got nineteen-year-tacks or leases only, although the Earl of Argyll gave in his time a small amount of land in feu.

The statement is also sometimes made that the Lowlanders got cheap land, but is difficult to see what this statement can mean. The average rent paid by the lairds for their Kintyre tacks in 1651 to 1652 was £32 Scots the merkland, and this had been the average rent for Kintyre in 1636, the year in which the Marquis took over the estate. These rents may have been lower than those in parts of the Lowlands, but it is not easy to prove that they were. That the rents of 1651 gave room for development would appear to be proved by the fact that, in thirty year's time, the merkland rent had risen to over £60 Scots, and this rise must have been due, in part at least, to increased agricultural production.

The reasons for a Lowland plantation were not, of course, so apparent to the native Highlanders, and for many years a good deal of animosity, no doubt arising out of misunderstanding on both sides, existed between them and the Lowland incomers. Writing as late as the first half of the nineteenth century Mr Kelly, parish minister of Southend, stated of the Lowlanders of his time: "They are a sober, hardworking, industrious class of people, who have rarely amalgamated themselves by marriages with the Highlanders. So far, indeed, do they carry this unsocial feeling, that they have a place of sepulture for themselves [in Southend] detached only by a strand from that of their Highland brethren."

In the century that has elapsed since Mr Kelly wrote, much of this old feeling has passed away, and to-day, inter-marriage has become so common that the two classes of the population can scarcely be distinguished from each other. The Kintyre plantation, of all those attempted, has, despite the fact that it was on a much smaller scale than that of Ulster, been perhaps the only one of which it can be truly said that it was a success, when viewed from the standpoint of its promoters.

CHAPTER XI
BIOGRAPHICAL NOTES ON THE LOWLANDERS

In the case of most of the Lowland planters, little or no information has survived which concerns them as individuals, although some account of the families to which they belonged may be found in such works as Robertson's *Ayrshire Families*, Paterson's *History of Wigtown and Ayr*, Craufurd's *Renfrewshire*, Pont's *Cunningham* (edited by Dobie), Wodrow's *History of the Sufferings of the Church of Scotland*, and other local and family histories. Some facts can also be found about them and their families in the Lowland congregation register, which opens in the year 1659, and in the Presbytery and Synod records. As these sources of information are, however, not available to the ordinary reader, we present here, in the case of those individuals concerning whom any facts of their lives have been ascertained, a few short notes which will enable them and their families to be identified, mentioning any incidents of their lives which appear worth recording, and which have survived the centuries.

WILLIAM RALSTON of RALSTON, or, according to the old style, Ralston of that ilk, was the living head of an ancient Scottish family, supposed to be descended from a certain Ralph, who was a son or brother of one of the ancient Celtic Earls of Fife. To this Ralph King David I gave a grant of lands and messuage in Renfrewshire, which became known as Ralph's town, so giving rise to Ralston, the surname of the family. John de Ralston was Bishop of Dunkeld in 1448, and Ambassador to England in 1451. Thomas Ralston was killed at Flodden in 1513, and Hew Ralston at Pinkie in 1547. William Ralston, the pioneer of the Lowland Plantation of Kintyre, was probably born about the year 1610. He was twice married, first to Ursula Muir of Glanderston, and secondly to Jean Dunlop, daughter of James Dunlop of that ilk, who was one of his fellow planters in Kintyre. He succeeded to the ancestral estate of Ralston in 1625, and later, in 1643, acquired the estate of Roughbank and Crumnock in the parish of Beith, and of Auchingown-Ralston in the parish of Lochwinnoch. At the time that he came to Kintyre he was the principal heritor in Beith parish.

He was a fervent Covenanter and, belonging as he did to the strictest sect, known as the Remonstrants, was no doubt, like most of them, somewhat fanatical in his religious and political opinions. He was, however, a resolute and courageous man who, although as far as is known, not a professional soldier, nevertheless did not hesitate to take up arms in the cause in which he found himself engaged. After the execution of King Charles I in 1649 he opposed the Cromwellian party, and in 1650 commanded a body of horse which attacked General Lambert at Hamilton, and he was one of the party which took part in the raid on the Duke of Buccleuch's estate, known as "the burnin' of the yetts of Drumlanrig," for which he was fined in £567 Scots. Later, following the example of his patron the Marquis of Argyll, he made his peace with the Cromwellian party, regarding the decision no doubt as the lesser of two evils, and in 1653 took up arms against the Royalists under Glencairn, for this purpose raising a body of horse, and holding the Castle of Lochhead.

When the troubles which led to the Pentland Rising began in 1665 he was arrested, as a possible leader of the rebels, by the Earl of Argyll, and spent two years in prison without charge or trial. He was released in 1667 and, as his tack of the Saddell lands had by this time expired, it was not renewed; but instead, he received from the Earl a new tack of a much more extensive holding, which included most of the best land in the Campbeltown and Southend parishes.

He appears to have settled in Southend, or at least died there in or about the year 1691. He is buried in Kilcolmkill, where a walled tomb marks his resting-place. It displays his family arms which were, "Argent on a bend Azure, three acorns in seed Or. Crest, a falcon looking to the sinister, and the motto *Fide et Marte*." An inscription, now nearly indecipherable, states that it was rehewed, or re-erected, by his great-great-grandson Gavin Ralston, in the year 1799. The family left many descendants in Kintyre, stated to be descended from David Ralston, a cousin of Laird William, and surrounding his tomb in Kilcolmkill there are the burying places of a number of these later Ralstons, who were tenants in Kintyre. There is a typescript family history of the Kintyre Ralstons in the Free Library, Campbeltown.

THE LAIRD OF DUNLOP was James Dunlop of that ilk, the estate of that name being in North Ayrshire. Like Ralston, he was a warm supporter of the Presbyterian cause, and was not only heavily fined, but also imprisoned for two years from 1665 to 1667. In view of the troubled nature of the times, he made a temporary alienation of his estates to the Earl of Dundonald, and his son Alexander did not succeed to the estate, but was a sufferer in the troubles of Bothwell Brig, and later was heavily fined and was forced to emigrate to Carolina, where he was appointed Sheriff. The estate was recovered at the Revolution by his son. James Dunlop, who received the Kintyre tack in 1650, was father-in-law of William Ralston, as the latter had married as his second wife, Dunlop's daughter Jean in 1674.

John Dunlop, a brother of Laird James, had purchased the estate of Garnkirk in Lanarkshire in 1634, and founded the family of Dunlop of Garnkirk. This branch was the most distinguished of the Dunlop clan, and produced in the next century professors and principals of colleges, men distinguished in naval and military circles, and others who took a leading part in the development of the City of Glasgow. John, the first Laird of Garnkirk, had only one son, James, who succeeded. James had several sons, one of whom, Alexander, died in Kintyre, and is buried in Kilkenzie churchyard. The date of his death is not recorded on the tombstone, which covers also the remains of John Maxwell of Southbar, who died in 1677, and it displays a shield bearing the Maxwell and Dunlop arms. A good many descendants of these families were in Kintyre as tenants during the eighteenth century, but their connection with the above-mentioned Dunlops has not been traced.

MASTER CUTHBERT CUNNINGHAM was a son of Sir Alexander Cunningham of Corsehill in Stewarton parish, Ayrshire, and was a brother-in-law of James Dunlop of that ilk, who had married his sister. "Mr Cuthbert Cunningham, son lauchful to Alexander Cunningham of Corshill" occurs in the testament of William Hume, chamberlain to the Earl of Eglinton, in February 1659. As his title of "master" implies he was a graduate, having matriculated at Glasgow in 1610, and taken his M.A. degree in 1614. There is no evidence that he was a minister, although it began to be usual about this date to bestow the title of "master" as an honorary designation on ministers, whether they were graduates or not. The Cunninghams of Corsehill were descended from a younger son of the Earl of Glencairn, and were therefore a cadet branch of that once important family. We have no further information about Cuthbert Cunningham, except the fact that he belonged to the Covenanting party. He does not appear to have left any descendants in Kintyre.

JOHN CUNNINGHAM OF HILL OF BEITH was, at the time of the Kintyre plantation, proprietor of the estate of Hill-of-Beith in Beith parish. Like the above, he belonged to a cadet branch of the Earls of Glencairn - the Cunninghams of Caddell - and he later became the proprietor of Caddell estate. He was a ruling elder in Beith parish in 1647 and 1649. His wife was Helen Knox of Ranfurly, and while he resided in Kintyre, as tacksman of Trodigal and Machrihanish, at least six children were born there, these being William (1673), Jane (1675), Elizabeth (1679), Helen (1680), Alexander (1682), and William (1683). Next to Ralston he was the most important of the Lowland lairds, and took a leading part in the public and ecclesiastical affairs of the district. In 1662 he was on the Commission appointed to deal with the question of Irish robbers. He appears to have been a Covenanter of a rather milder type than some of the others, and during the troubles of the Pentland Rising the Earl of Argyll testified that he was no fanatic. His second daughter, Helen, married Archibald Macdonald of Sanda in 1697, and so became an ancestress of all the subsequent generations of that family.

JAMES HAMILTON OF AITKENHEAD was proprietor of the estate of that name, which was situated near Langside, Glasgow. He was descended from a cadet branch of the ducal house of Hamilton and, like Ralston and Dunlop, was a staunch Covenanter who suffered much during the time of the persecution in Charles II's reign. He was before the Commission as early as 1664, and was fined twice in a quarter of his rents for refusing to accept the curate imposed on his parish. Later, in 1666, he was warded in Inverness for the same offence, and, on 11th July 1667, he petitioned the Privy Council to the effect that he had been there in ward for ten months, and that on payment of the third part of the fine imposed on him had been allowed to return to his own house of Aitkenhead, but not to go more than a mile from it, and that he has "continued ever since frequenting the public ordinances and living peaceably." He was granted permission to go to Edinburgh on his private affairs, under pain of a fine of 10,000 merks, to return home before the 1st day of August.

He is stated to have been three times married, and to have had thirty children. He was still alive when Wodrow was writing his history, as he says of him: "James Hamilton of Aitkenhead, near Glasgow, yet alive at a good old age when I write this, and attesting what I am giving, was among the first brought before the High Commission, and I shall give the whole detail of his sufferings at this time." He does not appear to have left any descendants of this name in Kintyre.

JAMES HAMILTON OF ARDOCH was the proprietor of the estate of that name in the parish of Kilwinning, which had been old Church land. His father, Gavin Hamilton, was also proprietor of the lands of Roughbank and Crumnock in Beith parish, which William Ralston subsequently purchased. James Hamilton married Barbara Mure of Caldwell in 1637.

WILLIAM HAMILTON OF BROWNMUIR, OR BRUMORE, was in Southend, probably as an associate or tenant of Ralston, at the time of the Atholl raids in 1685, when he was plundered. He was an elder in Southend in 1687, when he was sent to the Synod to protest against the induction of Mr John Darroch as minister of Southend. His Lowland estate of Brownmuir was part of the Barony of Beith, and his family were cadets of the ducal house of Hamilton. The estate of Brownmuir went finally to the Hamiltons of Wishaw, of whom Robert Hamilton married in 1686 Jean Hamilton, heiress of Brownmuir.

THE PORTERFIELDS OF HAPLAND had possessed the place of that name, which had been part of the estate of Dunlop, since the year 1612. John Porterfield of Hapland was a ruling elder in the parish of Dunlop, and a Captain in the Scots Army when Cromwell was in Scotland. He died unmarried, and was succeeded by his brother Alexander, who was the heir who had the Kintyre tack, in October 1653. The Porterfields were involved in the troubles of the Persecution, and some of the family sought a refuge in Holland.

CALDWELL OF THAT ILK represented the descendants of the original owners of the lands of Caldwell in Renfrewshire, but these lands, and the castle, had passed to the Mures by marriage, and the much more wealthy and powerful family of Mure of Caldwell founded. The head of the latter is known as the Laird of Caldwell, but the head of the Caldwells of that ilk, who had a small estate near that of the Mures of Caldwell, was known as the Goodman of Caldwell, a Goodman being originally a minor kind of laird.

William Caldwell of that ilk was in Kintyre at the time of the first plantation, and was an elder in the Lowland congregation at Saddell in 1658. It may be this man who is referred to as Caldwell, without mention of a first name, who was tenant of Laggan and Drumgarve in 1666. His son John was known as John, Goodman of Caldwell younger. He took an active part in the Pentland Rising of 1666, when his Lowland estate was forfeited. He would appear to be the same man who was in Laggan in 1685, and who was declared one of the Earl of Argyll's rebels in 1685, and was probably a brother of John. The Caldwells left descendants in Kintyre who continued there down to the middle of the nineteenth century, and were found mainly in the Southend parish at Christlach and Gartvain.

THE LAIRD OF HAZLETT, OR HAZELHEAD, near Beith, was Robert Montgomery. He was retoured heir to his father Robert on 6th April 1648, in the Temple lands of Cunningham. He was a representative of Ayrshire in the first parliament of King Charles II in 1661, and one of the Commissioners of Supply for Ayrshire in that year. He had only one daughter, who married MacAulay of Ardincaple, from one of the daughters of which union was descended Tobias Smollett the novelist. The family had taken a leading part in the Reformation in Scotland, having been supporters of John Knox. One of its representatives, about the end of the sixteenth century, was Alexander Montgomery, the poet, and author of "The Cherry and the Slae."

CAPTAIN PATRICK MONTGOMERIE, who received a tack of the forfeited lands of the Maceachrans of Kilellan, was the Laird of Blackhouse in the parish of Largs, to which estate he succeeded in 1657. His father, John Montgomerie, was killed at the Battle of Dunbar in 1650. Patrick Montgomerie's wife was Margaret Carse of Glasgow. He sold his property in 1663 and died in 1716.

A number of Lowland Montgomeries were in Kintyre, as tenants or business men in the town, during the succeeding two centuries, but whether they had any connection with the above cannot be said. The Kilellan estate was restored to Colin Maceachran by the Marquis of Argyll in 1659, and it is probable that Montgomerie's tack of it may have been annulled then.

CAPTAIN JAMES FORBES, who had the 20 shilling land of Langa, is uncertain, but may have been a member of the family of Forbes of Corse in Aberdeenshire. A note in the rental indicates that the terms of his tack had not been settled, and, as we hear no more of the name, it is possible that he may not have taken it up.

THE FORRESTERS found in Kintyre during the latter half of the seventeenth, and the first half of the eighteenth centuries, belonged to the family of Forrester of Arngibbon in Perthshire, and were descendants of Sir Duncan Forrester, or Forestare, Comptroller of the Household to King James IV, who received from that monarch the keeping of the Castle of Skipness and a grant of lands in Knapdale, in the year 1495. Arngibbon, by which is presumably meant Duncan Forrester the Laird of that place, had a tack of the five merkland of Beachmore in Kintyre from 1669. Alexander Forrester was tacksman of Knockrioch in 1666, and received a charter of the lands of Knockrioch, Cesken, and Strawachtrach from the Earl of Argyll in 1677. He was succeeded in that estate by his son James, whose wife was Finuel Macallaster of the Loup family, and they had a son Coll who married Talmash Muir, heiress of Kilkivan. Others traceable were Robert Forrester in Achachork in 1666, and John Forrester in Kileonan and Backs in the same year. Their exact relationship cannot be traced. Alexander Forrester of Knockrioch was examined by the Privy Council in 1685 for alleged compliance with the Argyll rebels, but was acquitted. The head family were at one time the King's foresters, and took their name from this office, which is signified on their coat of arms by three hunting horns. They do not appear to have left any modern descendants in Kintyre.

CAPTAIN JAMES BROWN, who appears in rentals of 1678 and 1684 as tacksman of Askomelmore, is of uncertain identity. A James Browne was one of the witnesses who attested the agreement for the repair of Saddell Castle by Ralston in 1650. In 1643 a Captain James Browne acknowledged the sum of nine hundred pounds odd due to him on account of the hire of a ship which had been used to convey soldiers and munitions of war, and some expenses incurred for a horse in a journey from Saltcoats to Edinburgh. In 1647 it was a ship commanded by Captain James Browne which conveyed old Colkitto from Islay to Leith. A James Browne was a ruling elder in the Lowland congregation at Lochhead in 1658, and a James Browne was surety for William Wallace in 1666. It is probable that all these references are to the same man, and that he was a naval captain who was employed by the Parliamentary Army during the Civil War. Whether the Browns found at later dates had any connection with his family is not known.

COLONEL ROBERT MUIR AND CORNET ALEXANDER MURE (or Mure, or Moor) were two younger sons of Sir William Muir, Laird of Rowallan in Ayrshire, and members of one of the most notable Ayrshire families, another member of which, Elizabeth Muir, was the first wife of King Robert II of Scotland. The two Muirs had been officers in the Covenanting Army, and, according to one account, Cornet Alexander was slain in Ireland, but the year is not stated.

CAPTAIN DAVID MUIR, whose wife was Margaret Drummond, was an officer in the Marquis of Argyll's regiment, who received a tack of Drummore in Kintyre in 1666, but was living there as early as 1659. His relationship to the last two is not known. At the time of the Pentland Rising, in 1666, he was imprisoned in Dumbarton Castle on a charge of re-setting William Wallace, son of Colonel James Wallace. He was also listed as one of the Argyll rebels in 1685. Many others of the name occur in Kintyre, in the seventeenth-century church registers and other lists, and some were proprietors of Kilkivan. The testament of a James Muir of Kilkivan is dated 1736.

THE MAXWELLS OF SOUTHBAR were the proprietors of the estate of that name in Renfrewshire. Crawfurd in his *History of the Shire of Renfrew* (1710) states of this family: "East of Dargevel stands the house and lands of Southbar, adorned with pleasant planting, the possession for well nigh three hundred years of a family of the name of Maxwell, descended of a youngest son of Lord Maxwell in the reign of King James III ... I can say little about them save that they were honoured by diverse matches with several ancient and honourable families ..." Of the Southbar Maxwells who came to Kintyre at the time of the Lowland Plantation the following have been traced.

John Maxwell of Southbar was probably the first member of this family who had, under the name Southbar, a tack of the four merkland of Ballivean, Knocknagour, and Drumlea, for twenty-one years from Whitsunday 1673. This John is buried in Kilkenzie, where his tombstone records that he died in 1677, at the age of 77 years. Along with him was buried Alexander Dunlop, son to the Laird of Garnkirk, to whom reference has already been made. The stone displays a shield with the Maxwell and Dunlop arms, those of Maxwell being "argent an eagle with two heads sable, beaked and membered gules, on his breast an escutcheon of the first, charged with a saltire of the second, for difference a fleur de lis."

In 1684 the above lands were possessed by James Maxwell of Southbar, probably son of John. In 1685 a son of James Maxwell, Thomas Maxwell of Milnehouse, was in the Southend parish, and was one of those robbed in the Atholl raids, but his exact location there is not stated. His Lowland estate of Milnehouse is near East Kilbride. His first wife was Anna Hamilton, who died in 1687, and was buried in Kilcolmkill. Her tombstone shows the Maxwell arms, and also those of Arran and Hamilton, indicating that she belonged to a cadet branch of the ducal house of Hamilton. Descendants of the Maxwells were in Kintyre as tenant farmers during the eighteenth century, and for the most part of that century occupied Cattadale in the Southend parish. They appear to have used the same burying ground as the Maxwells of Milnehouse. One of them was James Maxwell, Chamberlain to the Duke of Argyll in Mull, a daughter of whom married the Rev. Norman Macleod, senior, minister of Campbeltown in the early years of the nineteenth century. The Cattadale family emigrated to America about 1800, and at their departure presented to the newly erected Relief Kirk in Southend a pair of metal collection plates, which had the device of a full-rigged ship, probably emblematical of the fact of their emigration.

MR JAMES DRUMMOND, who had a tack of the lands of Kilmichell, Crossalbeg, and Kilchousland in 1666, was a minister of the Church. He had been chaplain to Margaret Douglas, Marchioness of Argyll. During the time of the persecution he was imprisoned for holding conventicles, but released in July 1674. On his release he again joined the field preachers, and in 1677 was imprisoned in the Bass, but liberated by order of the Privy Council in the same year, on condition that he would find caution to proceed to Kilmarnock and afterwards to Kintyre. After the Revolution he was minister of Kilconquhar in Fife. His wife was Marion Montgomerie, and the Lowland register records the birth of a daughter Jane at Crossibeg in 1673.

COLONEL ROBERT HALKET was in Kintyre as early as 1654, and was a ruling elder in the Lowland congregation at Lochhead in 1658. He received a tack of the two merkland of Kilmichell, the two merkland of Achalick, and the two merkland of Upper Balliwilling, for twenty-one years from Whitsunday 1669. He was a brother of Sir James Halket, laird of Pitfirrane in Fife, and a member of a family that had a long military record both at home and abroad. In the year 1643 Robert Halket is named as one of the captains in the regiment of French Guards which, as we have seen, was raised by Lord Kintyre in 1642. Halket was closely associated with Ralston, and like him opposed at first the Cromwellian party, and was engaged in the attack on Lambert's forces at Hamilton in 1650. He was a staunch Covenanter, and on several occasions was fined for attending conventicles. In 1665 he was, along with Ralston, taken prisoner by the Earl of Argyll, and spent two years in confinement. He was released in 1667, after finding caution in 5000 merks to keep the peace. The family is still in possession of Pitfirrane, but does not appear to have left any descendants in Kintyre.

COLONEL JAMES WALLACE is perhaps the most interesting of all the Lowland lairds who came to Kintyre at this time. There is no record of his having held a tack in Kintyre, but he was there at the beginning of the plantation, and was a ruling elder in the Lowland congregation at Lochhead in 1658. His son William was in Ballimenach, in Kilchousland parish, in 1666. Colonel Wallace was a member of the family of the Wallaces of Auchans, who were proprietors of that estate in South Ayrshire, but some time before he came to Kintyre he had disposed of the estate to the Earl of Dundonald. He matriculated at Glasgow University in 1627, but does not appear to have graduated. He was a professional soldier, and had been an officer in the Marquis of Argyll's regiment during the Irish rebellion of 1641 to 1642. He returned to fight against Montrose, and was taken prisoner at the Battle of Kilsyth in 1645. He was back in Ireland again in 1647, and in that year was appointed Governor of Belfast.

When Charles II was crowned King by the Covenanters in 1650 a new crack regiment of Life-Guards, the original Scots Guards, was formed in Scotland, and Lord Lorne, afterwards Earl of Argyll, appointed to be its Colonel, with James Wallace as his Lieut.-Colonel. He fought at Dunbar in 1650 and was taken prisoner there. Somewhat later we find Lord Lorne trying to obtain a pension for him out of the public revenues. He was of strong Covenanting sympathies, and, when signs of trouble became manifest in 1665, his arrest was ordered, at the instance of the Government, by the Earl of Argyll. Wallace, however, managed to escape to the Lowlands, where his military training and experience were placed at the disposal of the Covenanters, whose army he commanded at the Battle of Rullion Green in November 1666. The Covenanters lost the day, and James Wallace was forced to flee to Ireland. In his absence, sentence of death was passed upon him, and his estate ordered to be forfeited to the Crown, although the last part of the sentence does not appear to have been carried out. He finally found his way to the Continent, and, after many wanderings, settled at Rotterdam in Holland. There, he was an elder in the Scots congregation, and was a man universally respected by the Scots colony in Rotterdam. He appears to have been of a particularly amiable character, and even his opponent, Sir James Turner (of Dunaverty fame), whom he took prisoner just before Rullion Green, testified to this. He died in Rotterdam in 1678. Colonel Wallace left a diary, but it refers only to the part he played in the Pentland Rising, and makes no mention of his Kintyre connection, nor of any other incidents of his life.

Descendants of this family, probably of the two sons of William Wallace, son of the Colonel, whose names were James and John, were to be found as tenants in Kintyre during the subsequent two centuries. The Wallaces who were tenants in Machribeg during the eighteenth century had a burial place in Kilcolmkill, and there a stone displays the Wallace device of a horseshoe in the bill of an ostrich, and the Wallace motto *Sperandum est*. The Auchans Wallaces were connected with the family of the great Scottish patriot Sir William Wallace.

CHAPTER XII

SOME EARLY EVENTS OF THE PLANTATION

The first ten years of the main plantation, 1650 to 1660, coincided with the period of Cromwellian rule in Scotland. The Covenanters had opposed the execution of King Charles I, and had retorted on the English Parliament by choosing his son as the new king. Prince Charles landed at the mouth of the Spey on 23 June 1650 and, after undergoing an excessive amount of admonition and preaching at by the Covenanting ministers, had signed both the National and Solemn League Covenants. That done, there was no impediment to his coronation, which took place at Scone on New Year's Day 1651, the Marquis of Argyll placing the crown on his head. Many of the Covenanters, however, appear to have distrusted him, judging from his demeanour that his professions of friendship for their sect were insincere - a belief amply justified by subsequent events. Cromwell had put Scotland under his feet by his victory at Dunbar on 3rd September 1650, and exactly a year to a day later the Covenanting forces, which Charles led to the invasion of England, were routed at Worcester, and he was forced to go into exile on the Continent. A party in Scotland still held out for him, however, headed by the Earl of Glencairn, suppported by Lord Kenmore.

The position of the Marquis of Argyll was now one of extreme difficulty, and for a time he quitted public life and retired to Inveraray. He soon, however, made his peace with the Cromwellian party, and later collaborated with the English Government, an action which cost him his life ten years later, but for which, in view of his position and that of the country, he can scarcely be blamed. His son Lord Lorne, afterwards Earl of Argyll, took, however, the opposite side, and in spite of the warnings, and even of the curses of his father, joined the Royalist party under Glencairn. At this time the Chamberlain of Kintyre was Alexander Macnachtan of Dunderave, or the Laird of Macnachtan as he was called, and he too joined Glencairn's party.

The Cromwellians tried to get a footing in Kintyre in 1652, when an expeditionary force, comprising both foot and horse, came by sea from Ayr, led by Colonel Overton who commanded the English garrison there. This force, probably as a result of Macnachtan's influence, apparently made an unsuccessful attempt to land, and a contemporary historian tells us that, had it not been for assistance rendered to it by the Marquis of Argyll, Overton and all who were with him would have "gotten their throttes cut." The force had to return again amidst the jeers and laughter of the Highlanders.

The loyalty of Ralston and of the Lowland colony to the Marquis was now put to the test, and he apparently decided, more perhaps on grounds of expediency than of conscience, and as the lesser of two evils, to support the Marquis and the English party. Colonel Lillburne, the Commander-in-Chief in Scotland, in a letter to Cromwell, states that the Marquis of Argyll had informed him in an interview that Ralston proposed to raise a force of 220 horsemen, or three troops, but the exact number actually raised by him is uncertain. When Ralston's intentions of siding with the English, against whom he had borne arms only two years before, came to Macnachtan's ears, the latter swore vengeance against him and his Lowland following,

13. In Southend, the older part of the graveyard surrounding St. Columba's Church contains the Ralston monument and other 17th C. memorials. The church is adjacent to the site of 'St. Columba's footprints', and looks to Dunaverty and Sanda Island in the SE.

14. A headstone standing against the inner E. wall of St. Columba's Church is inscribed to Neil McNeil of Carskiey (d.1685) and carved with the shield of his Arms and the motto "Vincit aut mori(tur)".

15. A recumbent slab outside the E. gable of St. Columba's Church commemorates Ranald MacDonald of Sanda (d.1679 aged 34), his spouse Anna Stewart and other members of their family, and is carved with the armorial achievement of the MacDonalds of Sanda.

16. Dunaverty Bay, Southend, looking SE. to Sheep Island and Sanda. Little trace now remains of the castle of Dunaverty, with a first recorded mention in the early 8th C., and thereafter a chequered history of possession by the Crown and by the MacDonalds of Islay and Kintyre.

stating that if he was able to command one man he would not leave a reeking house among them. The Marquis dismissed him from his post of Chamberlain.

During the summer of 1653 Kenmore, accompanied by Lord Lorne and Macnachtan, the last being described as the ringleader of the expedition, marched into Kintyre with a military following. Kenmore belonged to the well-known Galloway family of the Gordons of Kenmore, or Kenmuir, and appears to have been a hot-headed and somewhat truculent man. It is related of him that, during this campaign, he had carried in front of him a "rundlett of strong waters," and this cask of brandy or aquavitae became known to the soldiers as Kenmore's Drum. Meanwhile, Ralston had taken possession of, and garrisoned, the Castle of Lochhead.

Kenmore and Lorne with their following arrived at Lochhead, and began to parley with Ralston. First they demanded that he should supply them with eighty horse and deliver up his arms and ammunition, which he had apparently received from the English garrison at Ayr. This he refused to do. They then requested that he should allow them to enter into the castle with a guard, to stay there all night, and to carry away in the morning six muskets and four or five pounds of powder. This demand was also refused, on which the invaders raided the Lowland population, driving away their cattle, and, according to one account, tearing the very clothes from off the backs of the people. This forced Ralston to make a sally from the castle, in the course of which he took Macnachtan prisoner, and held him so for a time.

In the long run, however, Ralston surrendered the castle to Lorne's discretion. This is clear from a letter written to Cromwell by one of his officers from Dalkeith, and dated 1st November 1653. In it he reports that "the Lord Kenmore fell upon a good honest party of Lowlanders in Cantire that opposed him, and hath one Laird Ralston prisoner, that was the chief of them, and had a very godly man whom he keeps in irons, yet he and the rest choose rather (I think) to suffer what is befallen them than to be beholding to us for assistance or to give us any timely intelligence." Baillie, a contemporary historian, states that "Ralston and the Remonstrant gentlemen of Kintyre seemed readie to arm for the English against the king's partie. Lorne and Kenmuir with the men they had raised went to Kintyre to suppress them. They, on the hope of the English assistance, fortified the Castle of Lochheid; but while neither Argyle nor the English appear in their defence they rander the house to Lorne's discretion. Kenmuir, thinking the besieged better used by Lorne than they deserved, fell in a miscontent and went from Lorne to Glencairn with many complaints."

It is quite possible that, if Kenmore had had his own way, Ralston and his followers would have met the fate of the Macdonalds at Dunaverty six years before, but it would appear that Lorne, despite his political opinions, shared his father's ideas about the value of the Lowland plantation to estates that would eventually pass into his own hands, and in this policy he apparently remained consistent, as subsequent events will show. The Marquis was much affected by these events, and in the interview with Lillburne mentioned above "spoke with much sadness, especially that Kenmore should make spoil upon those Lowland people in Cantire," and stated that he himself could do nothing to help, being unwilling to oppose his son. There can be no doubt, however, that had it not been for Lorne's intercession, the plantation in Kintyre might have come to a sudden end at this time.

In 1654 the King sent General Middleton to Scotland, but he was defeated at Loch Garry, and with his defeat the Royalist rising came to an end, after which the Kintyre colony was, for a time, left in peace.   After 1660 Alexander Macnachtan, the Chamberlain who had opposed them, lived at the Court in London, where he was a great favourite with King Charles II, who, at his death, had him buried in the Royal Chapel at his own expense. By 1656 the King, for whom many of the Covenanters had continued to pray, was nearly forgotten, and the English rule accepted. It was just, if foreign, and, as we have said, little or no interference with ecclesiastical affairs, except the banning of General Assemblies, took place, and the Presbyterian Church continued to extend its influence. Most of the rest of the history of this decade in Kintyre is concerned with ecclesiastical matters, a short account of which follows.

The first twenty years of Presbyterianism in Kintyre was a time characterised by a great scarcity of ministers. This was no doubt due, to some extent, to an actual shortage of suitable candidates for the ministry, but was accentuated by the fact that the twenty years, 1638 to 1658, were years of war, and that many of the parish ministers were called away from their charges to serve as chaplains in the army. Another fact to be recorded is that the older group of ministers, those who had served during what is known as the first period of Episcopacy, and some of whom were received into the Presbyterian church, were all dead by the year 1643. From that year to 1650 only three ministers are traceable in Kintyre. Mr Dugald Darroch, a member of an ecclesiastical family, had been minister of Kilcalmonell, in succession to Maurice Darroch who died in 1638, but in 1642 was called away to be chaplain to the Marquis of Argyll's regiment. He became the minister of Lochhead or Campbeltown in 1649. Another of this family, Mr John Darroch, was minister of Kilcolmkill (now Southend) from 1642 to 1646, but in the latter year was deposed for preaching to the Colkitto rebels, but reinstated later. In 1643 Mr Neil Campbell, who had been Bishop of the Isles, having accepted Presbyterianism, and having been duly disciplined into the new order, was presented to Lochhead by the Marquis.   He attended one meeting of the Synod in that year, but no further trace of him is found in the records, and the presumption is that he acted as minister there for a very short period only.

In 1644 there began the Colkitto raids, when the whole country was thrown into confusion, and sessions and presbyteries ceased for a time to function.   In the opening years of the next decade, 1650 to 1660, matters were worse still, and Mr Darroch of Lochhead appears to have been for a time the only placed minister in Kintyre.   In 1650 no Commissioner could be sent from that district to the General Assembly, because there was no Presbytery in existence to elect one.   The most glaring instance was afforded by the parish of Southend, which remained vacant from 1646 to 1672, a period of a quarter of a century. The Church, however, kept a vigilant eye on the vacant stipends, and these, under the authority of an Act of

Parliament of 1644, were devoted to the training of young men for the ministry which, under the circumstances, was a suitable and wise arrangement.

Such was the state of affairs at the time of the plantation of Lowland lairds and their followers, and to them, as devout Covenanters, the want of religious ordinances constituted a serious grievance. Tradition records that, for purposes of marriages, baptisms, and the celebration of communion, they made periodical journeys to their native parishes in the Lowlands, but this was an awkward and expensive arrangement.

The initial plantation was centred round Saddell, where the Laird of Ralston had his lands. Saddell had been annexed to Kilkenzie and Killean as a joint charge, but in 1642 an order of the Synod decreed it to be a separate parish, which, at the date we are now considering, was vacant. In 1653, however, the Lowlanders there gave a call to Mr James Gardiner, a young man licensed by the Presbytery of Paisley in the previous year, and sought the permission of the Synod to have him admitted. The Synod did not at once agree, for three reasons, viz., that the boundaries of the parish had not yet been properly fixed, that there were Highlanders in the parish to whom Mr Gardiner could not properly minister, he having no Gaelic and that they desired to test him before admitting him. He was, however, admitted in 1654 and, with Mr Dugald Darroch of Lochhead, had to take up the whole burden of attending to the spiritual wants of the Kintyre people, which for a time Mr Darroch had borne alone.

At its meeting in October 1654 the Synod enjoined on these two ministers that, in view of the absence of a presbytery, they and their two sessions should collaborate and "take inspection of the whole country, in so far as may be, for the bearing down of sin, and the good of the whole country," and Mr Gardiner was also requested to do what he could for the Lowlanders at Lochhead. His ministry at Saddell, however, owing to his lack of Gaelic, was not a success, and he himself put the matter in the Synod's hands and agreed to be recommended as transportable. This step, his transportation, at the request of Archibald Campbell of Glencarradale, the Synod took in 1660. After leaving Saddell, Mr Gardiner was for a time chaplain to the Marquis of Argyll, but after the death of the latter he was accused of seditious conduct, and ordered by the Privy Council to leave the country on pain of death. He went to Holland, but is said to have returned secretly to Glasgow, where he died some time before 1685. The ruling elders of his congregation at Saddell in 1658 were the following: William Ralston of that ilk; William Caldwell of that ilk; Archibald Adair; Harvie Kirkpatrick; John Ralston, Laird of Ralston, the last being apparently the then possessor of the original lands of Ralston near Paisley. This was the first Lowland congregation in Kintyre, but the centre of the plantation soon moved south to the Southend and Campbeltown parishes.

A Lowland congregation was formed in Lochhead in 1654. This differed from that of Saddell in that it was an entirely new congregation, and an addition to the one already in existence, which worshipped in the parish church of Lochhead, built, as we have stated, in 1643. It is strange that the Synod minutes contain no reference to the erection of this congregation, and to the circumstances which called it into being, beyond recording the fact that it was in existence, in embryo at least, in October 1654, and that Mr Edward

Keith, after being tested by the Synod as an expectant in October 1655, had been inducted as its minister, and attended the Synod meeting as such in May 1656.

Mr Keith was a son of the Provost of Montrose, and descended from a branch of the Earl Marischal's family. He was Lowland minister of Lochhead to 1662, when he was deprived, but later, in 1672, returned with an Indulgence. He died on 6th May 1682. The Lowland congregation built a new church known in tradition as the Old Thatched House or the Preaching or Meeting House. It was situated in Kirk Street, and a new church with slated roof, which still stands, was built on the same site in 1706. The ruling elders of the Lowland parish of Lochhead in 1658 were as follows; James Browne; Lord Neil Campbell (son of the Marquis); Nicholas Todd; Colonel Robert Halkett; Lieut.-Colonel James Wallace; John Cunningham of Hill of Beith.

Some provision for the Highland people of North Kintyre was made by the filling of the Killean vacancy in 1656, in the person of Mr David Simson. His career was somewhat remarkable. Born a Lowlander, he had no knowledge of Gaelic in his youth, but after leaving college he volunteered to do missionary work in the Highlands. In 1651, the year after he graduated M.A. at St Andrews, the Synod, approving of his proposal, granted him 400 merks yearly out of the vacant stipends, in order " to sett the said Mr David upon the best course for learning the Irish language." He proved such an apt pupil, that, three years later, he preached before the Synod in Gaelic, to their great acceptance, the Synod recording that "they did think much of his proficiencie in such a short time, he being formerlie altogether a stranger thereto." In 1660 Mr Simson was one of those chosen to translate the Scriptures into Gaelic, and had assigned as his portion the first book of Kings. These early translations have, however, been lost. He was deprived in 1662, being a man of strong Covenanting principles, but returned with an Indulgence to the parish of Southend in 1672, and was probably encouraged to take this step from the fact that the Laird of Ralston had settled there with a strong Covenanting following. He does not appear, however, to have adhered to the conditions of his Indulgence, for in 1684 he and several other ministers were called before the Marquis of Atholl at Inveraray, and confessed that they had violated their promises to the Government. Mr Simson was forced to emigrate to New Jersey, where he died before the year 1695, and is stated to have "continued stedfast in the faith till his death."

Shortly after the formation of the Lowland congregation at Lochhead an attempt was made to hand over to it the parish church there. This was the church built in 1643, and which became known as the Old Gaelic Church, and was situated, as already stated, on a spot near to where the New Quay Head is to-day. These proposals, which appear to show the hand of the Marquis, were actually approved by the Synod in 1658, and were to the effect that the Highland minister and his congregation were to be transferred to Kilkenzie and a new church and manse built for them there. In the meantime, however, and so long as any Highlanders remained at Lochhead, the minister was to preach there and in Kilkenzie on alternate Sundays, and to be allowed to retain the use of his manse in Lochhead. When, however, the Marquis of Argyll and his family were in residence at Lochhead the Highlanders were not to be allowed the use of their old church, but were to worship in the thatched house of the Lowland congregation. The Highland minister was also to have the legal stipend, because firstly, "the lowland plantation is more alterable and likelier to cease," and secondly, because the stipend of the Lowland minister had no authority from the Commissioners for the Plantation of Kirks. From this it is clear that it was not certain whether, at this date, the plantation was to be permanent or not. This one-sided arrangement, which shows how closely the Marquis had allied himself with the Lowlanders came, however, to naught.

Two years later the new era of Episcopalianism was inaugurated, and in 1661 the Marquis was executed. The Lowlanders had now not only lost their patron, but had to face a hostile government as well. Mr Dugald Darroch, minister of the Highland congregation at Lochhead, was deprived in 1662, and died shortly afterwards.

The Lowland congregation at Lochhead was supported partly by congregational contributions, and partly by help in the way of grants received from the Argyll family. Later there was an attempt to add to the Campbeltown parish a part of Kilkenzie as well, with the object of increasing the stipends of the two Lochhead ministers, and in 1672 the Laird of Ralston and Cunningham of Hill of Beith, two of the Lowland ruling elders, addressed a letter to this effect to the Earl of Argyll. As this is the only letter of Laird Ralston which appears to have survived, it is reproduced here, with its contractions expanded, and its spelling and punctuation modernised.

Machrihanish, 26 *November* 1672

RIGHT HONOURABLE,

I perceive the natives here doth not incline to enter into a joint submission with us who are Lowlanders. The bearer being in haste we could not get your Lordship's tacksmen's hands to a formal submission to be sent at time, but we do assure your Lordship you may dispose of us, as if you had an ample submission under our hands, for I know none of our Lowlanders will have any scruple except James Muir, (Tacksman of Knockstaplebeg in 1666), but I know if your Lordship declare your pleasure, he dare not refuse. We do likewise perceive that the natives is much reluctant to have any pairt of Kilhanzie jointed in to the four parishes, fearing the seat may be there for their preaching afterwards. My Lord, if a considerable pairt of Kilhenzie be not cast in to the other four, it will either occasion a very mean stipend to both ministers or else a very great burden upon the contributors. My Lord, as for coveting the old church of Campbeltown, we that are Lowlanders do not covet it. Your Lordship knows from the beginning we were ever cheerful to have contributed to our ability for Mr Edward [Keith] and purposes to continue so, or in case of his removing, by death or otherways, my Lord, our contributing will be only to these of a Presbyterian judgement, in whom we may have satisfaction. No further but we are,

    My Lord,
    Your Lordship's most humble Servants,
        W. RALSTOUN
        JO. CONYNGHAME.

In the case of the Lowland congregation at Lochhead, it is sometimes claimed that it was one of the first voluntary, and, in a sense, one of the first dissenting, congregations in Scotland. Neither of these claims have any historical foundation. That it was partly supported by voluntary contributions of its members is proved by the letter quoted above. It was not, however, entirely so supported. In a rental of 1678 it is shown that at that time the Earl of Argyll was contributing an annual sum of £133, 6s.8d Scots to its minister, Mr Edward Keith, this sum being paid out of the rents of the houses of Campbeltown. In what manner the addition from Kilkenzie to the four old parishes of Kilkerran, Kilchousland, Kilmichael, and Kilkivan, now united into the parish of Lochhead or Campbeltown, as proposed in the above letter, was intended to increase the stipends of the two Campbeltown ministers, is not clear. It may be that by this time payments were being allowed from the teinds to the Lowland congregation, or it may be that it was hoped that a larger population would mean larger stipends, by means of voluntary contributions. The principal of voluntary contribution was by no means unknown in the West Highlands at this time. In the year 1654 the people of Jura - a poor island - petitioned the Synod to be supplied with a minister, stating that, if the teinds of the island did not suffice for his stipend, they were prepared to make good the difference among themselves.

The statement that this congregation was the forerunner of dissent in Scotland has still less claim to our serious attention. Both Mr Gardiner and Mr Keith were ministers of the Church of Scotland, and admitted to their charges only after being tried by the Synod of Argyll, and their congregations were in full communion with that Church. Dissent in Scotland only began after the Revolution Settlement of 1690, when a small body of the strictest of the Covenanters, dissatisfied with the terms of that Settlement, founded the sect known as the Cameronians. Dissent, as it was afterwards understood, would have been unintelligible to the Kintyre Lowlanders in 1655.

Nor was it the case that these churches at Saddell and Lochhead had their origin solely in the exclusiveness of the Lowlanders, or in their contempt for Highland ministers. Mr Dugald Darroch was an able man, quite capable of commanding their respect, and quite competent to have preached to them in English, but his charge was so heavy that it was beyond his power to do so. Accordingly, the simplest course was to erect a new congregation, and to appoint an English-speaking minister. In this course it is quite clear that they had the backing of the Marquis of Argyll who, although he had himself been a ruling elder in the Highland congregation before the Lowlanders came to Kintyre, now openly associated himself with the Lowland colony in Church affairs.

CHAPTER XIII

THE PERSECUTION AND THE PENTLAND RISING

The news of the Restoration of King Charles II in 1660 was received with joy in Scotland, where the Covenanters acclaimed him as their covenanted King. They were soon to be disillusioned, for Charles at once made it clear that he meant to restore the arbitrary rule of his father. At his first parliament of 1661 legislation was passed which once more made Episcopacy the national religion, and it was no longer the mild Episcopacy of King James I's reign. The bishops were now placed in complete control of the lower courts of the Church - the kirk sessions and presbyteries - and these could not meet without their consent. "The old set of bishops," said Wodrow, "were but pigmies to the present high and mighty lords." By a proclamation of 1662, all ministers ordained since 1649 were required to seek collation from a bishop, and those who refused were deprived of their livings; 271 ministers, mainly in the west of Scotland, refused and were turned out. They lost their last year's stipends, and were often forced to wander about the country in bitterly cold weather, accompanied by their families. In their places were installed Episcopalian curates, hurriedly got together from wherever they could be found. Burnet the historian, himself an Episcopalian, described them as follows: "They were the worst preachers I ever heard; they were ignorant to a reproach, and many of them were openly vicious. They were a disgrace to orders, and the sacred functions, and were indeed the dreg and refuse of the northern parts." People who refused to attend their services were spied out and fined, and parties of soldiers were sent into the country to collect the fines.

Many of the outed Presbyterian ministers conducted secret services, known as conventicles, in houses, or in the fields. These were declared illegal, and were broken up by the military. In addition, many of the Presbyterian lairds in the west of Scotland were heavily fined for acts done during the Civil War and the Protectorate. When the Covenanters first came into power they had acted with a high hand, but they were now themselves the oppressed, and the fanaticism of Philiphaugh and Dunaverty was replaced by a burning passion to defend their personal and national liberty against the worst tyranny that Scotland had ever known. Its agent was the Privy Council of King Charles, which comprised the Earl of Rothes, a coarse and illiterate man; General John Middleton, described as a drunken debauchee; and the Earl of Lauderdale, a man of much culture and ability but who, in his zeal to serve his king, forgot his duty to his fellow countrymen.

Signs of rebellion in the west caused the Government some alarm in 1664, and in 1665 it became known that the Covenanters had made overtures to the Dutch, then at war with England. This, in the eyes of Government, was rank treason, and the arrest of those who might be potential leaders of a rebellion was ordered. Armed forces, accompanied by the sheriffs, were sent into the shires to disarm the people. It should be borne in mind, however, that only a small proportion of the Presbyterians took any part in this rising.

We have now to enquire into the state of affairs in Kintyre during this troubled period in our history. The execution of the Marquis of Argyll in 1661 had deprived the Lowland colony of their head and principal support. His son, the ninth Earl, had also been condemned to death in 1662, but the sentence was never carried out, and the family estates were restored to him in 1663.

In view of the fate of his father he had to walk warily. He had never been a Covenanter, nor was he even a staunch Presbyterian. It is related of him that Archbishop Sharp once commended him for his respectful demeanour towards bishops, when he replied that he had been at one time a Presbyterian, but had changed his mind after travelling in other countries, where the differences between various forms of Church government were not considered so important as in Scotland. To some extent he aided the Government in its efforts to suppress Presbyterianism, but he also advocated moderation. He was prepared to assist the Government to suppress armed rebellion when it occurred, but he refused to be a party to the grosser acts of oppression, and took no part in one of the most infamous of these - the Highland Host of 1678. He did not cut the same figure in the eyes of the Kintyre Lowlanders as his father had done but, as events will show, he was a good friend to them.

In 1662, when the ministers were outed, only three of the Kintyre parishes were filled, and all three ministers rejected the order to receive collation from bishops, and were deprived of their livings. They were Mr Dugald Darroch of the Highland charge of Lochhead, Mr Edward Keith of the Lowland, and Mr David Simson of Killean. Mr Darroch died shortly after, in 1664 or 1665, but Mr Keith and Mr Simson both returned to Kintyre charges later, with Indulgences, Mr Keith to his old congregation, and Mr Simson to Southend, in the year 1672. In an article "Church Life in Kintyre, 1600-1700," presented to the Kintyre Antiquarian Society in 1928, and based on research among the Presbytery records, the Rev. A.J. MacVicar, minister of Southend, has given us the names of some of the Episcopalian ministers sent to Kintyre at this time. They included James Campbell in Campbeltown, Irvine McLevine in Kilcalmonell, John McLevine in Jura, and Angus Macdonald at Killean.

These men left no parish records, but we are told that the outed ministers held conventicles in barns and in the glens, and even maintained a kind of secret presbytery. The clerk to the Presbytery in 1662 had been Mr Thomas Orr, who was a schoolmaster and notary in Lochhead; and after his death Mr Robert Duncanson, then minister of Campbeltown, endeavoured to recover, from his widow and his son Thomas, the Presbytery minutes from 6th March 1660 to November 1662, when the ousting took place, and after that the *private* minutes kept by the outed ministers, but they stated that they did not possess them. Hence the period 1660 to 1670 is largely a blank, both in the Presbytery and in the parish registers.

Turning from the ecclesiastical to the political aspect of affairs in the district, we find evidence that the Kintyre colony of Covenanters was being kept under the watchful eye of the Government. This is not surprising, when we consider that it comprised men like Ralston, Halket, and Wallace, whose previous records and political views must have been well known to the Privy Council in Edinburgh. Thus in the summer of 1665 the Earl of Rothes, in a letter to Lauderdale reporting the progress being made in the disarming of the people, states that it was going well in all the western shires, except in Kintyre, which he describes a "a nest of cneaves," that is of knaves. The inference to be drawn from this is that, in Kintyre, the authorities had either been unable or unwilling to put in force the repressive measures adopted elsewhere in the west of Scotland, and it does appear that the district escaped the worst features of the tyrannous government and persecution of this time. When, however, the arrest of potential leaders was ordered to be made, those in Kintyre did not get off so easily. The Earl of Argyll was called on to play his part in his own jurisdiction, and appears to have had sent to him a list of those to be arrested. In a letter to Lauderdale, dated 12th October 1665, the Earl reports that he had arrested Ralston and Colonel Halket, but that Colonel James Wallace had escaped. Ralston and Halket were confined in Dumbarton Castle, where they were kept for two years without charge or trial.

The escape of Colonel Wallace from Kintyre to the Lowlands had momentous consequences, for, when the Covenanters there decided to take up arms in the following year, the command of their army was given to him and it was his military training and experience that turned the rabble of lairds and their tenants into at least the semblance of a military force, which was capable of putting up several hours' fight against the Crown forces led by General Dalzell. This was at Rullion Green, on the southern slopes of the Pentlands, on 28th November 1666. The Covenanters were defeated, but Wallace had posted them so skilfully that not more than a hundred men were killed, although over a hundred more were taken prisoner, and hanged or transported. Wallace, as we have already seen, escaped to Holland, and died at Rotterdam in 1678. Of his leadership of the Covenanters Kirkton remarks: "Wallace himself was a gentleman godly and resolute, but such an undertaking was for a man of miracles."

When the fact of the rising of the Covenanters reached the ears of Government the levies of the shires were called out, and the Earl of Argyll is said to have been ready with a force of about 1500 men to aid the Government. He appears to have been much piqued that he was not called upon to use it, and in a letter to Lauderdale complains that "some good hand" had held back his orders. It is supposed that this was done on the advice of Archbishop Sharp, who was afraid that, if Argyll took his forces into the field, they might go over to the other side.

Some light is thrown on the state of affairs in Kintyre, immediately preceding the Pentland Rising, by the Earl's correspondence with Lauderdale. Argyll had been in Kintyre in May 1666, and writes from there as follows: "I am here, not only settling land, but breaking a club. I have now set most of my land, save a little of what the lowlanders possess. It is not money is the difference, but I will have every single tenant have his tack of me, with all necessary clauses, and not depend on one another, and remove or stay, and do everything as the word is given them." As we have seen the original number of tack-holders of the plantation was twelve only. These twelve were responsible for the rents, and their names alone occurred in the rentals. They were accompanied, however, by many more who either shared the holdings with them or were their sub-tenants.

The names of these latter were not known to the Earl, and he had no control over them. They had apparently, in his eyes, formed a club, that is a political society or clique of some sort and, as he states in his letter, he was determined to break this up, and to get control over these people by making each of them take out a written lease, whereby he, as their landlord and feudal superior, could control their political activities. There is, in fact, some reason to suppose that the Government at this time looked on Kintyre as a kind of Cave of Adullam for the disaffected, and as a possible focus of revolt. The new rental which the Earl prepared is extant, and reveals the names of some of the other Lowlanders who were in the district at this time. The new tacks would of course be given only to the more important of them.

Another indication of the suspicion that rested on the Kintyre colony is given by the fact that, although not invited by the Government to take the field against the rebels, the Earl, immediately after the news of Rullion Green reached him, proceeded to Kintyre, apparently on his own initiative. From his yacht at Tarbert he writes to Lauderdale on 3rd December 1666, that is four days after the battle, stating that "although I have not had the honour to endure blows for his Majesty's service ... I really am almost killed with toil and fatigue." He then reports that, having summoned the heritors of the county to meet him at Tarbert, "with a certain proportion of the best men, best armed" he marched into Kintyre, and made a round-up of the complete Lowland colony. "I went myself, day and night, forward to Kintyre, with a small party, and drove all, foul and clean, here before me." He reports that he found the place in no rebellious state, but that "in discourse I found them not principalled as I wished." This, of course, was what was to be expected, considering their origin and political and religious beliefs. He had, he states, put garrisons in the castles of Saddell and Skipness, making the Lowlanders pay their share of the expense, but refusing to have any of their men in them.

In a letter, dated 15th December 1666, he reports further on his enquiries into the behaviour of the Kintyre colony. William Wallace, son of Colonel James had, he states, returned to Kintyre, and had been carefully examined, the Earl coming to the conclusion that he had not taken part in the insurrection. He was released on bail, James Browne and John Cunningham of Hill of Beith going surety for him. Even his father the Colonel, the Earl thought, had not been in at the beginning, "but," he states "too many have been ready to rake when the fire was kindled."

Of the rest he mentions only one or two. John Cunningham of Hill of Beith he dismisses as innocent and no fanatic. Of the Goodman of Caldwell, who was one of his tenants, he is not so sure, as he was out of Kintyre at the time of the Rising. This man was undoubtedly implicated, and his name was excepted from the list of those who got a free pardon later, and his estate in the Lowlands forfeited. "I hope," said the Earl, "that Kintyre will not, after this, be so ill looked on: I am talked of for tenderness to them, and I deny it not, when I think it will do good, and no hurt, but if they abuse it, I hope they shall need no other to cut their throats." This statement provides clear proof of the suspicion under which the Lowland colony lay at this period, while the forcible language of the Earl was probably meant to provide some sort of compensation for his leniency towards them.

The Privy Council, however, was not disposed to be as lenient as he had been, and refused to accept his statement that William Wallace, son of the Colonel, had been innocent. Wallace was ordered to go to Edinburgh for further examination, and proceeded there without any guard, and while still on bail. On reaching Glasgow he met an Ayrshire acquaintance, Cunningham of Auchinyairds, who strongly advised him not to go, pointing out that no matter how innocent he could prove himself, he would be put to the torture of the Boot, an ancient form of torture long obsolete, but revived at this time to deal with the Covenanters. He therefore returned to Kintyre, where he spent one night on a remote part of the coast, and then, breaking his bail, and leaving behind him a letter protesting his innocence, fled to Ireland.

This appears to have greatly annoyed the Earl, who probably felt that his judgement and honour were at stake, and he accordingly made strenuous efforts to catch Wallace. All these failed, and he probably returned later when the general pardon to all the Rullion Green rebels was issued on 1st October 1667. His name was not among the list of those excepted, although that of his father was. In the spring of 1667 Argyll arrested Browne and Cunningham, who were Wallace's sureties, and also David Muir of Drumore, who was charged with re-setting him, and all three were lodged in Dumbarton Castle.

The Earl himself appears at this time to have been spied on, by the Government receiving information behind his back. In one of his letters to Lauderdale he states that, in February 1667, "one Mr McLoy, an Irishman of the age of 34 years or thereby, indifferent tall, very drunken faced in his ale, but otherwise of a pale complexion, came to Kintyre from Ireland. He gave out he was forced in by stress of weather, that he intended for Arran, that he was grievously opposed by the Marquis of Antrim, told a number of idle ranting news, and had a deal of odd discourses, ill knit together, which with his other extravagances, made him to be taken notice of everybody in the streets of Lochhead in Kintyre, whereupon producing several passes, wherein he was named McLoy, one in the company offered to prove one of the passes, pretended to be subscribed by the Governor of Derry, to be counterfeit. Whereupon next morning, before day, he stole away in a boat to Arran. If this be the informer, trust nothing but what he proves; let him condescend on persons and places, and all shall be tryed to the full."

Towards the end of the year 1667 the prisoners in Dumbarton Castle were set free. Ralston had petitioned the Privy Council to the effect that he had now been a prisoner for two years and more, "and as in the knowledge of his innocency he is confident he failed nothing, so he is most desirous to remove all suspicion of his carriage for the future ..." Accordingly the Lords of the Council, "with his Majesty's pleasure signified to them theranent ..." ordered his release, he to go at once to Edinburgh, and subscribe the necessary bonds to keep the peace in future. On 17th January 1668 Ralston signed a bond to keep the peace under a penalty of 10,000 merks, with Robert Hamilton, a clerk of session, and William Hamilton of Wishaw, as his cautioners. He also agreed that his tenants and servants, present and future, should sign a similar bond to keep the peace, under a penalty of paying the full value of a year's rent, or a year's fee respectively.

At the same time Colonel Robert Halket was also liberated, signing a similar bond for 5000 merks, Sir William Bruce of Balcaskie being his cautioner. At about the same time William Wallace's sureties and resetters were set free, Cunningham agreeing to sign a bond of 5000 merks, and Browne and Muir one of 1000 merks each, and to be answerable for their tenants and servants.

It is clear that, if the Earl of Argyll had harboured any ill-will against Ralston, he could easily have had him removed from Kintyre at this date. Ralston's tack of the Saddell lands, granted for nineteen years from 1650, was now due to expire. It was not renewed, and the lands of Saddell were granted in feu to Dugald Campbell of Lindsaig. Ralston, on the other hand, received a new tack of a holding nearly twice that of Saddell, and comprising all the best lands in the Campbeltown and Southend parishes. This tack was granted to him for the space of twenty-one years from Whitsunday 1669, and comprised the following holdings in Campbeltown parish: Crossibeg, Kilcousland, Smerby, Clackfin, Ballimeanoch, Barraskomill, or 18 merklands in all, and in the Southend parish Machrimore, Kilcolmkill (but reserved during James Omey's lifetime), Machricastell, Machribeg, Brunerican, Kildavie, Pollywilline, Dunglas, Kilblaan, Inchnareyll - in all 26 merklands, the total of his holding in Kintyre being thus about 44 merklands. Ralston, as already pointed out, appears to have been living in Southend at the time of his death in 1691, and is buried in Kilcolmkill.

Although there was an odd Lowlander in Southend before this time, the main plantation of that parish dates from Ralston's tack of 1669. It was very extensive, and in a return prepared in the year 1726, at the request of Edmund Burt, Southend is described as "a Lowland parish with some Highlanders." A hundred years later the position was reversed, and Highlanders were again in the majority. So common has intermarriage been between the two stocks in recent times that they are now scarcely distinguishable.

In the year 1669 the Government began to relax, for a time at least, in its treatment towards the Presbyterians, and granted an Indulgence to ministers of that order who were prepared to live and work peaceably in their parishes. A second Indulgence followed in 1672, and in that year four Presbyterian ministers returned to Kintyre. They were Mr John Cameron, who had been in Kilfinan, and who now became minister of the Highland charge in Campbeltown; Mr Edward Keith, who returned to the Lowland charge there after having been outed for ten years; Mr David Simson, outed from Killean in 1662, who now went to Southend, the parish having been vacant for a quarter of a century; and Mr John Cunnison, who had been in Arran, and who now became minister of Killean.

It is probable that the return of these ministers saved the district from the oppression that now took place in the Lowlands, for although there might be some slight stigma attaching to indulged ministers, it would not prevent the people from attending to their ministrations, and the necessity for conventicles would disappear. In the Lowlands, on the contrary, things went from bad to worse, and conventicles became the outward symbol of revolt against the Government. Legislation was introduced which at first made the convening of these meetings an offence punishable by death. Finally, the death penalty was decreed for any person attending them, and it is at this period that we read of people being shot or drowned by the military. Even if conventicles had been common in Kintyre, in the decade 1670 to 1680, it would have been difficult for the Government to have taken action there, without the support and active assistance of the Earl of Argyll, and, as we have seen, he was opposed to such persecution, both by conviction and family connections.

We think, therefore, that it is a fair conclusion to draw, that while some of the Kintyre Lowlanders took part in the Pentland Rising, and suffered on that account, there was no trouble in the following decade, and the district did become a place of refuge for the persecuted in Ayr, Renfrew, and other adjacent parts of the Lowlands, and that this was especially the case after the Highland Host had been let loose on these counties in 1678. Many Lowlanders must have sought refuge from this oppression by emigrating to Kintyre, some no doubt to join friends who were already there. We have only indirect evidence that this was so, and it is to be found in the register of the Lowland congregation, which reveals the fact that the number of separate Lowland names doubled between the years 1665 and 1685.

The influx appears to have been so great that, about the year 1683, a state of scarcity, amounting almost to famine, prevailed in Kintyre. In that year one of the agents of John Boyle of Kelburn, who had been appointed Crown Chamberlain of the forfeited estates of the Earl of Argyll, wrote to Boyle to the effect that he "would pity the case of this poor country as it now is, if ye knew it," and he beseeches him to try to get the ban on the importation of meal from Ireland removed. This last immigration may be considered to have been the third stage of the Lowland plantation. It was not planned, like the Burgh of Lochhead in 1609, or the plantation of lairds in 1650 to 1651, but was a spontaneous movement by the people themselves to escape from oppression in the Lowlands. It was the final stage of the plantation, which must have been fairly complete by 1685.

CHAPTER XIV

THE EARL OF ARGYLL'S REBELLION OF 1685

The unsuccessful attempt of the Earl of Argyll, in 1685, to overthrow the government of King James II is a matter of our national history. As, however, he began the enterprise in Kintyre, and as it had serious consequences to many Kintyre people, we propose to give a short account of it, in so far as it affected that district. The Earl had refused to subscribe the Test Act in 1681, for which he was proclaimed a traitor, tried, and sentenced to death; but, while awaiting execution in Edinburgh Castle he managed to make his escape, as the result of a clever ruse by his stepdaughter, Lady Sophia Lindsay. She came to visit him in prison, attended by a page of the same height and figure as the Earl, with whom the latter exchanged clothes, and left the Castle undetected. By morning he was over the border, and made his way to London, where his presence was made known to King Charles who, to his credit, refused to have him re-arrested. He escaped to Holland, and while there he hatched, along with Monmouth, the plot to invade this country which brought both of them to the scaffold.

The preparations being made in Holland by Argyll and Monmouth got to the ears of the Government during the summer and autumn of 1684, and steps were at once taken to deal with the threat. In Scotland, the Marquis of Atholl received two Letters of Gift and Tack, one bestowing on him the office of Lieutenant and Justiciar of the Shires of Argyll and Tarbert, and the other the gift of the houses, park, and mill of Inveraray. Boyle of Kelburn, who had been Crown Chamberlain of the Earl's forfeited estates, became Deputy Lieutenant, assisted by Patrick Stewart of Ballechin and others.

Atholl marched into Argyllshire with a force of 1000 men, and at once began the examination of suspected persons. The first and most important was Campbell of Ardkinglas, who acknowledged that money had been collected for the Earl in the year 1682, amounting in all to £50 sterling, of which Dugald Campbell, Baillie of Kintyre, had contributed £8, the Captain of Dunoon £5, and Dugald Campbell, brother to Glencarradale, 50 merks. An additional 300 merks was admitted to have been collected, but by whom Ardkinglas could not say. The Privy Council ordered the three Campbells above mentioned to be apprehended and sent to Edinburgh, and Argyll's charter chest and papers were also seized and taken there.

In addition to the above, some indulged ministers appear to have been suspect, and were called to Inveraray and examined by Atholl himself in September 1684. They were Mr John Duncanson of Kilbrandon, Mr Patrick Campbell of Inverarary, Mr Duncan Campbell of Knapdale, Mr Robert Duncanson of Campbeltown, Mr John Cunnison of Saddell, and Mr David Simson of Kilcolmkill or Southend. When interrogated as to whether they had obeyed the Council's instructions, they one and all confessed that they had broken and violated same, and they signed a declaration to that effect. Atholl thereupon declared their indulgences to be null and void, and prohibited them from preaching or exercising any part of the ministerial function in time coming, and caused each and all of them to give bond and sufficient caution to deliver their persons to the clerks of the Privy Council, to be disposed upon as the Lords of Council should think fit, and he ordained that they should go to prison until the caution money could be found. The exact nature of their offence is not revealed, nor is it clear whether they were involved in the Argyll plot or not.

Atholl next ordered the collection of all public arms, both King's and Militia, upon oath, these to be held at Inveraray. All those who refused to take the Test were also disarmed. About the same time he sent a force into Islay, and proceeded to disarm the inhabitants of that island. From the more important of its men he took bonds to keep the peace.

In the next year, 1685, after word had been received that Argyll had actually landed, Atholl was granted authority to raise a fresh force of 500. This was divided into seven companies, commanded by the Lairds of Grantully, Weem, Faskally, Ashintullie, Strowan, Macfarlane, and Leny. The castles of Skipness and Tarbert were garrisoned by Patrick Stewart, Atholl's deputy. Those of Lochhead and Dunaverty appear to have been occupied also by Boyle's agents.

Argyll set sail from Holland in three small ships - the *Anna, Sophia,* and *David* - on 2nd May 1685, with a company of about 300 men, including both Scotsmen and foreigners, and several thousand stand of arms. On Wednesday, 6th June, he touched at the Orkneys, where two of his chaplains, Dr Blackadder and Mr Spence, having gone ashore, were taken prisoner by order of the Bishop of Orkney, who, at the same time, dispatched messengers to inform the Government of the arrival of the expedition. From Orkney the ships proceeded down the west coast of Scotland, and touched at Islay for the purpose of obtaining recruits, but the reception of Argyll here appears to have rather been a cold one. In all, however, he obtained eighty recruits in Islay, apparently mostly voluntary men, but most of them deserted him later.

From Islay the ships sailed to Kintyre, and dropped anchor in Lochkilkerran on the morning of 20th May 1685. There were several reasons why Argyll should have chosen Kintyre as the place in which first to raise the standard of rebellion. Its situation was comparatively isolated, and so protected him from too early an attack by the Government forces, while at the same time it was close enough to the mainland to form a suitable jumping-off ground, should he find conditions for an immediate descent favourable. Another matter, and one which probably affected his decision more than anything else, was the existence of the Lowland colony of Covenanters, formed in Kintyre by his father and himself, and which, when it came to a struggle on behalf of Protestantism, might be expected to rally to the cause, and provide him with his first useful recruits.

In this matter he was not entirely disappointed, although he probably expected a greater response to his call than he actually obtained. As we have already said, he did not cut in their eyes the figure that his father the Marquis had done. He had never been a Covenanter, and he had handled them somewhat roughly at the time of the Pentland Rising. Young Erskine of Carnock, who accompanied Argyll as an Ensign, and whose *Journal* is one of our principal authorities for these events, tells us definitely that the Kintyre Lowlanders who joined the Earl did so on account of the religious principles involved, and not for his own sake. The expedition spent six days at Campbeltown and the principal events which occurred there were as follows -

After landing on the 20th May, Argyll and a party of his followers proceeded to the Cross, which stood in the Main Street, near to the Castle of Lochhead, and from there a *Declaration* was read with sound of Trumpet. This had the title: *The Declaration and Apology of the Protestant people, that is of the Noblemen, Barrons, Gentlemen, Burgesses, and Commons of all sorts now in armes within the Kingdome of Scotland, with the concurrence of their true and faithful Pastors, and of several Gentlemen of the English Nation joined in with them in the same cause, for defence and reliefe of their Lives, Rights, and Liberties, and recovery and re-establishment of the true Protestant Religion, in behalf of themselves and all that shall joyn with and adhere to them. Printed at Campbell-town in Kintyre, in the shire of Argyle.* Anno 1685.

On the following day, the 21st of May, a service was held in the parish church of Campbeltown, that is in the church built in 1643, when Mr Thomas Forrester preached from the text Exodus xxxiii, 14 and 15, and was reported to have spoken "excellently to the matter in hand." Mr Forrester was the outed minister of Alva in Stirlingshire, and probably a relative of the Kintyre Forresters. After the Revolution Settlement he became the Principal of the New College, St Andrews. After the sermon the Declaration read at the Cross on the previous day was again read in the church, and in addition a Particular Declaration of the Earl to his own people. This was entitled *The Declaration of Archibald, Earl of Argile, Lord Kintyre, Cowal, Campbell and Lorn, Heritable Sheriff and Lieutenant of the shires of Argyll and Tarbet, and Heritable Justice-General of the said shires, and of the West Isles and others.*

The Particular Declaration asserted that he had taken to arms for no private or personal end, and that in the event of his recovering his estate, he would pay all his debts in full. It protests his loyalty to his late Majesty (Charles II) but states that since his death the Duke of York (King James II) had thrown off the mask, and invaded the religion and liberties of the people. He therefore considered it to be his duty to God and to his country to use his utmost endeavours to oppose usurpation and tyranny, and to lead those good Protestants who had joined him to that end. He invited all such, and especially his own friends and blood relations, to concur in the Declaration, and he took this means to require all his vassals anywhere, with their fencible men within their command, to go to arms and join and concur in the Declaration, or be answerable at their peril, and to obey the orders received from him from time to time. After the reading of this Declaration the Earl himself addressed the congregation in a short speech, at which, Carnock tells us, "some seemed to be moved."

The above two Declarations were printed at Campbeltown, but not on a local press, and it is unlikely that any such existed at that time. The Earl had taken the precaution to bring with him a small press from Holland, and a Dutch printer, so that to save time copies of his Declarations could be put in circulation before he got control of any press in the Lowlands. This appears to have been one of the few pieces of foresight in all this hastily organised and ill-prepared attempt. Among those examined by the Privy Council in connection with the rebellion we find under the dates 22nd and 23rd June 1685 the following:

"Geeils Williamsone, printer, a Dutchmen, servant to Jacob Vandervelde, bookseller in Amsterdam, and was sent with Argyll by his master to attend him with a little press and some types and was hired for two ducats downs a week ... declares he knows not a word of English, and so he knew not what he was to do and that he printed these declarations at Campbeltown and Argyll himself corrected them and that he did cast off eight hundred copies."

This unfortunate Dutch printer, although his innocence must have been quite clear, was kept at least twenty-four weeks in the Tolbooth prison of Edinburgh, in a semi-starving condition, on an allowance of only one groat, or fourpence, a day. His ultimate fate is not recorded.

On the 22nd May a rendezvous of the recruits obtained up to date by the Earl was held in the park "at the town-head." This must have been a park near the Castle of Lochhead. The men were marshalled into two companies, of which James Henderson was given the command of one, and James Denham of the other, and Carnock was made Ensign to Henderson. To these companies two stand of colours were presented, that of Henderson's company bearing the motto *For the Protestant Religion*, and that of Denham's *Against Popery, Prelacy and Erastianism*. Some gentlemen, whose names are not disclosed, but who had withdrawn themselves at Argyll's first landing, came in to him on this day.

On the 23rd May these two companies, and several others formed by the Lowlanders (the exact number is not stated), again proceeded to the park, when arms were handed out to them; and on this day also a Mr George Barclay was sent to Carrick to rouse the people there, and David Dickson was sent on a similar mission to Cunningham, and to bring back information as to where the Government forces were.

On the 24th May there was more preaching. Mr Thomas Forrester preached in a "meeting house", which must have been the original building used by the Lowland congregation in Kirk Street, taking the same text, and presumably preaching the same sermon, from Exodus, as he preached in the parish church on the 21st. In the parish church the service on this day was taken jointly by Mr John Forrester and Mr Alexander Hastie, whose texts are not recorded. The former has not been traced, but Mr Hastie, who was an M.A. of Edinburgh, had been imprisoned after Bothwell Brig in 1680. He returned to Scotland again in 1687, and was minister of Torphichen, and of St Paul's, Glasgow. By his will he bequeathed half his estate to found the Hastie bursaries at Glasgow University, by which his name is still kept in remembrance.

It is not clear how many recruits Argyll got in Kintyre, but he had at least three companies of the Lowlanders, of which one at least was of horse, but the horses, Carnock states, "were but fit for dragoons," from which we may conclude that they were heavy farm horses. When he had got as far as Bute, two of the Macallasters, who were holding Skipness Castle for Atholl, reported to the latter, in a letter dated 2nd June, that his total force at that date did not exceed 1500 men. The eighty men got in Islay are stated to have enlisted voluntarily, but all had deserted, except twelve, by the end of his stay at Campbeltown. With the exception of the Lowlanders, the recruits he got in Kintyre were pressed, and even some of the Lowlanders, when examined before the Council later, pleaded that they had been dragged from their houses and forced to join against their wills.

So far as can be ascertained, none of the old Macdonald vassals of Kintyre joined Argyll. They had no doubt seen the scanty resources with which he hoped to conquer a kingdom, and, on the other hand, the careful preparations made by the government and, apart from hereditary inclination and ancient loyalties, were disinclined to embark on such a dangerous enterprise. Argyll had made a bid to win them over and, after reaching Campbeltown, wrote the following letter to, it is supposed, Macallaster of Loup.

CAMPLETOWN

May 22, 1685

LOVING FRIEND,

It hath pleased God to bring me safe to this place, where several of both nations doth appear with me for the defense of the Protestant Religion, our lives and liberties, against Popery and Arbitrary Government, whereof the Particulars and in two Declarations emitted by those noble-men, gentlemen, and others and by me for myself. Your father and I lived in great friendship, and I am glad to serve you his son in the Protestant Religion, and I will be ready to do it in your particular when there is occasion. I beseech you let not any out of fear or other bad principles perswade you to neglect your duty to God and your Countrey at this time, or believe that D. York is not a Papist, or that being one, he can be a righteous King. Then know that all England is in Arms in three several places and the Duke of Monmouth appears at the same time upon the same grounds as we do, and few places in Scotland but soon will joyn and the South and West waits but till they hear I am landed, for so we resolved before I left Holland. Now I beseech you make no delay to separate from those [who] abuse you, and are carrying on a Popish design, and come with all the men of your command to assist the Cause of Religion, where you shall be most welcome to

Your Loving Friend to serve you,

ARGYLL.

P.S. Let this serve Young Lorgie, Skipnage, and Charles McEchan.

The Macallasters of Loup and their adherents, however, were on the side of Atholl, as we have already seen, and the above letter appears to have been sent by its recipient to the Privy Council, as evidence against Argyll. We have no record of what Macdonald of Largie did on this occasion, but some of his relatives were on Atholl's side. He was Archibald Macdonald, and a minor. Four years later he managed to elude the Crown forces sent to prevent the Highlanders from joining Claverhouse, and is stated to have been killed at the Battle of Killiecrankie. Charles Maceachan, referred to in the postscript, was the Earl's vassal for his lands on Tangy, but did not join him and we find Atholl, towards the end of the year, requesting him to prepare a list of the Kintyre rebels. Another of the old vassals, Colin Maceachran of Kilellan, is found in the list of those taking part in the Atholl raids on the Kintyre people, to be described later, and he also took part in a raid on the estate of the Campbells of Auchinbreck, in which the Laird of Auchinbreck's uncle was killed. There is no mention of the Kintyre Macneils, and the side they took is unknown.

On the 24th May the expedition left Campbeltown, the men recruited being put on board the ships, and the Earl, accompanied by Sir John Cochran and some others, riding overland to Tarbert, for the purpose of obtaining more recruits. Over the rest of the events we need not delay, as they are detailed in our national histories. After some changes of plan the Earl landed on the coast of Renfrew, where he was recognised and taken prisoner by a man called Riddell, brought to Edinburgh, and at once executed by the Maiden, without further trial, on his previous sentence. It is stated that for long afterwards the Argyll family refused to have anyone of the name of Riddell in their employ.

Many of the inhabitants of Kintyre were involved in the aftermath of the rebellion, and the measures taken against the rebels were severe in the extreme. On 31st May 1685 the Secret Committee of the Scots Privy Council sent orders to Atholl which included the following: "Meanwhile destroy what you can to all who joined any manner of way with him. All men who joined, and are not come off on your or Breadalbane's advertisement, are to be killed, or disabled ever from fighting again; and burn all houses except honest men's, and destroy Inverara and all the Castles; and what you cannot undertake leave to those who come after you to do. But all this is with submission to your judgment, who are on the place. Let the women and children be transported to remote isles." There is no evidence that these orders were carried out in their entirety, but it is probable that it was at this time that the castles of Lochhead and Dunaverty were finally demolished; at least we find no further record of them.

Among the more important Kintyre people who were taken prisoner, and examined by the Privy Council, were the following:-

ALEXANDER FORRESTER was the proprietor of Knockrioch, and the Earl's vassal for its lands, for which he had received a charter a few years before this date. Evidence against him was given by Mr David Simson, minister of Kilcolmkill, Kilblaan, and Kilkivan, apparently the son and successor of the David Simson mentioned above, but, unlike his father, an Episcopalian. He testified that "he did see Alex. Forrester of Knockriochmore lying in arms with the late Earl of Argyll, and that he went with him in arms to Tarbert." The Council, however, discharged Forrester, "in all time coming in regard the said Forrester has proven he was forced out of his bed and carried prisoner by the rebels and was thereafter dismissed by them because he would not join with them and that there are several testificatts produced of his loyal and peaceable behaviour." From this case it is clear that even some of the Earl's Lowland vassals had refused to join him.

ALEXANDER ROWATT had been factor to the dowager Countess of Argyll in Kintyre, and deponed that he had been on duty there in May 1685, when the rising took place, and that he had been violently seized upon, and compelled to go along with the rebels, but at the first opportunity deserted them. He asserted that he had a just abhorrence of rebellious practices, and was ready on all occasions to serve his Majesty. He was acquitted, and given a safe conduct to Kintyre for another six weeks, to enable him to conduct his business there. He was an ancestor of the Campbeltown Rowatts of the next century.

At Inveraray, on 1st October 1685, MR THOMAS ORR, son to Mr Thomas Orr, schoolmaster at Lochhead, gave evidence before John Boyle of Kelburne and Patrick Stewart of Ballechin. He was described as an unmarried man, between 25 and 26 years of age. He stated that while looking over the shoulder of the Earl of Argyll he had read a letter from Ewan Cameron, chief of Locheil.

Among the humbler class of prisoners were the following: MURDOCH McISAAC in Machrimore was taken at Dumbarton, and declared that he was pressed. His fate is not stated. JOHN BUCHANAN, at the head of Lochhead in Kintyre, declared that he was pressed by Mr Charles Campbell, the Earl's son, and that his own two sons were with Atholl. They were, he stated, driven like sheep. JAMES BAIRD in Kintyre, who could not write, declared that he was seized and threatened with death, and that when he was taken he swore that he would never draw a sword against his Majesty. He was sentenced to banishment without stigma, this is without mutilation. DUNCAN FERGUSON, formerly a tenant of the Earl in Kintyre, deponed that he was pressed, but was sentenced to banishment. JAMES HALL, a tenant in Colin Mceachran's lands of Kilellan, stated that he was pressed, but was sentenced to banishment. WILLIAM MORE in Kildavie, and John Martin, servant to James Armour of Hillabee, both testified that they had been pressed. The former was sentenced to banishment, but the sentence of the latter is not stated.

DUNCAN McVICAR, son to the Bailie of Campbeltown, was a young lad about 16 years of age, "at school learning his grammar." He stated that he was pressed by Colonel Aileph, and that a whole company was made out of Campbeltown, being fifty-six men in all, and that they got collars with a motto on them for the Protestant religion. Another schoolboy examined was John Clark in Lochkilkerran, *alias* Campbeltown, and yet another Donald Thomson in Tarbert, described as a boy of 15 years and a packman. The fate of these youths is not stated. Samuel Huy in Kintyre, servant to John Huy, declared that he had been out with the Earl but forced to do so by threats. He refused to acknowledge the King's authority, and was sent to the Tolbooth to be put in irons. Later he was sentenced to banishment and to have his ears cut off. In all 177 men were banished, their destination at that period being the American colonies.

Among the lairds who suffered forfeiture were the Campbells of Auchinbreck, Melfort, Barbreck, Kilberry younger, Alex. Macmillan of Dunmore, Campbells of Carradale and Ottar, and also Captain John Hendry of the *Anna*, one of the Earl's transports. These sentences were of course revoked at the Revolution of three years later, and the tragedy of Argyll's attempt is that all that he tried to accomplish in 1685 was done in 1689, when King William landed at Torbay.

After the Earl left Kintyre in May 1685 the district was subjected to a systematic pillaging at the hands of Atholl's followers and others. These excesses, known as the Atholl Raids, were long remembered in Kintyre, but it is unfair to link them with the name of the Marquis of Atholl. As early as June, news of these happenings came to his ears, and he sent a letter of instructions as to how the malefactors were to be dealt with, to the Laird of Macnachtan, from Inveraray on the second day of that month. He had heard, he stated, that thieves and robbers, masquerading as soldiers, were committing thefts and robberies on his Majesty's loyal subjects. All such persons taken in the act were to be seized and sent to Inveraray for trial, and all stolen goods were to be returned to their owners, except "as much as will be meat to his men, since there is no other allowance for them."

This sentence is significant. The rebellion coincided with the last phase of the Lowland plantation of Kintyre when, as we have shown, the influx of people from the Lowlands had produced conditions bordering on famine, so that much difficulty must have been experienced by Atholl's men in getting supplies of food. A good deal of the robbery that took place may perhaps, therefore, have been done on the grounds of military necessity; but there is evidence that it exceeded the bounds of this, that Atholl's followings, despite the above instructions, got completely out of hand, and that the excesses were committed in a vindictive spirit against the Lowlanders. The fortunes of the Argylls were now at a low ebb, and it was but human nature that the old inhabitants should have endeavoured to get part of their own back, including a measure of revenge.

The robberies began in May, and continued to September 1685. After the Revolution an enquiry into the matter was held, and a list of those pillaged, and making claims for compensation, was prepared and printed in a curious old volume, entitled *Account of the Depredations on the Clan Campbell and their followers during the years 1685 and 1686 by the troops of the Duke of Gordon, Marquis of Atholl, Lord Strathnaver, and others.*

Whether those robbed received any compensation is not revealed. As the lists of stolen goods given in this book throw some light on the domestic furnishings and equipment of the period we give some extracts by way of example.-

John Langwill in Upper Balliwilling reported that he had been robbed, curiously enough by a Campbell, one Donald Oig Campbell from the bordland of Skipness, and had taken from him the following: cassicks or long coats, doublets, bonnets, four women's coats (two red and two brown serge), one coloured woman's plaid, "most sett to the green," green aprons, linen aprons, three pairs of women's stockings, of which two were knitted and the other plaiding, twenty-five suits of women's head clothes, "whereof nine were lace with hoods, the other sixteen neckcloths, two of them being laced," also twenty "craig cloaths and cravatts for men," twenty men's neckbands, some of them large and others little , and all of them "Holland and Caligo." In addition he lost a sword, and a wig costing £3 Scots money, his total loss amounting to £110 Scots "taken away by the said Donald Campbell and his accomplices and which can be verified and proven by famous witnesses and the said John Langwill his own oath in supplement, if required."

Some complained that they had been forced to pay money, and among these was Thomas Wilson in Smerby, who stated that he had been fined £22 by the Justiciars. Similarly, William Fulton in Campbeltown put in a claim for £19 which he had to advance to Boyle and his assistants. The same man had two bolls and two firlots of meal taken by Colin Maceachran of Kilellan, and William Campbell in Peninver claimed for eight cows taken away by Fergus McKay.

John and Donald McHutcheon in Campbeltown reported the loss of fishing gear taken by Donald Macdonald, uncle to the Laird of Largie. This included a large boat with sails, masts, cables, and compass square, valued at £266,13s.4d., nets valued at £80, fishing lines and household plenishing which included clothing, a saltfat or beeftub, a large looking-glass, and a brazen candlestick. They were also pillaged by Walter Lamont, a waiter or customs officer, who took from them riding coats and a box full of papers and accounts, and by Donald Macneil of Gallachalyie, who took a feather bolster, the pawn of a curtain, and - a much more unmanageable piece of loot if they contained their inhabitants - two bee scapes.

In the Southend parish James Maxwell in Pollywilline was raided by Donald Gorm Macdonald, John Mackay, Lauchlan McIntalyour, Gilniver Mackay, and others, and lost a half barrel of butter, a loaf of tallow, a barked hide, and several sacks of meal. William Hamilton, Laird of Brownmuir near Beith, then residing in Southend parish, had eighteen cows lifted by John Dow Macallaster, and "confest by the said John." Machrimore, then held in tack by the Laird of Ralston, and subtenanted by Alan Anderson, Alex. Picken, Robert Ross, and William Henrie, was raided by some men who came in a boat from the Isle of Skye, and beds, clothes, and household utensils carried off.

The places raided included Knockreoch, Upper Balliwilling, Askanelmore, Crossibeg, Gartgrellan, Smerby, Ardnacroish, Peninver, Pollwilline, Glenarkirdoch, Machrimore, High Barr, Barr, Chisken and others.

The lists of householding plenishing disclosed by this account suggest a fairly comfortable standard of living at this time in the case of the larger tacksmen and tenants, and of the burgesses in the town, and this receives confirmation from some Campbeltown accounts of the year 1672. In that year one of the most important merchants in the town was Donald Clark, a member of an old Highland family descended from the pre-Reformation parish clerks, and ancestor of the Kintyre Clarks of the following two centuries. He was at this date also proprietor of Drumlemble, which he held in feu from the Earl of Argyll.

The accounts show that in the year mentioned he stocked and sold agricultural necessities such as scythes, horseshoes, bridles, bits and saddles, tar, soap, candles, ropes, and paper, and in addition such articles of luxury as tobacco, French wines, sugar, wax and honey, dried fruits comprising prunes, raisins, and figs; spices, dyes and condiments comprising capers, mace, nutmeg, saffron, liquorice, aniseed, and indigo, also hops, gall, and cochineal. In the matter of clothing he sold gloves, ribbons, lace, pearling or embroidery, and silk. From these accounts it would therefore appear that the standard of living in the early years of the Lowland plantation, at least in the case of the better-off, compared not unfavourably with that of to-day, taking into account the interval of time between then from now.

The Atholl raids were not the first abuses of this kind to which the Lowland people of the district had been subjected, for in the early years of the plantation men armed with swords, dirks, and pistols, some of whom came from Ireland, and some from the north isles, violently attacked houses and threatened their inhabitants with death, unless they surrendered their goods and revealed where they kept their money. So great a plague did these caterans become that the people of Kintyre petitioned the Privy Council of Scotland for help, and in 1662 the Lords of the Council gave a commission to Gory McAllaster of Loup, Colin Campbell of Skipness, Archibald Campbell of Glencarradale, Neil Og Mcneill of Carskey, Lachlan Mcneill of Tirfergus, and John Cunningham of Hill of Beith to suppress and apprehend these robbers, to secure them until they could be tried, and to search after stolen goods and secure resetters. What measure of success attended this Commission's deliberations and actions is not revealed.

The Atholl raids appear to have been the last of these troubles, and there are no evidences of the district having experienced in the next century the cattle lifting and atrocious system of blackmail that prevailed in the Central Highlands during the times of Rob Roy and his like. Kintyre appears to have missed these outrages, as it did the worst features of the seventeenth century persecution in Lowland Scotland.

CHAPTER XV
THE RURAL SCENE: AGRICULTURE AND INDUSTRY

We do not possess any contemporary description of agriculture and rural conditions in Kintyre in the seventeenth century. Those who might have supplied it - the lairds and ministers - were too much absorbed in the political and ecclesiastical disputes of the age to have any time to bestow attention on it, and even if they had had the opportunity, would probably have thought it beneath their dignity to write on such a commonplace subject. It was only after the great agricultural revolution which began about the middle of the eighteenth century that educated men directed their attention to agricultural conditions and their improvement, and then a spate of writings on the subject appeared. Many of these, such as the *Old Statistical Accounts* and the *General Views of Agriculture*, describe conditions as they existed before the new agriculture was ushered in, and from these, supplemented by contemporary rentals, leases, and charters, we are able to reconstruct the rural scene of the seventeenth century.

One of the most fundamental differences between conditions then and now was the existence of the Tacksman system. The tacksmen were those who obtained tacks or leases (not necessarily, nor in fact usually, written leases) of land from the great landlord-chiefs. They were usually either the chief's near relatives, or persons holding offices such as those of Bard or Harper, but sometimes outsiders were permitted to hold land as well. The tacksmen's holdings in Kintyre were very large, generally speaking, and might extend to a 20 merkland or more. On the other hand, some were small, being only a merkland or less. (The merkland was a money valuation only and not a measure of acreage.)

There is no satisfactory evidence of the length of leases in Kintyre in the time of the Lords of the Isles, but we know that some attained the status of "native tenants," that is, had a hereditary or prescriptive right to their holdings. This status is said to have been acquired after a tenant had been in possession of a particular holding for three generations or eighty-one years. There are instances in Kintyre of very long occupancy of a holding by one and the same family. Thus Macnachtans occupied Gartavay in the Southend parish continuously from 1500 to 1800, and may have been there before the first of these years. When the lands of Kintyre fell into the hands of the Crown in the sixteenth century the Crown gave them out in three-year leases, but these appear to have been in general renewed to the original occupants. At the time of the coming of the Lowland lairds in 1650 the leases granted by the Marquis of Argyll were usually for nineteen years, and this became the common length of lease in the subsequent centuries.

Some examples of these large tacksmen's holdings in Kintyre during the sixteenth and seventeenth centuries were Kinloch, a 12 merkland; Kileonan, a 17 merkland; Machrimore, a 12 merkland; Carskey, a 12 merkland; the Bard's lands enumerated in chapter one, an 8 merkland; and the Harper's lands, a 4 merkland. These and other similar holdings consisted of several farms, generally for convenience a mixture of grazing and arable farms. Two of the largest holdings ever given in tack in Kintyre were the 53 merkland of the lands of Macdonald of Largie, set in tack to Campbell of Inveraw in 1651, and the holding of 44 merklands in the Southend and Campbeltown parishes given by the Earl of Argyll to the Laird of Ralston in 1669. It is perhaps true to say that Ralston was the last of the big tacksmen in Kintyre.

Although some of the smaller tacksmen may have been working farmers, the class in general were not, but gentlemen whose energies were taken up in the political and military activities of the age. They thus formed a kind of gentry who were the chief's council in time of peace, and his followers in time of war. They were also the capitalists, possessing most of the cattle, horses, and implements necessary for agriculture. They generally sub-let their holdings to the working farmers, who formed the commonalty, often lending out to them the above-mentioned stock and materials according to the old system known as *Steelbow*. The working tenant had to return the loans of cattle, horses, implements, and seed grain, known as the *Steelbow Strength*, at the end of his contract. This system of Steelbow was in use in Kintyre as late as the year 1710, in which year we find a good example of a Steelbow contract between Malcolm Macneill of Carskey and one of his tenants in his Compt Book, now in the Free Library, Campbeltown. The working farmers appear to have had little or no capital, and are often referred to as "poor tenants." They worked from year to year and had no tacks.

It was from the tacksman class that most professional men were recruited, because they alone were able to send their sons to the universities. Sons of tacksmen also took military service, and became officers in the armies of the Continent, and later in the British and Indian Armies. There is no doubt that they were a fine body of men, and of both chiefs and tacksmen Macaulay has said: "There was no other part of the Kingdom where such men had in such a degree the better qualities of an aristocracy, grace and dignity of manner, self-respect, and that noble sensibility which makes dishonour more terrible than death." When the lowland lairds came to Kintyre in 1650 the tacksmen system was still in full swing, and they simply took the place, as tacksmen, of the Highlanders who had formerly occupied the lands now set to them.

Yet the growing democratic trend of the age was against the system, and in favour of elevating the working farmers to the rank of tenants with some measure of security and better economic prospects. The presence of so many young men who had had military training and experience was also a menace to the peace of the realm, and in the time of John, Duke of Argyll and Greenwich, about 1730 to 1740, the system was abolished and leases given for the first time to the working farmers. To some extent, and in some respects, the large tenant farmer of to-day has taken the place of the seventeenth century tacksman. It is worthwhile noting that it was the abolition of the tacksmen that led to the first wave of emigration from the Highlands to America.

All the Kintyre rentals prior to 1700 are tacksmen's rentals, and from these it is possible to see the rents which the tacksmen paid to the chief, and which of course must have been paid in still greater measure to the tacksman by the working farmers, for the tacksman obtained his living from the difference between these two amounts. Land had not yet been surveyed in acres, and, in fact, such a survey was not accomplished until nearly the end of the eighteenth century. Farms were described as consisting of so many *merklands*, and it is necessary to explain this term. A merk was thirteen shillings and four pence, and a merkland was a holding originally valued at an annual rental of this amount. This valuation was probably made, in the case of Kintyre, during the thirteenth century.

Owing, however, to the great depreciation in Scottish currency, and to other causes as well, a general rise in the value of the merkland can be traced. Thus in Kintyre, at the beginning of the sixteenth century, a merkland was often rented at a pound, which represents a rise of 50 per cent. Later the rise became much more rapid, and at the time of the coming of the Lowland lairds in 1650, the merkland rental in Kintyre was standing at £32 Scots, or about fifty times its original valuation, or the old extent, as it was called. It must not, however, be supposed that rents were actually paid in money during this century, at least by the working tenants, who had little or no money. They generally paid in meal, cheese, malt, and marts or cows. Probably the tacksmen converted a good deal of these into money, before they paid their rents to their chiefs.

In addition to ordinary rents, a special rent called *Presents* was also required to be paid. The origin of this custom is obscure, but as these offerings, consisting of dairy produce, lambs, wedders, etc., had to be handed over by the tenant in person, they probably had their origin in some kind of feudal obeisance, and appear to have been parallel to the altar offerings of the church. There was a growing tendency to commute produce rents, and presents into money payments, and by the end of the century the usual value of a present in Kintyre was £7,10s. Scots, and we find tenants being required to pay a present, or a present and a half, or two presents, and so on.

Another charge on all lands was the *Teind*, or tenth part of all crops and animals due to the Church. Originally, this too was collected in kind, and the tenth sheaf of all grain crops had to be set apart in the fields, to be collected by the tacksman to whom the teinds had been set in lease. This was the usual practice, adopted in order to save the Church the trouble of doing the collection itself. In South Kintyre at least the teinds were valued as early as 1629, and in parishes where this had been done a fixed proportion of the constant rent, either in money or meal, was paid instead of the actual tenth sheaf.

Another burden was the *Calp* or *Hereyeld*, paid on the death of any tenant to his chief or landlord, and consisting of the best beast - horse or cow - in his possession. This was really an early form of death duty, and could be a most grievous exaction in the case of tenants who were under more that one landlord. *Calps* (from Gaelic *colpach*, a young cow) were abolished by Act of Parliament in 1617, but this Act would appear to have been a dead letter, for we have come across accounts of *Calps* of a much later date, and in fact the payment of the *Calps* or *Hereyelds* are specified in Kintyre charters of the 1670's.

Nor must we forget to enumerate the "services used and wont," required to be paid by the tacksmen to their chiefs, and by the working farmers to the tacksmen. These involved giving militiary assistance to the chief, attending him at his hunts, cultivating his lands, and carting his peats and manure. They gradually fell into desuetude, and at the end of the next century they were only taken by the smaller landlords who lived among their tenants. Dr Smith of Campbeltown, who wrote the very informative *General Views of the Agriculture of Argyll* in 1798, has some hard things to say about what he calls the "servitudes."

Where a particular holding produced some special commodity it was often called on to pay this as part of its rent. Thus, in 1505, the tenant of Balnabraid, on the Learside, had to pay "12 *le keling*," that is 12 dried cod-fish. In 1643 the tenant of Machrimore Mill had to pay geese and poultry as part of his rent - the only example encountered in Kintyre records, with the exception of the houses of Lochhead, of poultry paid as rent. In 1651 the tenant of Island Davaar possessed that holding in return for providing fish for the table of the Marquis of Argyll. In 1678 the tacksman of Machrihanish was required to supply two dozen rabbits, and in the same year the lessee of Carskey a barrel of salmon, and the tenant of Laggan two bee scapes. The burgesses of the town of Lochhead, who tenanted Crosshill jointly during a good part of the century, had to pay as rent for it six quarts of aquavitae. The tacksman of Kilchrist and Octoran in 1678 had to pay, in addition to a money rent, 200 loads of peats. All tenants at that time had to pay *straw*, then very important for thatching, and as winter feed for cattle. This was uplifted at the rate of two loads to each merkland. In the Carskey Compt Book it is referred to as "Duke's Straw," and must have been paid by feuars as well, as part of their feu duties.

The method by which a large tacksman worked his multiple holding was as follows. He lived at one of the farms - the principal or home farm - which he probably worked by means of hired servants and cottars or set out in steelbow. The other farms of his holding were sub-let to working tenants, and we have now to enquire into the methods by which these tenants worked their farm. It was rare to find one such farm tenanted by a single tenant, and in general several tenants worked the farm in communal fashion. All took part in each operation, and the rigs of the farm were drawn for by lot, each tenant receiving the produce of a number of rigs according to his share in the tenancy.

In order to ensure that each tenant got a fair distribution of good and bad land, the rigs apportioned to any one tenant were scattered throughout the farm, and this fact probably accounts for the word *Run-rig*, which was the name given to the system or method. It is perhaps from the Gaelic *roinn*, a division, and *ruith*, to run, and signifies that the rigs pertaining to a tenant ran or extended over all the arable area, and were not confined to one particular part of the farm.

The unit of cultivation was the farm that required a single plough, and, as the plough was drawn by four horses, it was known as a *Four Horse Ploughgang*. A farm employing such a plough was known in Islay as a *Leorthas*, meaning a whole or sufficient farm, from *leor*, meaning abundant. Less than this was merely a fractional farm, and the ordinary tenant had usually only a fraction of the Ploughgang for his share. Often there were four tenants, each supplying a horse for the common plough, so that the share of each such tenant was called a *Horsegang*. Sometimes there were more tenants, and we read of cases where a single tenant had only the share called a *Horse's Foot*. From the name this would appear to have been a quarter of the Horsegang, or a sixteenth part of the Four Horse Ploughgang. In the case of grazing, too, each tenant was allowed a number of animals proportionate to his share. The unit of grazing was the *soum*, which represented grazing for one cow or six sheep. The grazing of a horse was counted as two *soums*.

All the tenants in this communal system of runrig farming lived at one long, single-storied, thatched steading, or in a cluster of houses which must have been more like a small village than a farm steading of to-day. Under this system no improvement was possible, as no tenant had control of his own land. It probably worked best when all the tenants were near relations, but, when they were strangers, quarrelling and friction were frequent.

Runrig was common in Kintyre down to the middle of the eighteenth century, but, at the same time as the tacksmen were abolished, it was replaced by the system that gave each tenant his own separate holding and steading, and the old large runrig farms were divided up for this purpose. A lease of the farm of Ballivean, dated 1742, and given by the Proprietor, Alexander Macmillan of Dunmore, to William and John Fleming and Robert Dunlop, shows the change actually taking place. Ballivean had been a 4 merkland, apparently worked in runrig down to this time, but, by the terms of the lease of 1742, it was to be divided into three separate farms of (approximately) a 20 shilling land each. Two new steadings were to be built, making with the old one three in all, and the three farms were to be separated by march dykes to be constructed, as were the steadings, by the tenants. This was a fairly big undertaking, and the new lease was granted for forty-four years. In some parts of the Highlands this sub-division of the old common farms was pushed to an extreme degree, resulting in the crofter system, a minute subdivision of the land. In Kintyre, however, the crofter system never got a footing. Early in the nineteenth century, to meet the changed circumstances of the times, the process was reversed, and all over Kintyre several of these smaller farms were again combined to form one large modern farm.

On a typical seventeenth century farm all the best land lay next the steading. This was known as the *Infield* or *Croft*, and the latter name still survives as a field name in Kintyre. The infield received all the manure, and was all cropped every year with the only two important crops then grown, viz., *oats* and *bear*, or four-rowed barley. At this time potatoes, turnips, and artificial grasses were quite unknown.

The land farther away was called the *Outfield*. A piece of this was broken up each year, and cropped with oats or bear without manure for several years until the land was exhausted, when it was allowed to go back into grass again, and a fresh break of the outfield made.

This two-field system was the result of the difficulty experienced at that time in transporting heavy agricultural produce and materials like manures. Wheeled carts were then unknown, and all transport was by means of *slipes* or *slide cars*, or on creels on horse's backs. Hence the steading had to be in the centre of the work, and so arose the system of infield and outfield. The countryside presented a bare expanse unrelieved by fences, hedges, wayside trees, or plantations, the only diversification of the landscape being provided by the groups of high crooked rigs, some aligned in one directed and some in another, as the demands of draining dictated. Besides oats and bear a little flax might be grown to provide the family linen, and coarse meadow hay was raised on the lower lands near the streams, which at that date, by reason of the absence of underground drainage, were usually flooded swamps. A great deal of the arable cultivation was on fairly steeply sloping upland soils, where drainage, supplied by the high crooked rigs, was more easily obtained. Owing to the absence of rotations, returns were poor, that of oats being often no more than two or three-fold of the seed.

Implements were home made, and of very crude construction. The plough was largely made of wood, only the sock, coulter, and muzzle being of iron. The mouldboard, or wrest, was literally a board, or boards, as it was made of wood. It was drawn by four horse abreast. One man held the stilts, another held the reins and walked *backwards* in front of the horses, cheering them on by whistling. A third sometimes worked a pole attached to a ring in the beam near the muzzle, in order to regulate the depth of the furrow, and another man might be employed to dress the furrows with a spade. This was the *Old Scotch Plough*, probably introduced into Kintyre by the Lowlanders, for in the case of a farm pillaged in the Atholl raids, one of the items was "ane lawland pleuch," which shows that the Highland one had been different. Harrows were usually made of wood, if a bush tied to a horse's tail was not used.

The *Slipe* or *Slide Car* used for transporting sheaves at harvest consisted of two shafts to which a wooden frame, as in a modern hay waggon, was attached. A horse was yoked in the shafts, and the contrivance was pulled along the ground resting on the hinder ends of the shafts, or in some cases on a pair of runners or sleds attached to them.

All thrashing was done by the flail, and continued so during the next century. Mills were only introduced in Kintyre in the early nineteenth century. If grain was wanted in a hurry it was burned off by drawing a sheaf rapidly across a fire, or by setting fire to a loose heap of unthrashed grain. The kind of grain was partially burned, and produced meal which had a peculiar flavour, called in the Gaelic *gradan*. In John Slezer's *Theatrum Scotiae*, which first appeared in the last decade of the seventeenth century, some of the plates show these old implements in actual use, and depict the rural scene as it appeared to the author at that date.

Horses, cattle, sheep, pigs, and poultry were kept then as now. Kintyre had some very early connection with horses, for its ancient name, bestowed on it by Ptolemy, was *Epidion Akron,* or the promontory of the *Epidii,* the last word meaning horse people. Two well-known Kintyre names - Maceachan and Maceachran - both came from the Gaelic root *each,* meaning a horse. Cattle were the old black Highland breed. *Marts* or fat cattle were often included in the produce rents, and when the lands of Kintyre were in the hands of the Crown in the previous century, the King's marts were driven overland to Stirling Castle, the supervision being in the hands of the parish clerk of Kilkerran, who had a merk of land free of rent for this service. Sheep were the old white or yellow-faced, fine-woolled breed, and were kept in small numbers only. Most of the grazing on the hills was by cattle and horses. The Blackfaced sheep was not introduced until about the year 1780. The old breed was immune to the disease of Braxy, to which the Blackface is so susceptible. Pigs are included in most of the sixteenth-century rentals, so that there could not have been in Kintyre the prejudice against eating pork which existed, at least in more modern times, in many parts of the Highlands.

Poultry included fowls, ducks, and geese. They do not occur as part of the rents except in the case of some of the mills and of the houses of Lochhead. Bees were kept, and were among the loot taken by the Atholl raiders, and as already pointed out, were paid as rent in the case of one farm; but perhaps the "bee scapes" mentioned therein referred only to the honey.

Closely connected with agriculture and rural life is the question of roads. Roads such as we know to-day were unknown in the Kintyre of the seventeenth and eighteenth centuries. In the former century no wheeled vehicles were in use, so that the necessity for well-made, bottomed, and metalled roads did not arise, and such as did exist were merely bridle tracks. They did not always follow the alignment of the roads of to-day; for example, the old road from Campbeltown to Dunaverty - that along which Leslie's army must have marched - passed over Machrimore Hill.

Some attempt to improve the roads of Scotland was made in two Acts of Parliament passed in 1661 and 1670, which empowered the authorities to call out tenants and their servants and cottars to repair the roads "between bere seed time and hay time"; but these seemed to have had little effect in the West Highlands, for in 1674 King Charles II granted a special commission to the Earl of Argyll to have the law enforced in his jurisdiction, "owing to the slow progress made in the past." It was not until after the union of 1707 that an Act of the British Parliament, passed in 1718, enabled some real progress to be made.

During the seventeenth century the streams were unbridged, and fording had to be resorted to, but some bridges appear to have been built very early in the next century. Writing in the year 1702 to his friend Robert Wodrow the historian, the Rev. Lachlan Campbell, minister of the Highland congregation of Campbeltown, mentioned that there was at that time in Kintyre a certain Mathew Frew of Kilwinning, whom he describes as a noted engineer of coal works, who had come, he stated, as an undertaker in the building of some bridges there. Possibly some of the earliest bridges in Kintyre were constructed by Mathew Frew.

Of industries, in the modern sense of the word, there were none until the latter part of the century, but there were many home crafts connected with agriculture, which included milling, malt making, brewing of ale and distilling of aquavitae, dairying, weaving and, in addition, fishing, and we may consider each of these shortly.

Mills for the grinding of oats and bear meal and of malt were an essential on all estates, and Kintyre in the seventeenth century appears to have been quite well provided for in this respect, as we have traced mills at Saddell (1634), Kilkenzie (1633), Kileonan (1636), Kinloch (1636), Machrimore (1636), Kilellan (1659), Carskey (1651), and there may have been others as well. The dates are not to be taken as meaning any more than that the mills at these places were then working, and they no doubt were in existence much earlier.

Mills were erected at the expense of the landlord, who had to recoup himself by the *multure*, or milling charges, either directly through his own miller, or by leasing the mill to a tenant. Hence all the tenants and tacksmen on the larger estates were compelled to grind their corn at the estate mill, and were said to be *thirled* to it. The multure was paid in meal, and was usually a peck in the boll of meal milled, that is, a sixteenth part. If the miller kept a servant he was entitled to a small allowance of meal known as *Knaveship*. In the case of feuars who got charters from the Argyll family this condition was inserted in the charter. Thus when Lachlan Macneill of Tirfergus got a charter to the lands of that place in 1660 he was required to bring all his grindable corns to the mill of Kileonan, and pay *multure* and *knaveship* there, and a similar condition was inserted in the charters of Malcolm Macneill of Carskey and Malcolm Macoshenag of Lephenstrath, in 1700. Repair of the mill dam and lade, and help in bringing home the millstones, which were at that date all in one piece and quarried locally, were included in the "services used and wont" required of all tenants.

Malt was made at practically every farm in Kintyre in the sixteenth and seventeenth centuries. Both oats and bear were used, but bear malt was considered the best, and in the rentals, in which malt was always an important item of the produce rents, there was usually a stipulation that not more than a certain percentage of the malt was to be made of oats. It was ground at the mills, and used for the brewing of *ale*, which was in those days, for all who could afford it, the usual drink at table, taking the place that tea does to-day. The ale was made potable by flavouring it with local herbs, or with imported materials like liquorice and ginger. It was described as a wholesome drink, and only very mildly alcoholic. Ale-making was probably done at many of the farms, but we have evidence of professional brewers at work at Machrimore and Carskey in the early part of the succeeding century.

Aquavitae has been described as the parent of whisky. It was a distilled spirit, flavoured with herbs as in the case of ale. In sending a present of aquavitae from Argyllshire to the Earl of Lauderdale, in February 1667, the Earl of Argyll mentioned that it was a special kind, flavoured by the plant called in Gaelic *curmeil*, or wild liquorice. There was no duty in those days, and it was probably distilled at many of the farms, but there were also professional aquavitae-makers at work. A good deal appears to have been made at Lochhead, for, as we have seen, the rent paid by the burgesses of that town for the farm of Crosshill was six quarts of aquavitae.

Cheese and butter-making were, of course, home industries of unknown antiquity, and cheese, but not usually butter, was an important article of rent in the days of the old *Cain* or produce rents. It is of some interest to note that in Kintyre the season's make of cheese is still called the *cain* - the only use now of this old word, which is cognate with the Latin *canon* or law - and means the rent of the chief exigible by law. In the year 1325 the baillies of Kintyre paid in cheese as part of the Crown dues, to the Constable of Tarbert Castle. Compared with the cheese of to-day it was poor stuff for, as all or most of the fat was removed to make butter, it was hard and horny in texture. Kintyre butter of the succeeding century, on the authority of Dr Smith of Campbeltown, was excellent, and a great improvement in cheese-making took place when the Dunlop style was introduced from Ayrshire, having been invented by a farmer's wife in Dunlop parish, who had been a refugee in Ireland during the troubles of the persecution.

We have evidence that bees were kept and, as sugar was a very dear and scarce commodity, no doubt honey was largely used for sweetening purposes in cookery.

Herring fishing was practised at Lochhead in 1636, and of course no doubt long before that. In that year one of the burgesses paid a barrel of herring in lieu of a money rent for his house in the burgh. The salmon fishing on some of the waters was let, as in the case of Carskey already mentioned, and the Isle of Davaar was occupied in 1651 by a man named McEanvorran, in return for his supplying fish to the Marquis of Argyll when he was in residence in Lochhead Castle.

That there was a considerable herring fishing industry at Lochhead in the seventeenth century is proved by the fact that, in 1668, John Yuill had a tack of the Assize of Herrings there. This was a tax imposed by the Government of Scotland on all catches of herring landed, and dated back to the reign of King James IV. In 1663 the Earl of Argyll got a tack of the Assize of Herrings in all the western seas and, in the case of Lochhead in 1668, had farmed out the collection to Yuill. His rent is not stated, but it is clear that the industry must have been of such dimensions as to make the tack worth while.

A weaving industry was in existence in Lochhead towards the end of the century, but whether this had been introduced by the Lowlanders is not clear. The weavers there appear to have specialised in making horse rugs or sheets, which, at a time when horses were so much used for riding and carrying, must have been in great demand. In 1678, nearly all the burgesses of Lochhead who

17. The site of Dunaverty Castle looking W. to the Antrim coastline and to Borgadalemore on the Mull of Kintyre. A Royalist garrison, commanded by Archibald MacDonald of Sanda, was beleaguered and massacred by General Leslie's Covenanting troops in June 1647.

18. Rhunahaorine Point, in the parish of Kilcalmonell, Largieside; site of the engagement between Leslie's troopers and the forces of Sir Alexander Macdonald on the 24th May, 1647. The fate of the Macdonalds and the remainder of the campaign was effectively settled at this encounter.

19. The Glens of Antrim are some 15 miles across the North Channel from the parish of Southend, and the coastline is visible most days of the year. The commanding position of the Dunaverty headland can be seen in the centre of this view.

20. "The heavens declare the glory of God; . . " Ps.19.1. The Jura Bens outlined by a summer sunset.

Earl of Argyll, paid one or more horse sheets or rugs as part of the rent of their houses, the remainder being paid in eggs and poultry, so that poultry keeping in the burgh must also have been usual at that date. Two industries more nearly satisfying the modern definition of the word appear towards the end of the century, and their introduction is to be ascribed to the Lowlanders. They were coal-mining and salt-making.

The existence of coal in Kintyre appears to have been known, or guessed at, much earlier, however, for we find that in March 1498 King James IV dispatched to that district a collier named John Davison, described in the Treasurer's Accounts of that date as "a coll man to pas in Kintyr to vesy gif colys may be wonnyn thare," and the accounts show that he was paid certain sums to provide him with "werklums" or tools, and to pay for his other expenses. The coals would probably be meant for the use of the royal castles at Tarbert, Kilkerran, and Dunaverty, but we have no further record of the result of the experiment. Coal was being mined in Kintyre as early as 1670, when coal carriers are mentioned in the baptismal register, and in 1678 the farm of Ballygreggan was stated to be "parked for the colliers' horses." The parking or enclosing of a farm in those days was quite exceptional, and was only done for very special reasons.

At the same date, salt-making was done on the farm of Knockantimore, where two acres were reserved for the salt pans. This industry was carried on apparently during most of the next century, and its existence is commemorated in the local place-name Salt Pans, or The Pans. When William Dobie wrote his *Perambulations in Kintyre* in the year 1833, he recorded therein that the salt pans and the salt-making industry had closed down some sixty years before, that is, some time in the 1770's.

In the year 1678 the coal heughs, as the pits were called in those days, and the salt pans, were jointly tenanted by John Campbell, Chamberlain to the Earl of Argyll in Kintyre, and Alexander Forrester, proprietor of Knockrioch, who paid to the Earl for their tenancy the not inconsiderable sum of £1333,6s,8d. Scots.

No doubt other minor industries, such as boat building, may have been in existence, but no records of them have been found.

CHAPTER XVI
EDUCATION

We have no record of the existence of any school in Kintyre prior to the seventeenth century. Before the Reformation of 1560 the only schools in existence in Scotland were those at the principal burghs, and at abbeys or priories. There may have been a school at Saddell Abbey, which appears to have closed down about 1470, but if that was so it has left no records. The only people in the earlier days who could read and write were the professional classes - clerics, notaries, leeches, and others - and even the greatest chiefs in the Highlands were ignorant of letters. When Donald, Lord of the Isles, granted the well-known Gaelic charter to Mackay of Islay in 1408 he merely made his mark - a sword - and the other witnesses attested by representations of ploughs and other agricultural implements.

Even before the days of John Knox, however, the Parliament of Scotland had made some attempt to educate the ruling classes, and in 1496 an Act was passed ordaining that all barons and freeholders should send their sons to grammar schools at eight or nine years of age, and keep them there until they had "perfect Latin," and thereafter to schools of "art and jure" to learn law for three years. Heavy penalties were decreed for the non-fulfilment of this statute. Grammar schools were those in which language was taught - English or Latin or both - as opposed to "sang scules," which were for the purpose of training boys to sing in the Church choirs.

There appears to have been some more general diffusion of letters among the upper classes during the sixteenth century. As we have already pointed out, James McConnell of Dunnyveg was placed under the care of the Dean of Holyrood, to receive proper education as the presumptive leader of the West Highlanders. His grandson, Sir James Macdonald of Knockrinsay was, as we have already stated, a well-educated man, and deplored the loss of his books when he escaped from Edinburgh Castle in 1615. This same James had contracted a bond of friendship between his family and the Macneills of Kintyre at Kileonan, near Campbeltown, in 1594. In this case the two chiefs - James Macdonald and Hector Macneill of Carskey - actually signed the document, but the other seven Macneill witnesses all attested with their hands "led upon the pen," or "touching the pen." In other words, the notary signed for them, as they themselves were unable to write. The inference is, therefore, that about the end of the sixteenth century, while a sprinkling of the principal men in the Highlands could read and write, the majority of the smaller chieftains and the tacksmen were illiterate. It is perhaps this fact that accounts for the absence of tombstones in our old churchyards, of a date earlier than 1600. Those that do exist, and the Celtic crosses in other places, invariably commemorate leading men or ecclesiastics. As the mass of the people were illiterate, such memorials would have no meaning in their eyes, and were not therefore erected.

Further provision for the education of Highland chiefs was made by the Statutes of Iona in 1609. The sixth statute enacted that every gentleman or yeoman possessed of sixty cattle should send his eldest son, or , if he had no male children, his eldest daughter to school in the Lowlands, and maintain his child there till it had learned to speak, read, and write English. These statutes were drafted by Andrew Knox, Bishop of the Isles, whose name deserves to be held in remembrance as an early educational reformer of the West Highlands. The Bishop took a strict bond from each chief for the fulfilment of these statutes, to the existence of which Gregory attributes the beginning of the loyalty of the Highlanders to the House of Stewart.

Before we consider the state of education in Kintyre during the seventeenth century it is interesting to recall the fact that, long before that time, youths from the district attended the Scottish Universities. The earliest example of such was Cornelius Omey, a member of a local family which produced many pre-Reformation rectors, as well as Protestant ministers in later years. He graduated B.A. at the University of St Andrews in the year 1528, and was Rector of Kilblaan, now part of the parish of Southend, at the time of the Scottish Reformation of 1560. Another ecclesiastical family, with Kintyre and Islay connections, was that of the Obrolachans, and we find that Duncan Obrolachan, Rector of Kildalton in Islay, attended the congregation of the University of Glasgow held in the year 1453, that is three years after the foundation of the University. About the same time Neil Obrochlaan, probably a brother, was a priest in Kintyre.

During the first quarter of the seventeenth century several Protestant ministers in Kintyre, all natives of that district, or of the adjacent Highlands, graduated at Glasgow. Among these were Mr Donald Omey, minister of Kilkerran, who took his M.A. there in 1622; Mr Murdoch McWhirrie, minister of Killean, who graduated in 1621, and Mr John Darroch, minister of Kilcolmkill who took his M.A. in 1625. As all the teaching at the universities in those days was in Latin, these youths must have required considerable preparation in that language before they went up, and this they probably got by private tuition from some local clergyman, or by attending some grammar school in the Lowlands.

In Kintyre, as in other parts of Scotland, the first school of which we have any trace was a burgh school. As we have seen, a burgh at Lochhead, now Campbeltown, began to be founded about the year 1609, and a burgh school had been established there by 1622, the name of the schoolmaster being John Spang. Hence from this date onwards, English, and possibly also Latin, must have been taught in the burgh, and at least a proportion of the burgesses must have learned to read and write either or both of these languages.

The school was probably in continuous existence during the next twenty years, which, for this part of the country, were comparatively peaceful, for we find a reference to it in 1643, when Thomas Neere was schoolmaster there. We have no other information about it, for all local records of this period of our history have perished, and we do not know whether it had any endowments or not or, if it had, by whom they were made. This burgh school was dissolved during the disastrous Colkitto raids of 1644 to 1647, for we find that at its meeting held in May 1649 the Synod of Argyll recommended "to the right honourable the Lord Marquesse of

Argyll and to his deputs that there be a schoole for education of children erected and established at Lochhead in Kintyre," and this appears to have been done.

The next burgh schoolmaster whose name appears in the record is Mr Thomas Orr, who was a person of considerable importance during the early years of the Lowland Plantation in the 1650's. He is probably the same Thomas Orr who matriculated at Glasgow University in 1640, and graduated M.A. there in 1643. In addition to being the burgh school-master he was licensed at a "notar," that is a notary public, and as such practised in the burgh, his name occurring in several legal writs of the period. He was clerk to the Presbytery of Kintyre at the time of the outing of the Presbyterian ministers in 1662, and according to one account was himself suspected of prelatical leanings. His wife was Ann Montgomerie, and he had a son, Thomas, who was among the list of those examined at the time of the Earl of Argyll's rebellion in 1685. Thomas Orr, being the first of that name in the records, was probably the ancestor of the many Orrs found in Campbeltown during the next two centuries.

After the year 1686 the burgh school became known as the Grammar School of Campbeltown, the name "grammar" being now applied apparently more particularly to schools that taught Latin or, as we would now say, secondary schools. The first Rector of the Grammar School whose name occurs in the record as such was John Logan, and the Lowland congregation register duly records the fact that "John Logan Schoolmaster of the Grammar School ... took up the school the third of March anno 1686." Mr Logan was also Session Clerk of the Lowland congregation, and the register records also that this register is blank from 1st January 1684 to 18th June 1686, and that, in the interval between the death of Mr Edward Keith and Mr James Boes' ordination, it was kept by Mr John Logan, Grammar Schoolmaster. The Campbeltown Grammar School has therefore had a continuous existence from 1686 to the present day, and longer if we regard it as the lineal descendant of the school in existence in 1622.

It is clear from what has been said above that, so far as the burgh was concerned, reasonable provision for the education of children had been made early in the century, and continued down to its end. The same, however, cannot be said about rural education in Kintyre during most of the century, and to this aspect of the question we must now devote some attention.

It was John Knox's ideal that a school should be established in every parish in Scotland, but the troubles of the times prevented this ideal from being realised for more than a century and a half after his death in 1572. This ideal had never been forgotten, however, and we find the Scottish Parliament passing Acts in 1633 and 1646 intended to put it into effect. The Act of 1633 ratified an Act of the Privy Council, which declared that "every plough or husband-land according to the worth" should be taxed for the maintenance of parish schools, and that of 1646 decreed that there should be a school in every parish. It was, however, much easier in those days to get legislation put on the statute book than to have it enforced, and, during the first half of the century at least, it is clear that the great mass of the rural population was illiterate.

Kintyre does not appear to have been in this respect worse off than most other parts in Scotland. When the teinds were valued in the early years of King Charles I's reign the Teind Commissioners called for a report on the state of every parish in Scotland, to include the state of education in each. It is regrettable that, of the thousand or so reports that must have been prepared, only forty-nine have survived, and these, of the date 1627, were printed by the Maitland Club about a century ago. They are extremely interesting in many ways, and were in fact an early form of the *Statistical Accounts* of the eighteenth century. The forty-nine parishes reported on, of which the reports have survived, did not include any Argyllshire parish, but otherwise are a fair sample of Highland and Lowland parishes.

Out of the forty-nine some nine only had schools in 1647, and most of these school were reported to be in a moribund condition for want of funds. In the case of one Berwickshire parish, the minister stated that he was the only man in the parish who could read and write, and his fellow committee-man, either a laird or substantial farmer, made his mark - a sickle just as the Macdonalds and Mackays did in Islay in 1408. The conclusion to be drawn as to the state of rural education at this date is therefore obvious.

As soon as the Presbyterian Church was established in 1638 it made early and commendable efforts to deal with the question of rural education, activated perhaps mainly by the scarcity of ministers, and by the necessity of broadening the source of supply, so the Committee of Assembly approved, on the 17th or 18th December 1638, an overture "anent the planting of schools in landward." This was considered by the Synod of Argyll at its meeting in May 1640, which took action on it as follows. It proposed that a Grammar School be established at Inveraray to serve the whole province, and, in addition, that "at the least a schoole be in ilk presbytery seate, and ten marks to be allotted to the maintenance of the same by ilk minister within the presbytery out of his own stipend, with this caution, that seeing the schoole of Inveraray, to which maintenance is afforded by all the parishes within the province, holds at the presbyterie seat, that the other schoole agreed upon be erected at the next most considerable pairt within that presbyterie." This represented an attempt at a beginning, but it was very far removed from the ideal of a school for each parish.

As already pointed out there were, owing to the difficulty of obtaining a supply of properly qualified Gaelic-speaking ministers, many vacancies in the Kintyre parishes, and in those of other parts of the West Highlands, during the early years of Presbyterianism, so in May 1643 the Synod approached the General Assembly with a proposal to employ the vacant stipends for the ministry. As a result an Act of Parliament was passed on 23rd July 1644, authorising these stipends to be used "for trayneing up of youthes that have the Irish tongue in schooles and colleges."

This plan was upset by the disorders of the Colkitto raids, but when these were over in 1648, forty boys were selected who were regarded as suitable for the purpose, and were sent to be boarded in Glasgow to prepare for the University. Among them were the following from Kintyre: John Campbell, son to Donald Campbell, brother of Skipness; Angus Campbell, son of the Captain of Skipness; James Campbell, son to Glencarradale; John Macneill, son to the deceased Malcolm Macneill of Carskey; and Archibald Macneill, son to Neil Macneill of Carskey. They were, without exception, sons of lairds or larger tacksmen, from which classes, as has already been pointed out, all the professional men were recruited at this date. The clever sons of the poorer classes - those "lads o' pairts" which we hear so much of - did not get a chance to make their appearance at the Universities until the end of the eighteenth century.

One of the first systematic attempts at the establishment of parochial schools in Argyllshire arose out of the troubles of the Colkitto raids. It will be remembered that the Parliament recommended to the General Assembly that, in order to relieve the distress of the poor people of Argyllshire caused by these ravages, a collection should be taken for the purpose in every parish church in Scotland, and a scheme for its distribution was prepared in March 1647, two-thirds of the sum collected to go to immediate alleviation of the sufferers, and one-third to purchase seed grain. The Synod, however, apparently decided to set apart 11,000 merks of this money for the endowment of parish schools, but this proposal did not at first meet with the approval of the Committee of Assembly, which accordingly admonished the Synod, the minutes of which, of date May 1649, record the censure as follows:-

" it is fund that 11,000 marks of the voluntary contribution for the distrest people in Argyle is imployed to be a fundation for schooles. The assembly finds this worthy of rebuke and appoynts the money to be restored, recommending to the visitors to see to the distribution of it to the use it was destinat for."

There appears, however, to have been further discussion, and the approval of the Assembly was eventually obtained. The Synod therefore decided to use the amount to establish schools at Kilmadan, Kilfinan, Lochgoilhead, Glassary, Knapdale, Kilchrenan, Ardchattan, Kilmore, and Lismore. A school at Dunoon had already been established in 1641 out of the teinds of the Bishopric of Argyll. It is noteworthy that no rural school was proposed for Kintyre, but that at Lochhead or Campbeltown was to participate in the benefit. The scheme, however, miscarried to a great extent. The money was set out at interest to certain Argyllshire lairds; but owing to faulty drafting of the bonds, and failure to register them, added to the troubles and confusion of the times, some of the borrowers were able to default on both capital and interest, and the incident is extremely discreditable to those concerned. For our present purposes all we need to note is that no parochial school in Kintyre was founded at this date, from this allotment, and if from any other we have no trace of it.

At its meeting held in October 1650, however, the Synod of Argyll endeavoured to take some steps in lieu of the foundation of parochial schools, and moved the following:-

"Because the knowledge of the English language is so necessary for the weall of the Gospell, the scriptures not being translated in Irish, and seeing the country cannot have schools in every church for learning English, that therefore use be made of poor boys that can read and write English to teach the young and others that may be made willing in the parish to read and understand the English in the interim till schools may be erected, and the ministers to oversee and make report of their diligence and of the fruit of it to their several presbyteries and to the next synod."

The motion corroborates the conclusion already arrived at, that there were no parochial schools in existence at this date, and it proposes a makeshift arrangement whereby lads, who had learned to read and write at the burgh school at Lochhead or elsewhere, would go to the rural parts and act as amateur schoolmasters, perhaps getting fees, or a small pittance from the parents, for doing so. We have no presbytery records for the Episcopal period 1662 to 1685, but the oldest of our parish registers, that of the Lowland Congregation, records the names of quite a number of persons designated as "schoolmaster" in the 1660's and 1670's, and it is very possible that most of them were the amateurs mentioned above - "poor boys that could read or write English."

It may be of some interest to give here some of the names, and no doubt there were many more than those recorded in the parish registers:-

John Clark, 1661; John Whyte, 1664; James Houston, 1673; John Sheddan, 1676; Patrick Dunlop, 1676; James Bowman, 1676; James Stewart, 1676; William Reid, 1678; James Wilson, 1679; William Robertson, 1679; William Ralston, 1681; Andrew Adam, 1681; James Watt, 1682; and in addition Thomas Orr and John Logan, whom we know to have been burgh schoolmasters, and therefore holding office of a more permanent nature. So far as can be ascertained this system prevailed until after the Revolution of 1688.

The true origin of parochial schools in Kintyre is to be traced to an Act of the Scottish Parliament of 1690, which decreed that all vacant benefices of the several kirks in Argyll were to be applied "to educating youth for the purpose of planting and propagating the Gospel there." At or about the same time a sum of £150 sterling yearly was granted for the foundation of schools out of the now vacant Bishoprics of Argyll and the Isles. As a result of these benefactions, some forty schools were opened in Argyllshire. The sums allotted, however, appear to have been considered insufficient, and some representation in the matter must have been made, for on 28th February 1695 King William III addressed a personal letter to the Scots Privy Council on the subject.

The tenor of the King's letter was as follows. He had had his attention drawn to the prudence, moderation, and wise management of the ministry of the Synod of Argyll in connection with the vacant stipends placed at their disposal by the Act of 1690, by means of which, and the £150 mentioned above, they had already erected forty schools for the teaching of the English language. He had also been informed that some of their number had been put to considerable expense in publishing the

Psalms in Irish metre, and in translating the Shorter Catechism into Irish, that is Gaelic. He noted also the good example the Synod had shown "in assuming into their body of their own accord a number of the Episcopal clergy now equal to their own, and that they are willing to assume yet more," and he had been informed that, to meet these ends, the present allowances were insufficient. Hence, following the example of his grandfather King Charles I, he expressed his will and pleasure that the Synod should be allowed to collect the whole of the revenue of the Bishoprics "for the settling of schools, the repairing of churches, the educating and forming of ministers, the supplying of such of their number as have small stipends, and defraying the charges of the Irish Psalms and Catechism (that the same may be our free gift to the nation) and for such purposes as are ordinarily comprehended under the head of charitable and pious uses."

One of the earliest schools founded under these schemes was that of Southend, of which the first known schoolmaster was Mr James Boes. He had previously been schoolmaster at Glassary, in mid-Argyll, but must have come to Southend before 1694, for in that year he became minister of the Lowland Congregation in Campbeltown, and continued there until his death in 1749. He and his colleague Mr Lachlan Campbell of the Highland Congregation in Campbeltown were friends and correspondents of Robert Wodrow, the Covenanting historian. Mr Boes is said to be commemorated in Southend by the cave at the back of Dunaverty rock, which is still named Boes Chair, a place to which he is believed to have retired for purposes of meditation.

In an article entitled "Education in Kintyre, 1638-1707," by the Rev. A.J. MacVicar, based on a study of the records of the Kintyre Presbytery, which begin in 1655, the author has recorded the names of some other of the early parochial schoolmasters of Kintyre which appear in the records in the 1690's. Among these were Neil MacNeill, schoolmaster at Killean in 1697, John Peters, apparently Mr Boes's successor, schoolmaster at Southend in 1697, and Hugh McLean, schoolmaster at Kilkenzie in 1698. He records also that in 1695 James Forrester of Knockrioch addressed the Presbytery to have a school opened at Barr. From this time onward parochial schools were maintained, and the *Old Statistical Accounts* of a century later show that at that time every parish in Kintyre had a school, and some Church schools and S.P.C.K. schools as well, so that the district was as well served educationally as any similar district in Scotland, and much better than some.

In the seventeenth century, however, schoolmasters had no recognised status and no government protection. Many were students or probationers of the Church, or even, as we have seen, merely youths who had themselves barely mastered the rudiments of reading and writing. In the year 1696, however, the Scottish Parliament passed an Act which may be described as the schoolmaster's charter. It decreed once more that a schoolmaster was to be settled in every parish, that the heritors were to provide him with a "commodious" house, that he was to have a salary not less that 100 merks, nor more that 200 merks Scots, that is between £5,11s.1$^1/_3$d. and £11, 2s. 2$^2/_3$d. sterling money, but that this was to be "by and attour" any fees he might receive as a Reader of Scripture or Session Clerk. Powers were given to the Presbyteries to enable them to raise the amount from the heritors. This can scarcely be called a princely endowment, but it was at least a beginning.

During the succeeding century, however, owing to the rise in the cost and scale of living, this salary became utterly inadequate, and led to the office of parochial schoolmaster being sometimes filled by quite unsuitable persons, such as discharged soldiers and bankrupts. Dr John Smith of Campbeltown, writing in 1798, comments on this state of affairs as follows: "A schoolmaster should be a man of parts, learning, and virtue, and the man who is qualified and appointed for so important a business should be highly valued ... but instead of this, he is depressed and despised, and often obliged to subsist on an income inferior to that of a ploughman."

At long last the public conscience was aroused, and in 1803 a new Act was passed which doubled the maximum and minimum salaries fixed in 1696, and decreed that the heritors should provide him with a house of not less than two rooms, including a kitchen. Even this very modest improvement met with opposition, and the Lord Advocate who had charge of the legislation has left it on record that he had many complaints from lairds who objected, they said, to have to build "palaces for dominies."

The school buildings erected at the end of the seventeenth century were poor in the extreme, and continued as such during the next century. The Rev. James Giffen, a native of Southend parish, has left us an interesting description of the parish school of Southend when he attended it about the year 1812. It was a single-roomed house, with clay walls and clay floor. The windows were broken, and these probably helped to provide ventilation. In winter there was a fire of peats, which would, after the fashion of the times, be in the middle of the floor, and for this every boy was supposed to carry two peats from his home. Many, however, evaded this duty by taking them from the peat stack of some house near to the school. The place must have been horribly over-crowded, and we are not surprised to learn that on summer days the master often allowed his pupils to go out into an adjacent field, to con their lessons lying among the grass.

Yet these old parochial schools did good work, and kept the flame of learning alight in a dark age. They were attended by all the children in the parish, gentle and simple; by the sons of lairds, ministers, farmers, cottars, ploughmen, and herds alike, and a good part of our distinctive Scottish traits of character must have been formed in them.

They attempted to combine elementary and secondary education. In 1815 a schoolmaster for Southend was advertised for, and the advertisement stipulated that the successful candidate would be required to teach Latin, English, Writing, Arithmetic, Book-keeping, Geography, Navigation, Gaelic, and Church music. A few years later, Greek was added to this formidable list of attainments, for which the salary offered was £22, 4s. 5$1/3$d in addition to the fees. The master, of course, did not teach all these subjects to every pupil. Some took reading only, some reading and writing; to these some added arithmetic, or one or other of the subjects mentioned, and fees were paid for each individual subject, according to a scale approved by the heritors.

These schools set many a poor boy on the first rung of the ladder of success, and their establishment, at the end of the seventeenth century, was the true beginning of democracy in Scotland, which in the following century gradually replaced the state of close privilege which had preceded it. It is mainly to the efforts of the Church that we owe the parochial schools, and not infrequently the cause of education was upheld by the parish minister, against the opposition of the heritors. The schoolmasters, before appointment, had to be examined by the presbyteries, in order to satisfy the article in the Treaty of Union of 1707 which required that parochial schoolmasters were to be members of, and to accept the doctrines of, the Church of Scotland. This arrangement lasted down to the year 1861, when a new Act of Parliament permitted dissenters to hold the office of parochial schoolmaster.

APPENDIX 1
HIGHLAND PERSONAL NAMES

It is perhaps unnecessary to say that the principal, although not the invariable, characteristics of personal names derived from the Gaelic are the prefixes *mac*, meaning son of, and the now nearly obsolete *O*, from Gaelic *ua*, meaning grandson. Both to-day may be translated as "descendant of." Instead of *mac* the contracted form *Mc* may be used, and this in fact was the form almost invariably used by the scribes of the sixteenth century. The feminine form of *mac* is *nic*, used before female names.

In addition to the above there are two other prefixes often met with in the structure of personal names. When a saint's name was taken it was, out of reverence for the memory of the saint, invariably prefixed by a word meaning servant. The oldest, and Gaelic form, was *maol*, as in Maolcolm, becoming Malcolm and meaning servant of St Columba. It is from this word that the long series of Irish names beginning in *mul*, as Muloney, are derived. The later form, derived from the Norse, as *gille*, as in Gillecolm or Gillbride, servant of St Columba or of St Bride. These in their turn could be preceded by *Mac* or *O*, as in Macgillecolm, shortened to Macilcallum, and finally to the modern Macallum, and Omaolgherick, meaning descendant of the servant of St Cyric.

Two frequently-occurring suffixes, *ag* and *an*, may be noticed. They are diminutives meaning "little," but implying a sense of endearment. They are sometimes changed by scribes to *all* and *ell*, as McGugall for McGugan and McShenell for McShenag.

Many Gaelic-speaking people in Kintyre changed their names during the eighteenth century, either to English or other Gaelic forms. Thus McIlvrennenich became Arnot, Odrain became Hawthorn, Loynachan Lang, and Brolachan Brodie or Bradley. The change in some cases was into a Lowland name of somewhat similar sound; in others the new name was supposed, often erroneously, to be an English translation of the Gaelic word.

The names which follow have been taken from rentals and other lists of the sixteenth and seventeenth and sometimes subsequent centuries. In each case the date of the first appearance of the name in the record is given, and the name or names of the persons who bore it, with the localities where they lived. For the benefit of those who desire to make further studies into the subject of families and names it may be said that the sources made use of include the Kintyre rentals of 1505, 1506, and 1547, in the *Exchequer Rolls of Scotland*; the lists of tenants printed in *Highland Papers*, Vol. iii, of the Scottish History Society; rentals of 1633, 1636, 1643, and 1651 in the Regality Accounts of Argyll in H.M. Register House; rentals of 1684-85 in the Argyll Papers also there; the Registers of Testaments and Sasines; the Parish Registers and other sources. In the interpretation of the meaning of the names we have followed Woulfe and Alex. MacBain. Place names are spelt as they occur in the records.

McALLASTER; son of Alexander. The name appears first in the West Highlands about 1250, when Angus Mor of Islay named his eldest son after King Alexander II of Scotland. For Macallasters of Loup and Tarbert, see chap. I. Others were Roderick in Kilervan, 1505; Hector in Kildavie, 1596, and also in the Bard's lands of Cattadale, etc., see chap. I; Ronald in Achnaglach, 1596; Alaster in Dalnahauslek, 1596; Hector in Glak, Keprigan, Strone, Glenadale, Kilervan, Knockstaple, and Lonachan, 1605. Charles in Kildavie, 1632; Hector Nahinch, factor of the parsonage of Killean, 1636; Hector Macallaster and his two sons hanged at Lochhead by General Leslie in 1647 were probably belonging to one of the above families. Ronald and Charles in Kilervan, 1678; Doctor McAlester in Carskey Compt Book, 1725; Donald in Glenadil, 1716.

McCAIG; from *teague*, a philosopher or poet. Not found in earlier lists. Archibald in Achachocin in Kilkerran parish, rebel in 1685; in the eighteenth century in Pennyseorach, Coledrain, Penlachton, and Kilmanshenachan. Later in Inishrale.

McCARLY; probably from *mac* and *Sorley*, and meaning descendant of Sorley, Somerled, or Samuel. We find Gillaspey McCarly, tacksman of the 12 merkland of Gortinvale, Grennan, Speresak, and Crosak, 1541; Archibald McCarly in Grenen and Speresak, 1596; the name not found in later lists.

McCLEIREACH or CLERK; son of the clerk, that is the parish clerk, who was a person of some importance in pre-Reformation times. The English form Clerk only is found. Dugald Clerk, parish clerk of Kilkerran, 1505; he had remission of the rent of a merk of land for the service of supervising the transport of the King's marts to Stirling; Donald in Upper Ballemanach, 1505; John, wadsetter of Drumlemble, 1678; Donald, merchant in Campbeltown and proprietor of Drumlemble and Straichtrach, 1684, his first wife Giles Cunnison and his second Isabella Campbell, daughter of the Captain of Skipness; had daughter Catherine who married Lachlan MacNeill of Kilchrist, to whom and his wife the property of Drumlemble passed in 1745. The Highland Clerks of Kintyre must have been a branch of some of the old important families but took their name of Clerk from the office.

McILCHATTAN; a very rare name meaning servant of St Catan. Neil McGillechattan, tacksman of Iffernan in Saddell parish, 1634; Malcolm McIlchattan in Ballachgheran in Killean, 1676, his spouse Margaret Nic Stalker. The modern form is Hattan.

McILCHONNELIE or CONLEY; Woulfe gives the meaning as son of Connladh. Originally found near the Mull of Kintyre; McIlchonnelie (no first name) in Ballemakilchonnele, 1678, his place being named after him; Archibald and Malcolm in Borgadillmore and William and Donald in Mull of Kintyre, fencible men, 1692; Malcolm and Neil in Ballinamoil, 1720-22; John in Borgadillmore, 1716; Neil in Glenmanuil, 1735; Neil (perhaps same) in Muklach, 1736; Gilcum in Carskey, 1717-41; Neil in Cantaig, Learside, 1790-1830, elder in parish church; Donald his brother in Socach. They were not occupiers of land in 1857.

McCAMROIS, McCAMBRIDGE, McCAMBRIG; Woulfe gives the meaning as son of Ambrose, and describes it as a rare name of Scottish origin. Neil McCamrois was adjudicator of the court held by Lord Scone at Lochhead-Kilkerran in 1605; Gilinbro, witness to sasine of St Ninian's Lands to Alexander Macdonald of Smerby in 1620; Flora McCamrois is traditionally stated to have saved the life of Ronald Macdonald, the infant heir to the Macharioch estate, at the time of Dunaverty, in 1647, and to have married a McCaig to whom the Macdonalds later gave a farm; William and Gilneff, fencible men, 1692; John, in Ballegrogan, 1692; John Ban in Feorlin, Southend, died 1693; John, his brother's son and another John, his grandson; Anna, spouse to Malcolm McMillan in Borgadillbeg, 1686; John in Feorlin 1719, and Malcolm in 1739; McCamrois tombstone in Kilcolmkill erected in 1778 by Arch. McCambrig in Machrimore Miln in memory of his father Neil who died 1772. The name is now apparently extinct in Kintyre and probably in Scotland.

McCUALSKY, meaning uncertain; a Glenbreckrie name. Gilchrist in Achinsavill and William in Gartvain, 1692; Gilbert and Donald in Carskey, 1716-29; Neil in Carskey, 1712-20; tombstone in Kilcolmkill erected by Donald McCualsky in Darlochan in memory of his spouse Ann McNeill who died in 1771. Neil McCualsky was first schoolmaster of S.P.C.K. school opened at Culilongart in 1795.

McINDAYN; son or descendant of the Dean. A very rare name occurring once only in the records; Neil McIndayn, tenant of Ballegrogan, 1505, was surety for Gillecallum McMoylan in that year. In the same year McMartin, Rural Dean of Kintyre, was tacksman of Losset and Neil McIndayn may have been his son.

McEACHRAN; from Gaelic *each*, a horse, and *tighearna*, a lord, horse lord; for those of Kilellan, see chap. I; of others we find Andrew, rector of Kilcoman, erected the Campbeltown Cross to his father, Ivar rector of Kilrecan, about 1500; Gillespic, tacksman of 8½ merkland of Wegill, etc., 1505; John, in 12 merkland of Kinloch, 1505; a branch in Glenmanuil in the eighteenth century represented by Captain Colin McEachran, proprietor of Oatfield to his death in 1845, his wife Margaret, daughter of Rev. Dr Smith, minister of Campbeltown; Angus, in Kerranmore, died 1716; John, merchant in Campbeltown, son of John, merchant there, who died in 1715; Hugh, in Kilblaan, 1830, sons Angus and Colin also there. Many emigrated in first half of eighteenth century mainly to Ontario, Canada, and Michigan and Illinois, U.S.A.; representatives still in Kilblaan, Southend.

McDONALD or McCONNELL; apart from the leading families of Dunnyveg, Largie, and Sanda, this name was not borne by any occupier of land in the sixteenth-century lists. The lists of 1596 and 1605 contain a few of the name, but they are easily identifiable as belonging to one or other of the above three families. The name is derived from Donald, grandson of Somerled, and father of Angus Mor of Islay and Kintyre, and so dates back to the thirteenth century, but does not appear to have been in use as a surname till a much later period.

MACEACHAN; for those of Tangy, see chap. i. The main line of Tangy ended in 1709, but later branches descended from it are found. Hector, tacksman in Ardnacross, died March 1815 aged 84 years, his wife Agnes McNeill; their son Lachlan, farmer in Ardnacross, died March 1852 aged 82 years, his wife Flora McNeill and their family, Hector, Dugald, Mary; the last Hector's wife was Barbara Clark, a descendant of the Clerk, or Clark, family noticed before; he was tenant of Machribeg, Southend, about 1840, but later was ranching near Monte Video. The burying ground of the MacEachans is in Kilkenzie. Descendants are probably still in South America.

McFARLANE; son of Bartholomew. Incomers from Arrochar in the sixteenth century; characteristic names in this family are Andrew and Walter; Andrew, laird or chief of Arrochar, had a tack of Baraskomill, the Twa Narachans and Askomelmore, in all an 8 merkland, in 1506; Robert, Andrew, and Duncan Macfarlane of Arrochar received large holdings in tack in Kintyre in 1541; Tavis or Charles Macfarlane was in Glaknahall in 1596; John was in Glaknahall, Colelongart, Ballevianane, etc., in Southend in 1605; Walter in Pollywilline, 1796; Alexander in Pollywilline, 1857; Andrew in Keill, 1857.

McGOMRIE, McCOMRA, McCUMBRAY are different forms of the name borne by a family at the Mull of Kintyre; meaning unknown, unless Gaelicised form of Lowland Montgomery. Montgomeries of Eglinton had early connection with Kintyre; Alexander McGomrie de Ardrossan, Warden of Kintyre 1430; Sir Robert Montgomery, son of 2nd Earl of Eglinton, Rector of Kilblaan before 1538. The following occur: Gilpatrick in Mull of Kintyre, 1541; McCumbray (no first name) in Strone and Ballimacumbray, 1678; Malcolm in Ballimacomray, 1684; Patrick in Feorlin, 1713; Donald in Ballimacomra, 1723; Neil in Borgadillmore, 1733. After the Mull was put under sheep about 1780 they removed elsewhere, and we find Duncan, tenant in Kilblaan, 1782; Godfrey in Blasthill, early nineteenth century; Duncan, parochial schoolmaster of Southend, died 1883; Donald in Dunglas, to 1897. They all took the name Montgomery, but are not to be confused with Lowlanders of that name.

McGORRE, MAKQUHAR, McQUHORE, McWORY, McCOR, McWHIRRIE, McCURRIE; these names are either from Gaelic *guaire* meaning noble, or from Norse Godfrey, in which latter case they mean son of Godfrey. We find Donald McGillecallum McGorre, tacksman of 17 merkland of Kileonan in 1505; Gilcrest McCor in Kilervan, Knockstaple, and Lonachan, 1505; Gillaspic Makquhar surety for Kilkivan, 1505; Gillecallum McNeil McQuhore surety for MacMillan in Tirfergus, 1505; Lachlan McQuhurie in Gleneharvie, 1605; Mr Murdoch McWhirrie or McCurrie, M.A. Glasgow 1621, minister of Killean before 1640, died in 1648. Later forms are Currie; Mathew and widow Currie in Macharioch, 1811; Gilbert Currie there, 1823; Donald Curry in Ballewilling, 1830.

McGUGAN, McGOWGALL, MAKGOWGA; Woulfe gives it as a form of *eachagain*, a variety of *eachan*. The following occur: Maurice, a priest of Argyll, petitioned the Pope in 1420 to be presented to the vicarage of Kilkerran; John and Duncan, tenants in Kilwhipnach, 1541; Donald in Gartnagerach in Kilblaan parish in 1541;

Gillecallum More Makgowga in Kilwhipnach, 1596; Flaardoch Makgowgan in Gartnagerach, 1596; John in Gartnagerach, 1770, son Malcolm; Archibald, schoolmaster, in S.P.C.K. school at Mull of Kintyre, 1774.

McILHEANY; servant of St Kenny or Coinnich. Glenbreckrie name; Malcolm, fencible in 1692; John McIlheany, schoolmaster in Southend about 1718; John in Ballinacussaig died 1719, and had brother Donald in Strathgyle who died 1722. Later bearers are stated to have changed the name to Shaw. Donald Shaw was tenant in Keil about 1800.

McISAAC, McKESSAG, McESAK; son of Isaac; Lachlan McEsak surety for Gilcrest McCor in Kilervan, 1505; Donald in Kilervan, Knockstaple, and Lonachan, 1541; Donald in Feochaig, 1693; Angus in Feochaig, 1797, volunteer on horseback that year; another family in Corphen and Blairfarn on Learside. Member of Feochaig family Lachlan McIsaac, shipmaster in Campbeltown, and a later descendant John McIsaac in Dunglas in 1857.

McKAY; from old Gaelic *aodh* or *aedh* meaning fire; Latinised to Odo; in Ireland McGee, and in Lowland Scotland Mackie. For Mackay More of Ugadale and Arnicle, see chap. I. The branches of the Ugadale family were the most extensive occupiers of land in North Kintyre in the sixteenth century, but disappeared during the seventeenth. Some were probably killed at Dunaverty in 1647. Others in South Kintyre were Neil McAne McKay in Gartnacopaig, 1505; Gillespick or Archibald, tacksman in Colilongart, Ballyvianan, and Dalquirnock in Glenbreckrie, 1605; Neil in Brunerican, 1718; John and James in Achadaduie near Macharioch, end of eighteenth and early nineteenth centuries; John in Eridale in Learside, died 1816; his sons Donald and Neil in Eridale; Peter, son of Donald in Knockstaple, about middle of nineteenth century; his sons Archibald in Lephenstrath and Donald, one of the founders of the Campbeltown Shipbuilding Co.

McKIERGAN or McKERRAL; the first of these names is from St Ciric and means servant of St Ciric. An older form is Maolgirg to which the suffix *an* has been added. The corresponding Lowland name is Greig. McKerral, the form now used, may have been derived by phonetic change from McKiergan, as in the case of McGugall for McGugan, or by confusing St Ciric with one of the saints named Caireall. Of those who bore these names we find Angus, joint tenant with Hector McAllaster in Glak near Cattadale, Southend, in 1605. Tradition states that one of this family known as Gorrie Gow, or Godfrey the smith, was armourer to the Macdonalds and transported to France at the time of Dunaverty in 1647, but there is no written record of him; in the eighteenth century they were found at Drumavullin, Kilmanshenachan, Balnabraid, and Brunerican; Angus in Drumavullin, 1789; Hugh, tenant in Brunerican died 1811 aged 96; his son, grandson, great-grandson there, and his great-great grandson is still (1948) tenant; Malcolm, tenant in Balnabraid and Murrell, 1830, his brother Angus. A somewhat similar but different name is McIlchier, which means servant of St Ciar; Donald McIlchier, tenant of Cantaig in 1678.

McLARTY; from Gaelic *Flaithbheartach* meaning "princely bearing," A branch of Clan Donald claiming descent from the founder of Saddell Abbey. The following occur in the record: Gilbert in Kilwhipnach, 1678; James in Macharioch, 1692; Malcolm in Carskey, Donald in Lossett, Duncan and Murchie in Glacknahavill and Lagnacraig, and Iver in Campbeltown were all fencible men in 1692; tombstone of Iver in Kilcolmkill bears coat of arms. McLartys were tenants in Machrimore from 1730 to 1777; John, probably son of Iver, tidewaiter at Machrimore in 1749, had family John, James, and Alexander; Alexander, shipmaster in Campbeltown, 1758, his wife Jane Johnstone; Colin, eldest son of Alexander, graduated M.D. practised in Greenock and West Indies and purchased estate of Kilcolmkill in 1819; was three times Provost of Campbeltown between 1807 and 1820. McLartys sold Keil in 1865.

McMARQUIS or MARQUIS; son of Mark; other forms in Kintyre, McMarkische and Makmarkie. John McMarkische, tacksman in Kerranmore, 1506; Gilnow McMarquis in Laggan and Kerranmore, 1541; Donald Makmarkie in Laggan and Kerranmore, 1596; in 1658 the Records of the Synod of Argyll record that "John McMarques in Kintyre, ane old man and able in the Irish language" had been asked to assist in the syllabification of the Psalms in Gaelic; John McMarquis in parish of Kilkerran, rebel in 1685; Katherine McMarquis, wife of John McNeill in Cristlach, 1684; Mary Ann Marquis of Gigha and Cara, wife of Rev. John McKeich, parish minister of Southend, 1799-1815; she was tenant of Lochorodale in 1830.

McMATH; son of Mathew; Lowland Mathieson. Archibald in Largiebane, 1651; they occur in the list of fencible men of 1692 in Ballyvrennan, Glenadil, Largiebane, Achnaslishag, and Glenahantie. They were in the last place until recently; Archibald in Socach about 1820 was ancestor of many Mathiesons in Victoria, Australia. A McMath in Lochorodale in the early nineteenth century is said to have composed a number of Gaelic poems about Scotland; John and Dugald in Glenrea, 1830.

McMILLAN; older forms, McILMALEIN, McMOLAN, McMOYLAN. Gaelic speakers use McGILLEMHAOIL, from *maol*, meaning bald or tonsured; probably of ecclesiastical origin; Gaelic form curtailed to McGill, whence probably the Kintyre McGills. The McMillans were among the most extensive occupiers of land in Kintyre in the sixteenth century. Among them we find Gillecallum McMillan in Knockantimore in 1505; Duncan McGillecallum McMillan in Teyrargus, Largawayn, Pubill, Innergye, 1505; Gilbride in Ranadale, Donald in Knockantimore, Neil in Teirrarois, etc., Duncan in Glaknahawl, and Duncan (perhaps the same) in Mull of Kintyre and in Colilongart, Ballavenane, etc.; Gilcalum in Glaknahall in 1605; John in Enandownane, 1678; McIlmalein (no first name) in Ballemenoch, Kerrafuar, and Ballivrenane, 1678; Duncan in Borgadillbeg, 1678, Hugh there, 1717; Lachlan in Glenmanuil, 1719; Malcolm in Borgadillmore, 1719; John and Neil in Keil 1723; Ronald in Knockmorran, 1770; Hugh in Gartvain, died 1839, spouse Barbara McVicar, tombstone in Keil; John, son of Hugh, married Jean McNeill, daughter of Colonel McNeill of Carskey and with his wife inherited that estate taking name of McNeill; he died in 1859; Donald, son of Hugh in Gartvain, purchased estate of Lephenstrath in 1819; McMillan (no first name) in Machribeg, 1830; John in Coledrain from 1809, son John; Robert in Acharua, 1857.

McMURCHY or McVURICH; from *murcadh*, meaning sea warrior; name of the *seannachies* or bards of the Macdonalds in Kintyre. John the bard had rent-free tack of Cattadale, Gartvain, Keprigan, Brecklate, and Gartloskan, an 8 merkland, in 1505; Donald in Kildalloig and above Bard's lands, 1541; John Oig, doctor is Islay, 1615; Dr McMurchie's sons in Ballegregan in Kintyre, 1643; Neil in Corlich, Glenbreckrie, 1703; Angus, tenant of McNeill of Carskey, 1712; Archibald, in Glenadill, 1721, was in that year foster-father to Archibald, son of Malcolm McNeill, laird of Carskey; the deed of Fosterage witnessed by Duncan McMurchy in Glenrea, and Duncan McMurchy in Upper Glenadill; James in Backs, Campbeltown parish, 1812; James and son in Backs, 1853.

McNACHTAN, McNAUGHTON, McNAUGHT, McCRACKEN; Pictish name meaning pure; there was a St Nechtan. We find in the record Angus in Gartavay, Southend, in 1505; John in Gartavay, Keremenach, and Mucklach, 1541; Angus in Gartavay, 1596; John Dow in Keremenach, 1596; John in Keremenach and Gartavay, 1678; Donald in Kilbride and Kynochan in Kilkerran parish 1678; Neil in Gartavay, 1717; Archibald in Carrine, 1724; Neil McNaught in Machribeg died 1777 aged 77; tombstone next to that of McNeills of Carskey in Keil; his first and second wives both McNeills; Thomas his son in Drumavulline, died 1826; Daniel his son minister of Relief Church; Duncan in Ballivianan, Donald in Kilervan, Neil in North Carrine, and Thomas in South Carrine, 1830; Neil in Knockstaplebeg, wife Mary McMillan, son Rev. Colin McNaughton, minister of Tain, who died 1924.

McNEILL; from Gaelic *Niall*; for McNeills of Carskey see also chap. I. The Carskey line went as follows: Hector signed Bond with Macdonalds in 1594, and Keeper of Lochhead Castle, 1618; Malcolm died 1647; Neil Og, brother of Malcolm, tacksman of Machrihanish and Carskey, died 1685; John, son of Malcolm, tacksman of Carskey, 1678; Malcolm, son of John, received charter of Carskey lands, 1700; his Compt Book in Free Library, Campbeltown; Archibald, son of Malcolm, sasine 1752, married Penelope Macdonald of Sanda; Colonel Malcolm, son of Archibald, died *circa* 1824.

Others of the name, and probably same family, were Maurice, Rector of Kilblaan, 1433; another Maurice, also rector of Kilblaan, 1505; Malcolm McNeill *alias* Macpersone, probably son of last Maurice, tacksman of Cristlach, etc., 1541; Donald Dow in Kileonan, 1596; John in Ballegregan and Craigoch, 1605; Neil in Kildavic, 1605; John Kittoch in Cristlach, 1650, ruling elder; John in Cristlach, perhaps same, in 1678; Lachlan in Tirfergus and tacksman of Glenrea, 1651, received charter of lands of Tirfergus from Marquis of Argyll in 1660; Torquil married Barbara Mackay of Ugadale, *circa* 1690, and founded family of McNeill of Ugadale; Lachlan McNeill, wife Barbara Clerk, sasine of Drumlemble, 1745.

Early nineteenth century representatives were Neil in Ballevianan and Ormsary, 1830; Malcolm in Amod, 1830; family of McNeill of Lossit still extant.

MACOSHENAG, MAKCOCHENELL, McCOCHENNAN, SHANNON; the root is Gaelic *sean*, meaning old or wise. This family were harpers to the Clan Donald in Kintyre; in 1505 they had the 4 merkland of Brownherrekin, Amaid, Drumhereanoch, Dalsmeryl, Lagnadaf, and Innykew Callache, rent free for their services as harpers; Murdac in Macharebeg, 1505; Ivar in Lyel and Lephenstrath, 1541; Murdoch in the same, 1596; Mr Malcolm, minister of Kilkivan, 1635; Malcolm, tenant in Lephenstrath, 1678; the same proprietor of Lephenstrath from 1701; successors there, Hew, Archibald, Neil, Charles. They changed the older name to Shannon; in 1819 Captain Charles Macallister Shannon sold the estate of Lephenstrath to Donald McMillan.

McSPORRAN, McSPAIRAND; son of the purse-bearer. Duncan Roy McSpairand, tacksman of the Twa Duchries in North Kintyre, 1541; Duncan McSporran indweller in Kilcolmkill, witness to sasine of that place to Omey in 1622; Patrick Roy in Clachaig, 1615; Gormla, spouse to Donald McIlchier, in Muastill, 1678; Donald in Skipness, Argyll rebel, 1685; Donald in Borgadale, fencible, 1692; Gilbert in Carskey, 1694; Donald in Glenmanuil, 1716; More, servant to McNeill of Carskey, 1719.

McINSTOCKIR, McSTOCKER, STALKER; Gaelic *mac-an-stocair*, meaning son of the trumpeter; mainly in North Kintyre. Patrick in Kilmaloag and Malcolm his surety, 1506; John in Kilmaloag and Gilchrist in Stocadale, 1541; Donald Og in Kilmaloag and Gilbert in Stocadale, 1596; Robert and Donald, tacksmen of the 3 merkland of Tortastill in Saddell parish, 1633; Margaret, spouse to Malcolm McIlchatten in Killean parish, 1676; Barbara, spouse to Donald McIlglas in Clachaig, Killean, died 1690; Donald Stalker, late merchant in Campbeltown, test. Sept. 1772; Duncan Stalker, sometime of the island of Tobago, late resident in Killean, test. Oct. 1798.

McINTAYLOUR, TAYLOR; son of the tailor. John, son of Gilbert, witness to sasine of St Ninian's Lands, 1620; Duncan, tenant in Achnaglach, 1651; Lachlan, tacksman in Remulichtrach in Glenbreckrie, 1678; Lachlan involved in Atholl raids at Macharioch, 1685; Catherine spouse to John McEachan in Killocra, 1687; Neil, tenant of Knockantimore, 1691; Janet, spouse to Neil McEachran in Kilellan, 1768; Lachlan, tenant in Eden, Southend, 1771; Lachlan, probably same, in Blasthill, 1779; Lachlan, flax spinner in Campbeltown, died 1794 aged 63, buried in Kilkerran; wife, Mary McIsaac; sons, Neil and Lachlan, of whom Neil carried on flax-spinning business; Neil's son, James, tenant of Argyll Hotel, Southend; Lachlan, tenant in Sanda about 1830.

McVICAR; son of the vicar; mainly at Mull of Kintyre in early records. Gilquhane, joint tenant of Mull, 1541; John, tenant in Ballimacvicar, Southend, 1678; Patrick in Gartvain, 1678; Andrew in Balnaglek and "officer" of North Kintyre, 1685; Duncan, son of above, examined at time of Argyll rebellion; Archibald, merchant in Campbeltown, test. June 1686; Hew and Dermond, fencibles, 1692; Neil in Lailt, Southend, 1717; Dermond and John in Borgadillmore, 1717; George, son of Barbara, aunt to Malcolm McNeill of Carskey, 1717; George, probably same, merchant in Campbeltown 1725; Hugh in Lailt, 1769; Hugh in Dunglass, probably grandson, 1830; Hugh's son John in Dunglas emigrated to Canada, 1835; John's sons Professor Donald McVicar (1831-1902), Principal of Montreal Presbyterian College, and Professor Malcolm McVicar, President of Virginia Union University, Richmond, Virginia, U.S.A. Charles McVicar was proprietor of the estate of Kilellan during the first twenty years of the nineteenth century.

McILVRENNENICH; servant of St Brennan or Brendan. The place Ballybrennan in Southend is supposed to be named after a family so called; Gilbert in Corphyn and Blairferne in the Learside, 1596; Duncan McIlwrindie (corruption) in Gartnagerach and Corphyn, 1605; the form O'Brennan also found; Donald O'Brennan in Campbeltown, 1685; Donald O'Brennan in Carskey Book, 1736; name changed to Arnot in eighteenth century; Neil Arnot in Pennyland Mill, 1802; Donald Arnot, wife Katherine Ferguson, in Auchencorvie, 1811.

OBROLACHAN or BROLOCHAN; probably from Gaelic *brolach*, the breast. Name of an Irish ecclesiastical family which came to Scotland in the twelfth century. Duncan Obrolachan, rector of St Molruba in Islay, attended congregation of Glasgow University, 1453; Neil Obrolachan, priest in Kintyre, petitioned Pope in 1466 against rector of Kilmichael and vicar of Kilcolmkill, who had misconducted themselves "to the shame of the priestly dignity." John, rector of Kildalton in Islay, died 1548; Neil, rector of Kildalton and Kilneachtan in Islay, died 1592; Patrick, tenant in Arinascavach, 1687; Gilbert, fencible in 1692; A. and J. Obrolachan, tenants in Kilchattan, Southend, 1830.

The name was changed to Brodie, or Broadley. The Rev. Neil Brodie born in Campbeltown, 1813, was later Free Church minister at Pollokshaws, Glasgow, and one of the reputed authors of the song *Flory Loynachan*.

ODRAIN; Woulfe derives it from Gaelic *drean*, meaning wren, but Kintyre family apparently regarded it as from Gaelic *droighinn*, meaning hawthorn, and took the name of Hawthorn. Malcolm in Carrine, Southend, 1676; Archibald in Carskey, fencible in 1692; in Carskey Book, Mary, Charles, and Malcolm in 1719, Effreck in 1721; Donald dochrich Odrain in Glenadale, 1721; John in Strone, 1735; John in Glenehervie, 1830; Donald, elder parish church, Southend, 1818; Daniel, tenant in Catadale and Lepencaver, 1830; his grandson Daniel in Crossibeg, 1853; James, elder in Relief Church, Southend, 1853.

OLOYNACHAN, LOYNACHAN; probably from Gaelic *flann*, meaning ruddy. Duncan in Machrimore, spouse Margaret McMillan; she died 1694; children Neil, Margaret and Iver; Katherine, sister of Donald Oloynachan, and spouse to Donald McKissag, died March 1694; Donald Oloynachan, tenant in Shennachie, now Glenehervie, end of eighteenth century; John, son of above, also tenant there to 1825. Flora, daughter of John, is heroine of the well-known Kintyre song *Flory Loynachan*; she emigrated to Ontario, and married Donald McGillivray.

OMEY or OMAY, aspirated form OFEY; probably from Gaelic *miadh* meaning respect or esteem. Borne by a Kintyre family of whom many were ecclesiastics, both in pre-Reformation and Protestant times. We find the following; John Ofey, tacksman in Cristlach, etc., in 1505; Gilchrist also in Cristlach and surety for John in that year; Cornelius, graduated B.A. St Andrews, 1528, and rector of Kilblaan *circa* 1560; Duncan, principal surgeon to King James V, received a grant of lands in Perthshire, after which the name begins to appear there. James, rector of Kilcoman in Islay, 1542; Duncan, minister of Kilcolmkill and Commissary of Kintyre, 1611; Donald, minister of Kilkerran, died 1640; Duncan, tacksman of Glenehervie and Kilkivan, 1596 and 1605. Duncan, probably same, received charter to the 20 shilling land of Kilcolmkill from the Bishop of Argyll, 1622; James, tacksman of the teinds of Kilkivan in 1635. The Omeys were proprietors of Kilcolmkill, or Keil, from 1622 to 1819, and of these the following have been traced: Duncan, 1622; James, 1659; James, 1682; Duncan, 1725; James, 1754; Archibald, 1772; Archibald, 1781. Samuel, the last, sold Keil to Dr Colin McLarty in 1819, and went to live in Edinburgh. The Keil family, after the first Duncan, were descended from Mr Donald, minister of Kilkerran.

APPENDIX II

LOWLAND NAMES

The names borne by the incomers from Ayrshire and Renfrewshire, and other parts of the Lowlands, were derived either from Gaelic, or Norse, or English. Examples of Gaelic, or at least Celtic, names of Lowlanders are McNair, McTaggart, McColme, Dunlop, Orr, Muir, Giffen, and Wallace. From the Norse are derived Caldwell, Langwill, Maxwell, while names like Reid, White, and Porter are English, although their bearers may have been originally Gaelic-speaking. The names given below have been taken from old Kintyre rentals, from the Parish Registers, and from other sources such as the Registers of Testaments and Inventories and the Sasine Registers. In each case the earliest date of occurrence of the name in the record is noted, and also the locality of its bearers then, and at subsequent dates. The notes are meant to be illustrative and selective, not exhaustive. Place names are in general spelt as they occur in the records.

ANDREW: James in Ballimenoch, 1692; David in Eden, 1784; his family John, Archibald, Elizabeth, Mary, Agnes, Jean and David; David in Glenemucklach, 1798; his family Janet, Jane, John, Mathew, David; a David in Kildavie married Janet Huie and had family Jean, Robert, James, Mathew, Janet, Archibald; David and William Andrew signed Southend Relief Call in 1799; John in Glenemucklach, wife Mary Brown, 1830; later Hugh in Keprigan and his son David in Knockstaplebeg.

BOES: Mr James Boes, schoolmaster of Glassary, and of Southend about 1690; became first minister Lowland Congregation, Campbeltown, in 1694; continued in that charge till death in 1749; wife Mary Spence; daughter Mary born 1698; son Robert born 1703.

BROWN: James in Ballagir, 1685 and 1692; John in Kildonan, 1692; Andrew in Cristolach, 1692; Robert in Knockriochbeg, 1692; Edward in Kerranbeg, 1756; Thomas in Machrimore, 1770; Edward in Machrimore, 1776; George in Kilblaan, 1795; Archibald, Robert, Thomas and Charles signed Relief Call, 1799; James, Charles and William in Machrimore, 1800-20; Mathew, son of James, in Southend village in nineteenth century.

BRECKENRIDGE: Robert in Craigs, 1666; James and Jane Kilpatrick in Craigs, 1675; James, rebel in 1685; David in Lepinmore, 1685; William in Drum, 1692; David and James in Craigs, 1692; James in Ardnacroish, 1692; Hugh in Kilblaan, 1797; Andrew and Hugh signed Relief Call in 1799; John in Kileonan, 1830.

CALDWELL; for Caldwell of that ilk see chap. xi. Of others, probably descendants, we find John in Ardnacroish, 1692; James in Ballagir, rebel, 1685; Caldwells in Cristlach, 1755-93; James signed Relief Call in 1799; James in Cristlach, 1830; John in Lower Gartvain, 1857.

COLVILLE; John Colville and Betty Armour in Gartgreillan, 1663; John in Crossibeg, 1692; William in Trodigal, 1692; William in Glenmanuil, 1799; Robert in

Machrimore Mill, 1830; James in Upper Ranachan, 1830; four of the name Provosts of Campbeltown, viz. John in 1842, David in 1848, Duncan in 1881, and John in 1919.

CORDINER; Andrew and James in Carrine, 1692; William and Jean Ald in Kilblaan, 1695; James in Glenemucklach, 1786; they were in last place down to 1874. Mathew signed Relief Call, 1799; Mathew in Glenemucklach, 1857; Alexander in Machrimore to 1898; Rev. Robert, his brother, U.P. minister of Lesmahagow; Rev. Robert, son of Alexander, minister in Australia.

CUNNISON: Mr (Rev.) John Cunnison, minister of Kilbride in Arran, came to Killean with Indulgence in 1672; outed again, 1684; had tack of Feochaig in 1678; his son James, Chamberlain of Kintyre and Provost of Campbeltown in 1712; Rachel Cunnison married Donald Clerk, proprietor of Drumlemble; daughter Beatrice born 1680.

CUTHBERTSON or CULBERTSON; James Cuthbertson and Agnes Templeton had son James born in Peninver in 1663, and daughter Mary born in Killownan in 1673; Robert Cuthbertson and Ann Breakenridge had two sons and two daughters born between 1687 and 1695; Robert Cuthbertson and Agnes Harvie had family, William born 1753, Robert 1755, Robert 1758, and John 1760. Robert Cuthbertson in Callyburn paid for eight sittings in Longrow Church 1767; Robert Cuthbertson in Craigs (apparently same as in Callyburn), tombstone in Kilkivan, died 1799 aged 77. Some emigrated to America towards the end of eighteenth century; a living descendant (1948) of these is Colonel William Smith Culbertson of the U.S. Diplomatic Service.

DUNLOP; for lairds of Dunlop and Garnkirk, see chap. xi. Others were Normand Dunlop and Jean Muir in Gartgreillan, 1676; Hugh in Ballegregan, 1685; John and Betty Wylie in Rannachan, 1670; Patrick and Mary Orr, 1695; James, elder and senior, and Alexander in Peninver, 1692; Robert in Kildonan, 1692; Robert in Cristolach, 1692; Hugh in Glenemucklach, 1692; Patrick and Mary Love (no location), 1724; Alexander in Ballevean got fifty-seven years' lease of that in 1786; James in Macharioch, 1857.

FERGUSON: Duncan, prisoner in Argyll rebellion, 1685; Hew Ferguson and Elizabeth Stewart in 1686; William married Jean Andrew, 1703; Andrew in Achilochy in 1777 and in Kilervan, 1794, his wife Eliz. Huie; son David, grandson Andrew, great-grandson Andrew, whose family still there (1948); David, smith and merchant in Campbeltown, wife Margaret Fleming, died 1813.

FLEMING; James, tacksman of Ballevean, 1666; David in Brecklate, rebel 1685; Archibald in town, rebel 1685; John in Ballevean, 1692; David in Kilellan, 1692; William in Garvochie, 1692; John in Kileonan, 1692; Fleming in Ballybrenan, Southend, 1730; in Glecknahavill, 1752 and 1772; in Kilchattan, 1756; in Kilervan, 1775, 1795; James signed Relief Call, 1799; in Gartnagerach, 1875; Captain John Fleming, R.N., of the Ballivean family, "was one of Nelson's captains and received sword of honour from City of London." He was proprietor of Muasdale and Glencreggan, and built Fleming's land on the Castlehill, Campbeltown; his mother Jean Porter of Crossibeg family.

GIFFEN; John and William in Machribeg, 1692; Ralston and Giffen in Brecklate, 1730; Alexander, maltster in town, 1761; John and James signed Relief Call in 1799. James was one of first founders of Southend village; his son the Rev. James Giffen, U.P. minister of Saltcoats, died 1870; John, watchmaker in town, 1821; Alexander, draper in town mid-nineteenth century.

GREENLEES; family said to have come from Lochwinnoch, probably with Laird Ralston. John and Isabel Finlay in Pennygown, Southend, 1671; John in Acharua, 1692; John in Upper Gartvain, 1720; Archibald in Southend married Marion Love, 1734; Greenlees in Machribeg, 1774, 1795, 1830; George, Edward, William, Robert, John (twice) and Thomas signed Relief Call in 1799; John, son of George in Machribeg, founded Argyll Settlement in Illinois, U.S.A., in 1836. William in Darlochan, James in Smerby, James in Peninver and Isca, and J. and R. Greenlees in Putchanty, in 1830; Charles C. Greenlees, Provost of Campbeltown, 1875.

HALL; Robert in Eden, 1692; James in Cattadalemore, 1692; in Benton or Pirlieknowe, 1780, tombstone in Keil; in Glenehervie, 1794; James signed Relief Call in 1799; Robert in Glenehervie, 1830; Peter in Polliwilline, 1830.

HARVIE or HARVEY; Alexander, indweller in Lochhead, 1636; James and Agnes Ralston in Smerby, 1678; James in Lailt, fencible 1692; William in Kilblaan, 1724; James, shipmaster in Campbeltown, 1767; Archibald, merchant in town, 1767; Andrew, merchant in town, 1767; William, shipmaster in town, 1767, wife Agnes Orr; the last became first keeper of the Mull of Kintyre Lighthouse, erected in 1788, and succeeded by his son Mathew. Andrew and Margaret Orr in Skeroblin, 1791; Andrew, maltster in town, 1800; Nathaniel in Laigh Remul, 1830; James in Park farm later.

HOWIE, HUIE, HUY; John in Lochhead, rebel in 1685; Samuel, servant to John Huy, examined by Privy Council in 1685 and sentenced to transportation; Alexander and Sibella Dickie, 1686; Robert and Susanna Allan married 1686; John, fencible in town, 1692; John in Machrimore, fencible, 1692; Huie in Kerranmore, 1816; Huie in Benton, 1759-88; Huie in Kildavie, 1775-1807; John in Kildavie, 1830; Alexander in Auchincorvie, 1825; William in Polliwilling, 1830; James in Knockruan, 1830; James and William in Durry, 1830; Peter, David, Robert, John, and William signed Southend relief Call in 1799.

KEITH; Mr Edward, first minister of Lowland Congregation of Campbeltown; son of Sheriff of Montrose; inducted 1655; died 6th May 1682. Wife Jane Campbell; at least two children, William and Mary (twins), born 1672.

LANGWILL; John and Margaret Mitchell in Straw, 1671; James and Agnes Glasgow in Upper Balliwilling, 1671; John and Isobel Watson in Straw, 1676; William and Patrick in Balloch, 1692; John and Agnes Millin, 1717; Patrick and Mary McMillan, 1731; John and Marion Fleming, 1727; Alexander and Martha Lindsay, 1726; Edward and Isabel Turner, 1787; Langwill in Brecklate, 1778; James in Brecklate, 1787; Anne, wife of John McMillan in Coledrain, 1809; Alexander, shipmaster in town, 1767; John, tenant in Kilkivan, 1767; Rebert, tenant in Crosshill, 1767; James and John signed Relief Call in 1799.

MAXWELL; for those of Southbar and Milnehouse, see chap. xi; William and James in Macharioch, 1692; John and Elizabeth Johnstone in South Ballegregan, 1674; James and Bridget Crawford in Ballegregan, 1674; Robert and Mary Robertson in Southend, 1705; James Maxwell married Jean Maxwell, 1729; James in Cattadale, Southend, 1771; James, Provost of Campbeltown, 1785; Robert in Ballochgair, 1767; Thomas, merchant in town, 1767; Robert in Ballochgair, 1830. Maxwells in Cattadale emigrated to America about 1800.

MONTGOMERY; for planter lairds, see chap. xi. John, James, and Neil, fencibles in town, 1692; John Montgomery and Mary Anderson in Ballimenach, 1682; John married Ursula Muir, 1688; Hugh Montgomery, proprietor of Broomlands in Ayrshire, Collector of Customs, Campbeltown, early eighteenth century, Provost of Campbeltown 1725; his wife, Mary Boes, daughter of Rev. James Boes; his daughter, Elizabeth, wife of Rev. David Campbell minister of Southend, 1742-92; Montgomeries in Cristlach, 1774; Robert in Cristlach signed Relief Call, 1799; Mysie in Cristlach married Neil McKay, Erridale, 1806; Robert in Cristlach, 1830; James in Southend Village, 1857.

MUIR, MORE, MOIR, MOORE; for planter lairds, see chap. xi.; John Moir in Kildavie, 1666; James Muir in Knockstaplebeg, 1666; William and Mary Melville in Craigs, 1673; William in Kildavie, rebel, 1685; Alexander, rebel in town, 1685; James and Mary Huie, 1689; James Moir in Laggs, 1682; Moores in Brunerican, 1735; Samuel Muir, maltster in Campbeltown, 1767; Samuel and Daniel, coopers in town, 1767; John in Ballenatoan, 1767.

MITCHELL; Mary Mitchell, wife to John Langwill in Strath, 1671; Thomas, maltman in town, 1679; James and Archibald in town, fencibles, 1692; Thomas in town died 1698; James, maltster in town, test. 1725; Thomas, late merchant in town, 1773; Archibald Mitchell junior, tenant in Clochkeil, 1767; William, tenant in Ballemenach, 1767; David, merchant, and Lionel, wheelwright, in town, 1767; Mitchell in Dalbuie, 1775; James Mitchell in Largiemore, 1830; Hugh, Provost of Campbeltown, 1896.

McCOLME; Andrew and Janet Fleming, 1683; Andrew junior and Isobel Fulton in Kilblaan, 1692; Andrew, fencible in town, 1692; James, fencible in town, 1692; Robert, physician in Campbeltown early eighteenth century, joined Town Council, 1704, Provost, 1709, member of Council to 1764, Provost six times, wife Rachel Cunnison; Francis McColme, merchant in Campbeltown, 1767; tombstone of Andrew McColme in Kilkerran bearing Fleming arms.

McINTAGGART, McTAGGART; John in Crosshill, spouse Mary Martin, 1694; John and Agnes Thomson, son Archibald, 1724; William in 1728; some of them may have been Highland. Daniel, Proc. Fiscal, 1815; son Charles and grandson Daniel also in that office; Col. Charles McTaggart, son of last, C.S.I., I.M.S. The well-known artist, William Mactaggart, R.S.A., was born in Campbeltown of Kintyre stock.

McNAIR; Nathaniel, weaver, and Isobel Ramsay, son John, 1682; Nathaniel in Upper Balliwilline, son Joseph, 1696; Nathaniel, fencible, 1692; Robert, tenant in

Chiscan, 1767; Archibald, tenant in Kildonall, 1767; John, merchant in town, 1767; Nathaniel junior, shipmaster in Campbeltown, 1767; Nathaniel senior, merchant in town, 1767; James, maltster in town, 1767. Nathaniel McNair & Sons, wood merchants and ship owners, owned the *Gleaner* which carried emigrants direct from Campbeltown to America, bringing back timber for shipbuilding. This firm cast, in their own foundry in Campbeltown, the iron street lamp-posts when gas was introduced in 1830, and the first iron water pipes in 1834.

ORR; Thomas, schoolmaster and notary in Lochhead in 1650's; clerk to Presbytery, 1662, wife Anne Montgomerie, son Thomas examined time of Argyll rebellion, 1685; Peter in Skeroblin and Mary Montgomerie, 1683; John and Mary Alexander, 1682; Archibald and Janet Greenlees, 1703; John in Glenemucklach, Archibald in Pennygown, and Edward in Cattadalemore, fencibles in 1692; Edward, bailie in town, wife Elizabeth Wylie, daughter Elizabeth, 1743; Edward in Knockrioch, 1758; John in Knockrioch, 1767; David and Robert, merchants in town, 1761 and 1773; Agnes, wife of William Harvey at Mull of Kintyre, 1788; Robert, distiller in Campbeltown, late nineteenth century.

PICKEN; Thomas in Pollywilline, rebel 1685; William in Gartgreillan, rebel 1685; Thomas, John, and John junior in Kilervan, 1692; William in Kileonan, 1692; John Picken and Isobel Omey, 1773; Pickens in Gartloskan, 1755, 1778; Alexander in Kildavie, 1775; William in Erridale, 1758; John in Machrimore, 1787; John, Alexander, James, and Archibald signed Relief Call, 1799; James in Kilervan, 1833.

PORTER; Robert and Janet Wilson, 1673; William in Crossibeg, rebel 1685; William in Baraskomill, 1692; John and Jane Colville, 1694. John Porter in Crossibeg wrote or inspired the book known as *Porter's Prophecies* in 1737; John and Agnes Longwill, 1760; Isobel and Daniel McMillan, 1761; Hugh and John, tenants in Crossibeg, 1767; John and Janet McNair, 1817. Lieut.-Col. John Porter, of Crossibeg family commanded a regiment of Argyll Fencibles during Irish rebellion of 1798, later lived at Drumore, was Provost of Campbeltown in 1794.

RALSTON; for Ralston of that ilk, see chap. xi. Kintyre Ralstons of eighteenth and nineteenth centuries said to be descended from David Ralston, a cousin of the laird, but his name does not occur in the record. James in Eden, rebel 1685; Patrick in Ballimenach, 1685; John in Crossibeg, Alexander and James in Eden, fencibles 1692; Patrick and William in Brecklate, 1692. Ralstons were in Brecklate and Knockstaplebeg during the eighteenth and first half of the nineteenth century, and in Achnaglach in 1756. Thomas and Peter in Brecklate, 1830; heirs of Gavin Ralston in Upper Gartloskan, 1830; Andrew in Dalbuie, 1830; Thomas in Homeston, 1830; John Ralston's heirs in Brecklate, 1857. Surrounding the tomb of Laird Ralston in Kilcolmill are burial places of Ralstons who had been in Dalbuie, Trodigal, Brecklate, and Knockstaple.

REID; for Reids of Barskimming, see chap. i. Alexander in Knockstaplemore from 1671; John in Macharioch, 1692; John in Blasthill, 1692; Hew in Polliwilline, 1692. Reids were in Kildavie and Polliwilline during the eighteenth and most of the nineteenth century. Jean, widow of Walter Macfarlane, in Kildavie, 1700; John (twice), Alexander, Mathew, Hugh, David, Andrew, and William, signed Relief Call in 1799; John in Kildavie and Andrew in Polliwilline, 1830; John's heirs and Peter Reid in Langholm, 1857; Walter in Polliwilline, 1857.

ROWATT; Alexander Rowatt, factor to Marchioness of Argyll in Kintyre, was taken prisoner and examined by Scots Privy Council at time of Argyll rebellion in 1685; his descendant, Dr Charles Rowatt, physician in Campbeltown, and one of the founders of the Longrow congregation.

RYBURN, REYBURN, RAEBURN; a family named Ryburn owned estate of that name in Dunlop parish, Ayrshire. In 1638 Neil Ryburn of that ilk sold this estate to Porterfields of Hapland, who were among the planter lairds of Kintyre. Ryburns of Kintyre most probably of this family. John Ryburn and Janet Jamieson in Backs, 1659; John, tacksman in 1666, name of holding indecipherable, but probably Backs; Patrick and Jane Baird in Garvachie, 1673; John, tenant in Aros, 1678; Mathew Ryburn and Elizabeth Ryburn, 1702; John Ryburn and Mary Dunlop, 1701; William Ryburn, tenant in Drumlemble, 1830.

WALLACE; for Colonel James Wallace, see chap. xi. His son William, tacksman of Ballimenach, 1666; William's wife Elizabeth Drummond of Concraig; two sons James and John from whom probably later Wallaces descended; a John in Brecklate, rebel in 1685; William in Lochhead, rebel 1685; Hew in Lochhead, fencible 1692; John in Kileonan, fencible 1692; William and Gavin in Kildavie, 1685. During eighteenth century Wallaces were in Machrimore, Dunglas, and Machribeg. Mary Wallace in Machribeg married John Greenlees, 1774; Gavin in Kildavie died 1775 aged 52, wife Janet Morrison; William in Machribeg signed Relief Call, 1799; William's heirs in Machribeg, 1830. Tombstone in Kilcolmkill has Wallace crest and the motto *sperandum est.*

WHITE; John in Blasthill 1685 and 1692; John in Campbeltown, 1685; William, senior and junior, in Kilblaan, 1692. Whites were in Machribeg from 1730 to 1774 and later; William Wallace married Mary White in 1784; Samuel, tenant in Peninver, 1767; John, tenant in Dalbuie, 1857.

WYLIE; Betty Wylie, wife of John Dunlop in Rannachan, 1670; John Wylie and Margaret McKinnie, son Nathaniel, 1686; Joseph and Mary Niven, 1695; John, senior and junior in town, rebels 1685; John, elder and junior, tenants in Kilkeddan, 1692; Archibald, tenant on Carskey estate, 1712; John in Arinascavach, 1767; David signed Relief Call, 1799.

(Note to above: 'Rebel' means implicated in Argyll's rebellion of 1685).

APPENDIX III

OLD LAND MEASURES

In modern times we are accustomed to describe an estate or a farm as consisting of a certain number of acres, but this usage is of quite recent origin and does not date any further back than the close of the eighteenth century. The use of the acre in Scotland was known from the twelfth century, but was applied only to small areas of land. Thus we read of village acres, town acres, vicar's acres, baillie's acres, these being what we would nowadays call small holdings. The reason why large farms were not described in acres was that the art of surveying large areas of land was not known, and therefore could not be practised.

Hence in all rentals prior to the early nineteenth century we find an older nomenclature of *pennylands* and *merklands*, and their multiples and fractions, and their occurrence is apt to prove a stumbling-block to the proper understanding of rural conditions in days gone by. We therefore propose to explain very shortly the meanings of these old terms, and their relations to modern conditions. The names employed are derived from the languages spoken by the various peoples who have occupied our country, and may be classified in three groups in historical sequence as (1) Celtic, (2) Norse, and (3) English or Scottish.

In purely Celtic times the people lived in groups of about twenty houses each, which in Ireland and Dalriada were known as "ballys." This word still persists in place-names such as Ballymenach, Ballygreggan, and others, Each of these ballys consisted of a piece of land, which probably belonged to a leading man or chief, and which, as time went on, became divided up among his family. The usual division was into quarters, eighths, and smaller fractions, for which the Gaelic words were *ceathramh, ochdamh,* etc. This system had ceased to be used in Kintyre before our historical record begins, but the existence of the *ceathramh* or quarterland is commemorated in place-names like Keromenach (middle quarter) and Kerafuar (cold quarter). In Islay and the Isle of Man the *ceathramh* or quarterland was in practical use as a land name down to the early nineteenth century.

Norse names were introduced during the occupation of Kintyre by the Norsemen from approximately A.D. 800 to 1100. The Norse overlords did not make any attempt to change the Celtic system, but apparently made use of it, and imposed a tax or scat of one ounce of silver on each of the Celtic ballys or townships. These therefore became known as *Ouncelands,* or in Gaelic *Tirungas,* sometimes written *Terungs* or *Tirungs.* The Gaelic word is from *tir,* land, and *unga,* and ounce. The ounce was the English ounce of 20 pennyweights, and as there were usually about twenty houses in each bally, the share of the individual house was one penny. It should be remembered that this was not a copper coin as it is to-day, but the old silver penny which was the only coin in circulation in Scotland down to the time of King David II (1329-1370). Hence the land pertaining to the individual house became known as the *pennyland.* The half-penny, or *leth-pheighinn* in Gaelic, and the quarter penny or farthing, in Gaelic *feorlin,* are also found as elements in our place-names.

There is only one authentic instance of the use of the *pennyland* as a practical measure of land in Kintyre. It occurs in a charter of King Robert the Bruce, granting the lands of Ugadale to Gilchrist Mackay, in the year 1329. The grant was of four pennylands, which must have been individual farms, for they are detailed in the charter under individual names, which do not occur in any map of Kintyre, and which must now be obsolete. In other parts of Argyllshire, and in the Island of Mull and other isles, the pennyland was, however, in use down to the eighteenth century. In Kintyre its former use is now commemorated in place-names such as Pennygown, or Smith's pennyland, Peninver, or Ivar's pennyland, Lephenstrath, or the strath of the half-pennyland, and Feorlin, or the quarter penny or farthing land.

We now come to the *Merkland*, which is the denomination by which land in Kintyre is described in all extant rentals down to the late eighteenth century. A mark or merk was eight ounces of standard silver, which was coined into 160 silver pennies, or 13 shillings and 4 pence. The merkland was most probably introduced into Kintyre during the century 1200-1300, and was certainly in use in 1329 when Mackay of Ugadale got his charter from Bruce; but, as it was deemed necessary in that charter to specify the extent of the grant in both merklands and pennylands, it is clear that the newer denomination of the merkland was just supplanting the older pennylands at that date, and we do not hear any more of the latter in Kintyre.

The merkland was probably introduced as a result of the feudal system, whereby proprietors held their land in return for providing armed knights or other forms of military aid to the Crown, or in lieu of these, a sum of money, usually assessed in merks. Hence a valuation in merks of all the land under the authority of the Crown had to be made by the sheriffs or other officers of the Crown, and this is known as the Old Extent, or old valuation. In Kintyre it was probably made between 1222 and 1264, and there the valuation appears to have been, in some cases at least, at the rate of 10 merks to the ounceland or bally, that being the yearly rent to be paid therefrom. In other parts of the West Highlands the rate was as low as 4 merks to the ounceland. A *merkland* was therefore a piece of land which had been assessed as paying an annual rental of one merk or 13 shillings and 4 pence at the time the Old Extent was made, and so is usually referred to as a *merkland of old extent*.

We meet also with its multiples and fractions. Thus 1½ merklands amounted to 13s. 4d. + 6s. 8d or a 20s. land; 2 merklands were a 26s. 8d. land, 3 merklands a 40s. land, and so on. A half-merkland was 6s. 8d. land, a quarter merkland 3s. 4d. land. Other extents arose by adding together two or more holdings, or by dividing them up in certain proportions. Thus, if the "bally" had been assessed as a 10 merkland of 133s. 4d. land the *ceathramh* or quarter would be 33s. 4d., the *ochdamh* or eighth 16s. 8d. land, and so on for smaller fractions such as 4s. 2d. land which last, in English money, was practically the equivalent of the English groat of 4 pence, and so became known as the *Groatland*.

Clearly the merkland was a money valuation only, and therefore did not denote a fixed number of acres, for the richer the land the smaller would be the area of the merkland. In Kintyre, about the time that it was supplanted by the acre valuation, it appears to have been a one-plough farm. In our old rentals the extent in merklands of any particular holding, of which the boundaries had not been altered, remains constant throughout the centuries, but the actual rents paid show a constant increase. This was due to various causes, one of which was the great deterioration of the Scottish currency. In the reign of Alexander III, English and Scottish currencies were at par, but at the date of the Union of the Crowns in 1603 a Scottish shilling was only worth an English penny. This represented a 36-fold depreciation. Hence, if no other causes had been at work, a merkland of Old Extent would have been paying a rent of 36 merks in 1603. In Kintyre, in 1678, some merkland farms were actually paying as much as £80 rent. Some of this increase must have been due to increased agricultural production as well as to depreciation of the currency.

In the late eighteenth century the Duke of Argyll employed an English surveyor, Lieut. Langlands, to survey his estates in acres, after which the merkland passed out of use, and is now practically forgotten except by students of history and antiquities.

Note: prior to decimalisation of British currency in 1970, monetary units were in pounds, shillings and pence (pennies, and fractions thereof; farthings, quarter pennies). 4 farthings = 1 penny (d.); 12 pence = 1 shilling (s.); 20 shillings = 1 pound (£). eg. 1 shilling = 5p. (5 'new' pence).

Similarly; as a measure of land area, the acre had given way at the close of the 20th Century, to the hectare. 1 hectare is equivalent to 2.471 acres.

APPENDIX IV

A STEELBOW CONTRACT OF 1710

[From the Compt Book of Malcolm MacNeill of Carskey in

Free Library, Campbeltown]

"Conditions agreed on betwixt Malcolm McNeill in Carskey and Neill Dow McNeill in Lailt. I the said Malcolm McNeill setts to the said Neill McNeill the merkland of Carskey on the following conditions: *Imprimis.* The said Neill is to get from me one half merk of the foresaid merkland stocked. Ten bolls of corn for seed corn and two bolls of Barley for seed barley and ten tydy cows, with Timber, Iron, Horses for to work the said ½ merkland.

"For which the said Neill Binds and Oblidges him and his to pay to me or mine yearly Ten Bolls of Corn and Six Bolls of Barley att ilk term of Candlemas, and that sufficient and merchantable att the usual measure of Kintyre, also for the Ten Kows oblidges him and his to pay to me or myne Eight stones the couple with a stirk, which is in all fortie stone of Cheese, or the current pryss of what is unpaid of the said Fortie stone, and five stirks sufficient according to the custom of the country."

[The system of tenancy by Steelbow was common all over Scotland in ancient times.]

INDEX

A

Adamnan, his name for Kintyre, 1
Agricola, supposed visit of, 1
Ale, 117
Alt-na-sionnach, northern boundary of Kintyre, 24
Antrim, Earl of, 14, 31, 34, 37
    estate of Glens of, 5, 14
Aquavitae, 34, 118
Ardcardle, fort of, 5
Argyll, Archibald, 2nd Earl of, 6, 13
    Archibald, 7th Earl of, 17, 18, 20-22
    Archibald, 8th Earl and Marquis of, 37-39, 43, 51-59, 68, 69, 82, 87-88, 90
    Archibald, 9th Earl of, 94, 95-99, 100-109
Askamylnemoir, fort of, 34, 46
Askomel, house of, 16
Atholl, Marquis of, 54, 90, 100, 101, 105, 107
Atholl Raids, 107-109

B

Baillie, Principal Robert, 42, 62
Baird, James, Argyll rebel, 106
Ballimenach, William Wallace son of Col. James Wallace tenant in, 81
Bar, Barony of, 14
    Ward of Barony of, 14
Bard's Lands in Kintyre, 11
Barley or Bear, 114
Bede, Cuthbert, 56, 60
Bee Scapes, paid as rent, 113, 116
    stolen in Atholl Raids, 108
Bishop of Argyll, 6, 12, 18
    of the Isles, Mr Neil Campbell, 88
    Andrew Knox, 125
Bishopric of Argyll, Saddell lands annexed to, 6
Bishops' War, 32, 34
Bissett, John, 48
    Marjorie, 5
Boes, Mr James, 126, 130, 143
    Chair at Dunaverty, 54
Borgadale, fort at, 1
Boyle, of Kelburn, 21, 54, 99, 100
    Finella, 22
Boyll (Boyle), John of Ballachmartin, 21, 23
Breckenridge, name of, 143
Bridges in Kintyre, 116-117
Brown, name of, 143
Browne, Capt. James, 58, 79
    James, elder at Lochead, 90
Bruce, King Robert, 4, 11
Burgesses of Lochhead, earliest Low-land, 33
Butter, 118

C

" Cain " rents, 118
Caldwell, name of, 143
    John, Younger of, 77, 96
    William of that ilk, 77, 89
Calps, see Hereyelds
Cameron, Mr John, minister of Campbeltown, 98
Campbeltown, Neolithic workshop at, 1
    earliest mention of name, 21, 22
    Cross of, 11
Campbell of Argyll, see Argyll
    Agnes, Lady of Kintyre, 14
    Archibald of Glencarradale, 89
    Archibald of Lawers, 51
    Aylis, daughter of Mathew of Skipness, 49
    Colin of Lundie, 24
    Colin of Skipness, 109
    Mr David, minister of Southend, 49
    Dugald of Inverawe, 45, 70
    Dugald of Lindsaig, 98

Sir Duncan of Auchinbreck, 34, 05
Sir Hew of Cessnock, 71
James of Ardkinglas, 42, 52
John of Calder, 15, 16, 18, 21, 24, 38
Sir John of Lundie, 21
John, Chamberlain to 9th Earl of Argyll, 124
Mr Lachlan, minister of Campbeltown, 116
Mathew of Skipness, 49, 50
Mr Neil, Bishop of The Isles and Minister of Lochhead, 40
of Kilberry, 25
miscellaneous tacksmen of name, 70
Carnock, Erskine of, Ensign to Earl of Argyll, 102
Cars or slipes, use of, 115
Carskey, Macneills of, 11
mill at, 117
Castlehill, castle built at, 24
church at, 35
Castle Mail, 24
Cave, men found in at Dunaverty, 51
Cheese, 118
Church at Kilkerran, 24, 35
at Lochhead, 35
at Kilblaan, Kilcolmkill, Kilchousland, Kilmichael, 35
Clanranald, *Red Book of*, 6
chief of, 35
Clerk (Clark), name of, 134
Donald, accounts of, 109
Coal, mining of in Kintyre, 123
Colville, name of, 143
Cordiner, name of, 144
Cunnison, name of, 144
Mr John, minister of Killean, 99
Cuthbertson (Culbertson), name of, 144

D

Dalriada, kingdom of, 1
Darroch, Mr Dugald, minister of Lochhead, 40, 49, 88-89, 91, 92
Mr John, minister of Kilcolmkill, 41, 88, 125
Mr Maurice, minister of Kilcalmonell, 35
Dick, Captain Louis, 43, 46
Dobie, William, author of *Perambulations in Kintyre in 1833*, 123
Drummond, Mr James, 80
Dunaverty (Aberte), castle of, 2, 4, 5, 24, 31
siege and massacre at, 48-54
Duncanson, Mr Robert, minister of Campbeltown, 94
Dundonald, castle of, 4
Dunfermline, abbey of, endowed with Kintyre tithes, 3
Dunlop, name of, 144
Alexander of Garnkirk, 75
Laird of, 69, 75
Robert, obtains lease of Ballivean, 114
Dunluce, Viscount, lands of Kintyre sold to, 31
Dunstaffnage, Captain of, 57
execution of Colkitto at, 58-59
Duns, or forts, in Kintyre, 1

E

Education, Act of 1496, 124
state of in sixteenth century, 124
Statute of Iona relating to, 124
early Kintyre graduates, 125
see also under Schools
Epidii, ancient tribe inhabiting Kintyre, 1
Epidion Akron, Ptolemy's name for Kintyre, 1
Episcopalianism, first period of, 34
second period of, 93
ministers, 93-94, 130

F

Fergus, King of Scots, 1
Ferguson, name of, 144
Fleming, name of, 144
    John and William in Ballivean, 114
Florida, ship of Spanish Armada, 14
Forbes, Captain James, 70, 78
Forestare (Forrester), Sir Duncan, Comptroller, 5, 13
Forrester, of Arngibbon, 78
    Alexander of Knockrioch, 78, 105, 123
    James of Knockrioch, 130
    John and Thomas, chaplains to Earl of Argyll, 103
French regiment, raised by Lord Kintyre, 32, 51, 80
Frew, Mathew, bridge engineer, 117
Fulton, William, robbed in Atholl Raids, 108

G

Gabran (Gowran), Dalridic tribe of, 2
Gallowhill, the, 26
Gardiner, Mr James, minister at Saddell, 89
Giffen, name of, 145
Rev. James, his account of Southend, 131
Gigha, General Leslie's dispatch from, 56
Gilleasbeg Grumach, name given to 7th Earl of Argyll, 20
Gillebride, father of Somerled, 3
Glencairn, Earl of, Royalist leader, 82, 87
    master of, Governor of Kintyre, 13, 49
Greenlees, name of, 145
Guthry, Henry, Bishop of Dunkeld, 42, 52

H

Halket, Colonel Robert, tack in Kintyre, 80-81, 98
Hall, name of, 145
James, Argyll rebel, 106
Hamilton, James of Aitkenhead, Kintyre tacksman, 69, 76
    James of Ardoch, Kintyre tacksman, 69, 77
    William of Brownmuir (Brumore), Kintyre tacksman, 77
    Anna, spouse of Thomas Maxwell, 80
Harper's Lands, 12
Harvie, name of, 145
    Alexander, indweller of Lochhead in 1636, 33
Hastie, Mr Alexander, chaplain to Earl of Argyll, 103
Henderson, Alexander, Dean of Holyrood, 14, 124
Hereyelds, 112-113
Herring fishing, 21, 33, 118
Highland Host, 94, 99
Hill, Rev. George, author of *Macdonells of Antrim*, 23, 31, 72
Holyrood Abbey, endowed with Kintyre tithes, 3
Horsegang, a share of a farm, 114
Horse Sheets, as rents, 118, 123
Hostages taken from Kintyre, 15
Howie, name of, 145
    Samuel, banished as rebel, 107

I

Implements, agricultural, 115
Infield, 114
Illiteracy in Kintyre, 124, 127
Iona, church lands of at Kilchenzie, 13
    Statutes of, 124
Ireland, 1-2
    meal from, 99
Irish, troops under Sir Alexander Macdonald, 45
Islay, Alexander of, 3-4
    Angus Mor, Lord of, 3-4

Angus Og, Lord of, 4
Donald, Lord of, 3
Isles, John, 1st Lord of the, 4
John, 4th Lord of the, 4-5
Donald, 2nd Lord of the, 124
James III, King, creates Stewardry of Kintyre, 5
James IV, King, fortifies castles of Skipness and Ardcardle, 5
visits West Highlands in 1493, 5
stays at Dunaverty Castle in 1494, 5
his governor of Dunaverty hanged, 5
erects new castle at Kilkerran, 6
erects lands of Saddell Abbey into temporal lordship to be annexed to Bishopric of Argyll, 6
James V, King, arranges for education of James Macdonald of Dunnyveg, 14
orders re-building of Dunaverty Castle, 49

K

Keith, Mr Edward, first minister of Lowland Congregation at Lochhead, 90, 92, 98-99
Kelly, Rev. Daniel, minister of Southend, 53, 73
Kenmore, Lord, Royalist, 82,87
Kilblaan, old parish of, 35
waste land in, 62,67
Rector of, 12
Kilcalmonell, 24, 45
Kilchousland, old parish of, 35
Kilcolmkill, old parish of, 35
waste land in, 62,67
Kilellan, Maceachrans of, 11
Mill at, 117
Kileonan, Bond of Friendship between Macneills and Macdonalds signed at, 12, 124
Mill at, 117
Kilchenzie (Skierchanzie), proposal to transfer part to Lochhead, 90
proposal to transfer highland congregation to, 90
Kilkerran, castle erected at, 6
parish church of, 35
Kilmichael, old parish of, 35
Kinloch (Lochhead), castle erected at, 18
Mill at, 117
Kintyre, James Lord, 20-25
Knapdale, 14
Knaveship, payment to miller's servant, 117
Knox, Andrew, Bishop of The Isles, 125
John, reformer, 124, 126

L

Lamont, Walter, Customs Officer, in Atholl Raids, 108
Langwill, name of, 145
Lany, John De, Constable of Tarbert, Castle, 4
Largie (Largy), estate of, set to Campbell of Inverawe, 70
Bond of Maintenance, 40
see also Macdonald and Macrannaldbane
Lephenstrath, Macoshenags of, 12
Leslie, General Alexander, 42
General David, Kintyre campaign, 42-47
massacre at Dunaverty, 48-54
return march and Islay campaign, 55-59
Lochhead (Kinloch), erection of burgh at, 20-26, 31-36
Lowland congregation formed at, 89
Old Gaelic Church of, 35
Castle erected at, 18

Logan, John, first Grammar Schoolmaster, 126
Lorne, Lord, afterwards Marquis of Argyll, 24
    afterwards Earl of Argyll, 33, 80
    Marquis of, 61, 67
Loup, Macallasters of, 6, 104, 109
    Tutor of, 16

M

Macallaster, name of, 134
    of Loup, 6, 104-105
    Charles MacAlexander, Steward of Kintyre, 5
    Hector, hanged at Lochhead, 56
McCaig, name of, 134
McCamrois (MacCambridge, MacCambrig), name of, 135
McCarly, name of, 134
McCleireach (Clerk, Clark), name of, 134 see also under Clerk
McColme, name of, 146
Macruarie, Amie, wife of John, Lord of The Isles, 4
McCualsky, name of, 135
Macdonald (Maconnell, Macdonell), name of, 135
    Sir Alexander, 37-41, 42-45, 59
    Angus of Dunyveg, 14-16, 19, 22, 26
    Coll (Colkitto), 37-41
Macdonald, James of Dunyveg, 14
    Sir James of Knockrinsay, 15, 16-19, 23, 25
    Sir James of Dunluce, 16
    Sir John Cathanach of Islay, 5
    of Largie (Macrannaldbane), 6, 12, 40, 45, 105, 108
    of Sanda, 23, 40, 41, 46, 50-51
Maceachan, name of, 136
    of Tangy, 11
    Charles, 104-105
Maceachran, name of, 135
    of Kilellan, 11
    Angus, killed at Dunaverty, 40, 51
    Colin, 105
    John, hostage, 15
Macfarlane, name of, 136
    of Arrochar, 12
McGomrie, name of, 136
McGorre, name of, 136
McGugan, name of, 136-137
McHutcheon, John and Donald, plundered in Atholl Raids, 108
Mclain, John of Ardnamurchan, 5
McIlhattan, name of, 134
McIlchonnelie (Conley), name of, 134
McIlheany, name of, 137
McIndayn, name of, 135
McInstokir (Stalker), name of, 140
McIntaylour (Taylor), name of, 140
    Lachlan, in Atholl Raids, 108
McIntaggart, name of, 146
Macintosh, Peter, author of a *History Of Kintyre*, 56, 60
McIsaac (McKessag, McEsak), name of, 137
Mackay, name of, 137
    of Ugadale, 11
    of Ardnacross, 56
    of Islay, 124
    Adam and Duncan, in Crossibeg, 41
    John and Gilniver, in Atholl Raids, 108
McKiergan (McKerral), name of, 137
Mackoul (Macdougal), John, sole survivor at Dunaverty, 50, 52
McLarty, name of, 26, 138
Maclean, of Duart, Lachlan, 14
McMarquis, name of, 138
    John, to assist in translation of Psalms into Gaelic, 138
McMath, name of, 138
McMillan, name of, 138
McNachtan, name of, 139
    Alexander, Chamberlain of Kintyre, 82-88

McNair, name of, 146-147
Macneill, name of, 139
   Hector of Carskey, hostage, 15
   keeper of Lochhead Castle, 25
   signed Bond with Macdonalds, 12, 124
   Malcolm of Carskey and son John, 128
   Neil of Carskey and son Archibald, 128
   Malcolm of Carskey, his Compt Book, 111, 152
   Colonel Malcolm of Carskey, 11
   Lachlan of Tirfergus, 109, 117
Macrannaldbane, Donald, 6, 11
McSporran, name of, 26, 140
McVicar, name of, 140-141
   Rev. A.J., minister of Southend, 94, 130
   Duncan, in Atholl Raids, 106-107
MacVurich (McMurchy), bards of Macdonalds, 6, 11, 139
McWhirrie, name of, 136
   Mr Murdoch, minister of Killean, 35, 125
Machrihanish, 5, 76, 91
Machriemore, mill at, 26, 117
   Ralston's tack of, 98
Magnus Barefoot, King of Norway, claims Kintyre, 3
Malt, made in Kintyre, 117
Marts, paid as rent, 116
Maxwell, name of, 146
   John of Southbar, 79
   James of Southbar, 79-80
   James, in Pollywilline, robbed in Atholl Raids, 108
   Thomas of Milnehouse, 80
Menzies, Colonel, arrests Colkitto, 57
Merklands, 112, 150
Mills, in seventeenth century, 117
Mitchell, name of, 146
Montereul, Jean de, French Ambassador, 42, 50, 51, 53
Montrose, Marquis of, 37-38

Montgomery (Montgomerie), name of, 146
   Captain Patrick, 70, 78
   Robert of Hazelhead (Hazlett), 69, 78
Muir (More, Moir, Moore, Mure), name of, 146
   Colonel Robert, 70, 79
Muir, Cornet Alexander, 70
   David, 79
   James, 91
Multure, charge for milling, 117

N

" Native " Tenancy, 110
Neere, Thomas, schoolmaster at Loch-head, 36
Nevay (Nevoy), Mr John, chaplain to Marquis of Argyll, 44, 52
Norse, settlement in Kintyre, 2

O

Oats, 114
Obrolachan, name of, 141
   Duncan, rector of Kildalton, 125
   Neil, priest in Kintyre, 125
Odrain (Drain), name of, 141
Oloynachan (Loynachan), name of, 141
Omey (Ofey), name of, 141-142
   Cornelius, rector of Kilblaan, 12, 125
   Mr Donald, minister of Kilkerran, 31, 35, 40, 125
   Mr Duncan, minister of Kilcolmkill, 12
   Duncan, received charter of Kilcolmkill, 12
   Samuel, of Kilcolmkill, 12
O'Neill, Turlough of Tyrone, 14
Orr, name of, 147
   Thomas, schoolmaster and notary at Lochhead, 94, 126
   Thomas, his son, 94, 106
Outfield, 115

P

Paisley, grant of church of Kilkerran to Abbey of, 3
Parishes, boundaries of, 4
Pennylands, 150
Pentland Rising, 93-99
Picken, name of, 147
Picken, Alexander, plundered in Atholl Raids, 108
Pigs, paid as rent, 116
Pipers, 26
Pirate Ship, capture of by Lord Kintyre, 31
Plague, epidemic of in Kintyre, 60-67
Plantation of Lowland lairds, 68-73
Plough, Old Scotch, 115
Ploughgang, Four – Horse, 114
Pont, Timothy, cartographer, 23-24
Pork, prejudice against, 116
Porter, name of, 147
    John, author of *Porter's Prophecies*, 147
Porterfield, John of Hapland, 69, 77
Potatoes, 114
Poultry, paid as rent, 116
" Presents ", paid as rent, 112
Ptolemy, his description of Kintyre, 1

R

Ralston, name of, 147
    William of that ilk, receives tack in Kintyre, 69
    occupies Lochhead Castle, 82, 87-89
    his letter to Earl of Argyll, 91
    imprisonment, 95, 97-98
    tack in Campbeltown and Southend parishes, 98
    tomb and arms in Kilcolmkill, 74-75
    John, Laird of, 89
Rathlin, island of, 14

Reginald, son of Somerled, 3
Reid, name of, 147-148
    Sir Adam of Starquhyte and Bar skimming, 5
Remonstrants, 69, 74
Rents, in seventeenth century, 72-73, 113
Rhunahaorine, battle at, 45
Roads, in Kintyre, 116
Robbers, in Kintyre, Commission on, 109
Roman Catholics, 39
Rowatt, name of, 148
    Alexander, Chamberlain to Countess of Argyll, 106
Rullion Green, battle of, 81, 97
Runrig, 113
Ryburn, name of, 148

S

Saddell, Abbey of, 3, 6, 13
    Castle of, 6, 69
    mill at, 117
    parish of, 89
Salt Pans, at Knockhantimore, 123
Sanda, island of, 2
    Macdonalds of, 40
Schools, at Lochhead, 125
    parochial, 126-132
    Grammar School, 126
Schoolmasters, earliest parochial, 130
Scone, Lord, King's Lieutenant at Lochhead, 17
Scots Guards, Lord Kintyre's regiment of, 32, 51
Scrymgeour, John, builds Dunaverty Castle, 49
Sealbach, of Dalriada, 2
Services (servitudes), of tenants, 113
Sheep, 116
Simson, Mr David, minister of Killean and Southend, 90, 94, 99, 100
    Junior, 106
Sinclair, Alexander, 53

Skipness, lands and castle of, 5, 13
Skierchanzie (Kilchenzie), church lands of, 13
Smerby, Angus Macdonald prisoner at, 16
Smith, Rev. Dr. John, minister of Campbeltown, 35, 131
Somerled, 3
Soum, a unit of pasturage, 114
Southend, parish school of, 130, 131
　Ralston's tack in, 98
Spang, John, schoolmaster at Lochhead, 36
Spaniards, employed as mercenaries, 14
St Ninian's Lands of Kintyre (Macharioch), 13
Steelbow tenancy, 111, 152
Steward, Robert the (King Robert II), 4
Stewardry, of Kintyre created, 5
Stewart, Archibald of Blackhall, 32
Stewart, Sir William of Houston, King's Lieutenant, 15
Stirling, William of Auchyle, occupies Castle of Lochhead, 32
Strachan, Colonel in Leslie's army, 46
Sussex, Earl of, 49
Sweyn, Castle of, 45

T

Tacksman system, 110
　holdings in Kintyre, 110-111
Tangy, Maceachans of, 11
Tanister, John Mor, 5
Tarbert, Castle of, 4
　Constable of, 4

Sheriffdom of, 5
Leslie sails from, 55
Teinds, 112
Tolbooth, at Lochhead, 33
Tuath, ancient division of land, 2
Turner, Sir James, 37, 40, 43, 44, 48, 49-56
Turnips, 114
Uigle (Wagill, Wigill), lands of, 2, 21
Ulster, *Annals of*, 5
Urry, Colonel in Leslie's army, 47

W

Wallace, name of, 148
　Colonel James, 81, 95
　William, his son, 81, 96, 97
　James and John, sons of William, 81
Weaving, industry at Lochhead, 118
Whithorn, Priory of, 13
Waste land, in Kintyre, 15-16, 67
Watson, Prof. W. J., Celtic Scholar, 1, 2
White, name of, 148
William III, King, letter of *re* schools, 129
Williamson, Geeils, Dutch printer to Earl of Argyll, 103
Wodrow, Rev. Robert, Historian, 93, 116
Wylie, name of, 148

Yuill, John, tacksman of the Assize of Herring at Lochhead, 118